Peterson's®

MASTER THE™ AP® ENGLISH LANGUAGE & COMPOSITION EXAM

3RD EDITION

About Peterson's

Peterson's®, a Nelnet company, has been your trusted educational publisher for over 50 years. It's a milestone we're quite proud of, as we continue to offer the most accurate, dependable, high-quality educational content in the field, providing you with everything you need to succeed. No matter where you are on your academic or professional path, you can rely on Peterson's for its books, online information, expert test-prep tools, the most up-to-date education exploration data, and the highest quality career success resources—everything you need to achieve your education goals. For our complete line of products, visit www.petersons.com.

For more information about Peterson's range of educational products, contact Peterson's, 3 Columbia Circle, Suite 205, Albany, NY 12203, 800-338-3282 Ext. 54229; or find us online at www.petersons.com.

Previously published as *Peterson's AP English Language & Composition* © 2005. Previous edition © 2007.

ISBN-13: 978-0-7689-4185-2

Printed in the United States of America

10 9 8 7 6 5 4 3 2 1 20 19 18

Third Edition

Petersonspublishingcom/publishing updates

Check out our website at www.petersonspublishing.com/publishingupdates to see if there is any new information regarding the test and any revisions or corrections to the content of this book. We've made sure the information in this book is accurate and up-to-date; however, the test format or content may have changed since the time of publication.

OTHER RECOMMENDED TITLES

Peterson's Master the™ AP® English Literature & Composition Exam

Peterson's Master the™ AP® U.S. History Exam

Contents

PART III: THREE PRACTICE TESTS

Before You Begin

HOW THIS BOOK IS ORGANIZED

Whether you have five months, nine weeks, or just two short weeks to prepare for the exam, Peterson's *Master the™ AP® English Language & Composition Exam* will help you develop a study plan that caters to your individual needs and timetable. These step-by-step plans are easy to follow and remarkably effective.

- **Top 10 Strategies to Raise Your Score** gives you tried and true test-taking strategies.
- **Part I** includes the basic information about the AP® English Language and Composition Exam that you need to know.
- **Part II** provides the review and strategies for answering the different kinds of multiple-choice questions on nonfiction prose and numerous opportunities to practice what you are learning. It is a good idea to read the answer explanations to all of the questions because you may find ideas or tips that will help you better analyze the answers to questions in the next Practice Test you take.
- **Part III** includes three additional practice tests. Remember to apply the test-taking system carefully, work the system to get more correct responses, and be careful of your time in order to answer more questions in the time period.

SPECIAL STUDY FEATURES

Peterson's *Master the™ AP® English Language & Composition Exam* was designed to be as user-friendly as it is complete. It includes several features to make your preparation easier.

Overview

Each chapter begins with a bulleted overview listing the topics that will be covered in the chapter. You know immediately where to look for a topic that you need to work on.

Summing It Up

Each strategy chapter ends with a point-by-point summary that captures the most important points. The summaries are a convenient way to review the content of these strategy chapters.

Bonus Information

You will find three types of notes in the margins of the *Master the™ AP® English Language & Composition Exam* book to alert you to important information.

NOTE

Margin notes marked "Note" highlight information about the test structure itself.

TIP

Tips draw your attention to valuable concepts, advice, and shortcuts for tackling the exam. By reading the tips, you will learn how to approach different question types, pace yourself, and remember what was discussed previously in the book.

HOW TO PLAN FOR YOUR TEST USING THIS BOOK

This books consists of a section on the content, structure, scoring of as well as useful strategies for success on the exam followed by three chapters of content review and three full-length practice tests with full explanations. Each content chapter also provides review exercises and walkthroughs designed to help you get up to speed.

You may already know what you know and don't know. If not, and frankly even if you think you do, we'd recommend taking any of the three full-length tests first, without studying, as a "diagnostic test" (with the proper timing, using a bubble sheet, at 8AM, in a testlike environment, etc.) in order to see where your weaknesses lie. Let your results guide your use of this book. After reviewing your test results, note what content you need to work on and study for first.

For more specific test-prep timeline information, see our "Building an Effective Study Plan" section on page 24.

YOU'RE WELL ON YOUR WAY TO SUCCESS

Remember that knowledge is power. You will be studying the most comprehensive guide available, and you will become extremely knowledgeable about the exam. We look forward to helping you raise your score.

GIVE US YOUR FEEDBACK

Peterson's publishes a full line of books-test prep, education exploration, financial aid, and career preparation. Peterson's publications can be found in high school guidance counselor offices, college libraries and career centers, and your local bookstore and library.

We welcome any comments or suggestions you may have about this publication. Please call our customer service department at 800-338-3282 ext. 54229 or send an email to custsvc@petersons.com.

WORKS REFERENCED

The following list represents all the works of literature discussed in this book, broken out by chapter.

Chapter 2

Excerpts from essays by Michel de Montaigne

Excerpt from *NASA Confirms Evidence That Liquid Water Flows on Today's Mars*, NASA.gov

Excerpt from *Six Months in Mexico*, by Nellie Bly

Excerpt from *The Autobiography of Benjamin Franklin*

Excerpts from essays by Leo Tolstoy

Excerpts from essays by George Eliot

Excerpts from *History of the Impeachment of Andrew Johnson, President of the United States*, by Edmund G. Ross

Excerpt from *The Personal Memoirs of General Ulysses S. Grant*

Excerpt from *Magmas to Metals*, USGS.gov

Chapter 3:

Excerpt from *The Life and Work of Susan B. Anthony*, by Ida Husted Harper

Excerpts from "Protected Bicycle Lanes in NYC", New York City Department of Transportation (2014)

Excerpt from *Testing of investigational inactivated Zika vaccine in humans begins*, nih.gov

Excerpt from *An Estimate of the True Value of Vaccination as a Security Against Small Pox*, by T. M. Greenhow

Excerpt from "Controversies and challenges of vaccination: an interview with Elizabeth Miller," nih.gov

Eulogy for Chief Justice of the Supreme Court Joseph Story, by Daniel Webster

Except from *Rethinking the National Parks for the 21st Century: A Report of the National Park System Advisory Board*, nps.gov

Excerpt from *The Book of the National Parks*, by Robert Sterling

Chapter 4

Excerpt from "A Plea for Captain John Brown" by Henry David Thoreau

Excerpt from "Louis Pasteur and His Work" by Patrick Geddes and J. Arthur Thomson

Excerpts from an essay by *Robert Louis Stevenson*

Excerpts from essays by *George Eliot*

TOP 10 STRATEGIES TO RAISE YOUR SCORE

When it comes to taking an AP® Exam, some test-taking skills will do you more good than others. There are concepts you can learn and techniques you can follow that will help you do your best. Here are our picks for the top 10 strategies to raise your score:

1. **Create a study plan and follow it.** The right study plan will help you get the most out of this book in whatever time you have.
2. **Choose a place and time to study every day,** and stick to your routine and your plan.
3. **Complete the diagnostic and practice tests in this book.** They will give you just what they promise: practice—practice in reading and following the directions, practice in pacing yourself, practice in understanding and answering multiple-choice questions, and practice in writing timed essays.
4. **Complete all of your assignments for your regular AP® English class.** Ask questions in class, talk about what you read and write, and enjoy what you are doing. The test is supposed to measure your development as an educated and thinking reader.
5. **If the question is a *main idea* or *theme* question,** look for the answer that is the most general and can be supported by evidence in the selection.
6. All elements in an answer must be correct for the answer to be correct.
7. **Don't rely on your memory; refer to the passage.** For poetry, read a line or two above and a line or two below the reference.
8. **With *not/except* questions, ask yourself if an answer choice is true about the selection.** If it is, cross it out, and keep checking answers.
9. If you aren't sure about an answer but know something about the question, eliminate what you know is wrong and make an educated guess.
10. **Finally, don't cram.** Relax. Go to a movie, visit a friend—but not one who is taking the test with you. Get a good night's sleep.

PART I

AP® ENGLISH LANGUAGE AND COMPOSITION EXAM BASICS

All About the AP® English Language and Composition Exam

Chapter 1

OVERVIEW

- **The AP® English Language and Composition Exam: An Overview**
- **Exam Registration Essentials**
- **Getting Ready for Exam Day**
- **Building an Effective Study Plan**
- **Summing It Up**

We understand *exactly* why you're here and why you're reading this book—you're a high-achieving student with the goal of getting your best possible score on the AP® English Language and Composition Exam. Your reasons for setting this goal are likely twofold:

- Getting a good AP® Exam score (typically a score of 3 or higher out of a range from 1 to 5) will help you earn valuable college credit while still in high school, allowing you to potentially place out of introductory-level undergraduate courses in that subject area.
- A good score looks great on your college application, and will allow you to be more competitive and stand out amongst the pool of qualified applicants to the schools to which you're applying.

These are great reasons to take your AP® Exams *seriously*—which means making the most of your preparation time between now and exam day to ensure that you do your best.

You've undoubtedly taken your academic career seriously thus far, which is why you decided to take this AP®-level course in the first place. The last thing you want to have happen now is to get this close to your goal of acing the exam and to not do your absolute best because of a failure to plan appropriately!

We *completely* get it—and if this description sounds like you, then here's some great news: you have already made an excellent decision and have taken a wise step forward in your exam preparation by deciding to purchase this book. We're here to help make your goal of a great score on the AP® English Language and Composition Exam a reality. So keep reading!

Peterson's *Master the™ AP® English Language & Composition Exam* is your comprehensive study resource, all-in-one test prep coach, effective preparation guide, and indispensable companion on your journey to getting a great AP® exam score. Every facet of this book is designed by AP® Exam experts with one singular purpose: to help you achieve your best possible score on test day.

This effective test prep tool contains all of the following helpful resources—and more:

- **Complete coverage of the AP® English Language and Composition Exam:** You'll get a thorough insight into every aspect of this important exam—from structure and scoring to what to expect on exam day and how to effectively tackle every question type. After reading this book there will be no confusion or surprises about the exam, and you'll have a great head start on the test-taking competition!
- **Comprehensive AP® Exam review:** This study guide will take you step-by-step through the entire exam, with an analysis of each section of the exam, along with helpful sample passages and questions that mirror those you'll encounter on test day.
- **Effective strategies, tips, and advice from AP® experts:** You'll be ready for *anything* on test day once you're equipped with the expert tools this book provides for crafting an unbeatable study and attack plan and achieving test success. The creators of this book know exactly what it takes to earn a top score on the AP® English Language and Composition Exam—and now that knowledge is in your hands!
- **Proven AP® Exam practice to build your test-taking skills:** This book provides sample questions for every section and question type you're likely to encounter on test day, along with comprehensive answer explanations that will help you learn from your mistakes, build your skills, and get you in elite test-taking shape.
- **Practice tests that mirror the actual exam:** Chapters 4, 5, and 6 of this book are full-length practice exams with detailed answer explanations that look and feel just like the AP® Exam you'll take in May. In addition, this book gives you access to two online exams. You'll be more than ready to take the real thing after you've made your way through these practice tests and read over the detailed explanations for every answer choice.

We know how important doing well on this high-stakes exam is to you—and we're here to help. The tools you need for test-day success are in the helpful pages that follow—so let's get started!

THE AP® ENGLISH LANGUAGE AND COMPOSITION EXAM: AN OVERVIEW

It's perfectly natural if you're eager to skip over this chapter and get straight to the test prep—we completely understand! However, we suggest that you take some time to review the information here. Gaining a clear understanding of the structure and format of the AP® English Language and Composition Exam and the test fundamentals you should know is an important first step along your journey to exam success.

EXAM ESSENTIALS

Test Focus: This exam is designed to test your skills in close reading and rhetorical analysis, as well as your ability to critically engage with expository, argumentative, and personal texts from a range of authors and time periods. You will also be asked to craft written arguments in response to and incorporating nonfiction source texts, including science, journalism, autobiography, and criticism.

Length:
3 hours and 15 minutes (with a break between Sections I and II of the exam)

Format:
2 sections:

Section I: 55 multiple-choice questions (1 hour; 45% of your exam score):

You'll encounter a variety of published excerpts from different academic disciplines, sociocultural positions or periods in the evolution of written English.

- Each excerpt will include a set of multiple-choice questions or prompts based on what you've just read and designed to test your comprehension of the literal meaning of the text, ability to infer writer's intended meaning from the formal features of the text, and ability to use basic academic terminology to discuss features and functions of written English.
- You'll be given an answer sheet to record your answers to the questions on this section of the exam.

Section II: 3 free-response questions (2 hours and 15 minutes; 55% of your exam score):

You'll encounter 3 essay prompts and will be tasked with crafting written responses. Expect to encounter prompts that involve the following writing skills:

  - A synthesis prompt that requires you to address an issue by synthesizing information from multiple texts
  - An analysis prompt that requires you to analyze the rhetoric of a single text
  - An argument prompt that requires you to compose an argument supported by evidence and reasoning drawn from your own reading, observations, and/or personal experiences

- Your essay responses will be written in the exam booklet provided for this section of the exam.

Now that you know that you'll have just over three hours to complete the two sections that comprise the exam, we recommend that you devote some time between now and test day to get comfortable with the timing, in order to develop an effective test-taking pace.

A great way to do this is to take the practice tests in this book under simulated and timed test-like conditions, and to get comfortable with completing each exam section in the time provided. You certainly don't want to be caught by surprise on test day and hear "time's up!" before you've had the chance to finish!

AP® Exam Question Types—A Closer Look

Now you know that on exam day you'll be tasked with utilizing what you've learned throughout your academic year—along with the breadth and scope of knowledge you've acquired throughout your entire academic career—to demonstrate that you've successfully mastered the skills covered in your AP® course.

As mentioned, the exam consists of two sections—a multiple-choice section and a free-response section. Subsequent chapters will delve deeply into each section, and will provide comprehensive review, practice, strategies, and advice for earning your best possible score on exam day. Here, we'll take a quick look at each question type, so you'll have a better idea what you can expect when you face the exam.

Section I—Multiple Choice

Section I of the exam will consist of 52–55 multiple-choice questions based on several nonfiction passages. You may or may not recognize the passages and authors that you'll encounter on exam day; regardless, you'll have 60 minutes to complete this section, and you'll need to make the most of your critical reading and analytical abilities.

Answer All Multiple-Choice Questions!

Your score on the multiple-choice section of the AP® Exam will be based on the number of correct answers you earn.

This means that you should make every effort to answer each question on exam day. If you're stumped by a question, use effective strategies, including eliminating incorrect choices and educated guessing, in order to increase your chances of answering it correctly—and to increase your score.

TIP

You will *not* lose points for incorrect answers and you will not earn points for unanswered questions! So, be sure to answer every question—even if you have to guess.

Let's take a look at a sample passage and question from the *Personal Memoirs of General U.S. Grant:*

> When I had left camp that morning I had not expected so soon the result that was then taking place, and consequently was in rough garb. I was without a sword, as I usually was when on horseback on the field, and wore a soldier's blouse for a coat, with the shoulder straps of my rank to indicate to the army who I was. When I went into the house I found General Lee. We greeted each other, and after shaking hands took our seats. I had my staff with me, a good portion of whom were in the room during the whole of the interview.
>
> What General Lee's feelings were I do not know. As he was a man of much dignity, with an impassible face, it was impossible to say whether he felt inwardly glad that the end had finally come, or felt sad over the result, and was too manly to show it. Whatever his feelings, they were entirely concealed from my observation; but my own feelings, which had been quite jubilant on the receipt of his letter, were sad and depressed. I felt like anything rather than rejoicing at the downfall of a foe who had fought so long and valiantly, and had

> suffered so much for a cause, though that cause was, I believe, one of the worst for which a people ever fought, and one for which there was the least excuse. I do not question, however, the sincerity of the great mass of those who were opposed to us.
>
> — General Ulysses S. Grant, (1822–1885)

1. Which of the following descriptions effectively captures General Grant's feelings during the meeting with General Lee?
   - **A.** Begrudging and respectful
   - **B.** Cautious and optimistic
   - **C.** Hearty and friendly
   - **D.** Relieved and sorrowful
   - **E.** Resentful and disappointed

This passage is from a scene in General Grant's memoir, which took place just before General Lee surrendered. This meeting put in motion the end of the U.S. Civil War in 1865. It highlights the complexity of the feelings both men must have felt, confronting the end of such a long, costly conflict. Grant employs a variety of rhetorical strategies in this short piece of writing, including evidence of his authority as a narrator, descriptive prose, personal reflection, and nuanced perspective.

Were you able to identify the correct combination of feelings Grant recounts himself as experiencing amongst the answer choices? **The correct answer is D**; it reflects Grant's positive feelings about the war ending, but his compassion for his opponent.

Use What You *Don't* Know!

Use the questions in this book—especially the ones you answer *incorrectly*—to help you focus and refine your study plan as you prepare for test day. Incorrect answers will help you determine the subject areas in which you need more practice.

Make sure you make careful note of any possible test weaknesses you may have as you answer the sample practice questions in this book, and be sure to make time in your study plan to address them and build your skills.

Section II—Free Response

Section II of the exam will consist of 3 free-response questions, for which you'll have 2 hours and 15 minutes to answer. You'll encounter 3 essay prompts that will task your ability to effectively engage with various types of texts and rhetorical assignments. The essays will test your skills with the following types of writing:

- Synthesis
- Rhetorical analysis
- Argument

Let's take a look at a sample prompt. As a point of reference, we suggest you spend about 40 minutes on a prompt like this. This question would count as one-third of your total essay section score.

Question: Rhetorical Analysis Essay

The following passage is from John Locke's *A Letter Concerning Toleration* (1689), in which Locke discusses the virtues of tolerance. Read this excerpt from the letter carefully. It's not the letter in its entirety. Then write an essay in which you analyze how Locke argues that tolerance must be a cornerstone of anyone professing to be Christian, and what rhetoric of evidence and logic he uses to persuade his reader and convey his own authority on the topic.

Honored Sir,

Since you are pleased to inquire what are my thoughts about the mutual toleration of Christians in their different professions of religion, I must needs answer you freely that I esteem that toleration to be the chief characteristic mark of the true Church. For whatsoever some people boast of the antiquity of places and names, or of the pomp of their outward worship; others, of the reformation of their discipline; all, of the orthodoxy of their faith—for everyone is orthodox to himself—these things, and all others of this nature, are much rather marks of men striving for power and empire over one another than of the Church of Christ. Let anyone have never so true a claim to all these things, yet if he be destitute of charity, meekness, and good-will in general towards all mankind, even to those that are not Christians, he is certainly yet short of being a true Christian himself. "The kinds of the Gentiles exercise leadership over them," said our Savior to his disciples, "but ye shall not be so" (Luke 22. 25). The business of true religion is quite another thing…

If the Gospel and the apostles may be credited, no man can be a Christian without charity and without that faith which works, not by force, but by love. Now, I appeal to the consciences of those that persecute, torment, destroy, and kill other men upon presence of religion, whether they do it out of friendship and kindness toward them or no?

Your written responses on the AP® English Language and Composition Exam will be evaluated by expert AP® Exam readers for **content**, **style**, **organization**, and **mechanics**.

High-scoring AP® English language essays offer an effective, well-constructed, and persuasive analysis in response to the prompt, with a convincing point of view that thoughtfully addresses all the relevant evidence from the passage under discussion. You should take care to make appropriate references and examples throughout your essay to support your argument. Finally, you should exhibit a mastery of English language usage and mechanics, and overall the piece should be well edited and largely free of errors.

For example, a successful response to this particular prompt might begin by first explaining Locke's purpose in writing the letter, including the definition he provides for belonging to the "true Church."

The evidence he presents includes quotations from religious texts and an "if/then" logical construction to argue that nobody who commits harmful acts can possibly be doing it in the name of Christianity.

Bottom line: Make sure you have developed a versatile set of planning, writing, and revision tools that will help you generate ideas, organize them, and polish them into a final draft in the time allotted—which means getting as much practice writing well-crafted essays as possible between now and test day.

Scoring

Your AP® English Language and Composition Exam score is designed to reflect the knowledge you've acquired as a result of taking this college-level course and how well you can apply this knowledge to the questions you encounter on the exam. The score you earn will be a weighted combination of the scores you achieve on the two exam sections—the multiple-choice section and the free-response section—and will be based on the following 5-point scale:

1 = no recommendation

2 = possibly qualified

3 = qualified

4 = well qualified

5 = extremely well qualified

The multiple-choice questions on Section I of the exam will be machine scored, and your free-response essays will be scored by expert AP® Exam Readers.

So, what exactly do these scores mean? The colleges you have decided to apply to, and to which you send your official AP® score report, will use your score to determine whether you qualify for course credit and have achieved advanced placement—allowing you to skip the equivalent college course.

Typically, a score of 3 or higher indicates that you have achieved a sufficient level for advanced placement and course credit consideration.

Earn an AP® Scholar Award!

The College Board and the AP® Program have created the AP® Scholar Awards in an effort to recognize talented students who have demonstrated exemplary levels of achievement by doing well in AP® courses and exams. For more information, visit ***https://apscore.collegeboard.org/scores/ap-awards/ap-scholar-awards.***

NOTE

AP® score reports are cumulative, which means that they will include all scores from every AP® Exam you've taken, unless you have specifically requested that one or more scores be withheld or canceled.

Register for a College Board account via the official website in order to access your score, which will only be available online. You'll also receive an email update regarding when you can access and review your score, typically in July of the year you take the exam.

Once you access your score report via your account, you'll have the option to view and send your score to the college indicated on your answer sheet. You can also opt to send your score report to additional colleges, for a fee.

You will have several options for reporting your scores to the schools and scholarship programs you hope to pursue. In addition, each college has its own set of criteria for granting course credit and advanced placement. For a complete set of guidelines, options, and fees for score reporting and earning college credit, visit ***https://apstudent.collegeboard.org/creditandplacement.***

NOTE

Currently, there is no limit to the number of AP® Exams you can take, and you are not required to take an AP® course prior to taking an AP® Exam—although it is strongly encouraged to ensure test-day success.

EXAM REGISTRATION ESSENTIALS

We know that you're undoubtedly focused on making sure your English language and test-taking skills are at peak form for test day. However, you also need to have a good handle on the test essentials in order to be fully prepared—from registering to fees, to what you can and cannot bring on test day, and everything in between.

This section provides a comprehensive rundown of exactly what you need to know, so keep reading.

Registration

AP® Exams are typically administered in May each year. Once you register for an AP® course at your school, it is the responsibility of your school's AP® Exam coordinator to keep you informed regarding exam essentials and to notify you when and where to report for the official exam. Your exam coordinator is also responsible for collecting all exam fees and ordering the exams. He or she will also help with scheduling if you are planning to take multiple AP® Exams that are scheduled for the same time period.

Speak to your AP® Exam coordinator or visit the official AP® website for additional information if you have special circumstances that need to be addressed or accommodated, including a disability, or if you are home schooled or are an international student.

Fees

The current basic fee for taking an AP® Exam in the United States is $94. There are options available for fee reductions and wavers, typically based on financial need.

To determine if you're eligible for a fee adjustment, contact your school's AP® Exam coordinator. For a comprehensive list of fees, guidelines, and available options, please visit the official College Board website for AP® students.

GETTING READY FOR EXAM DAY

We know that after preparing diligently and making the most of this study guide, you'll be totally ready to tackle every AP® English Language and Composition Exam section and question. Knowing test-day fundamentals, including what to expect when you arrive for the exam, what to bring, and what to leave home, will help you avoid surprises, reduce anxiety, and stay ahead of the competition.

First Steps

Make sure you arrive for the test early, with plenty of time to spare in case there are any unforeseen delays. When you arrive on exam day, you'll be asked to review the policies and procedures regarding test security and administration—which includes everything from maintaining exam integrity and good conduct to your right to have a fair and equal testing experience, and more. You'll be asked to complete and sign your registration answer sheet, indicating that you have reviewed and agree to all of the AP® Exam policies and procedures.

Test Day Checklist: What to Bring on Exam Day

Use this helpful checklist to know what you should bring with you on the day of your AP® English Language and Composition Exam:

- ☐ Your AP® Student Pack, which you should receive from your AP® Exam coordinator
- ☐ A school-issue or government-issue photo ID (if you are taking the exam at a school you do not currently attend)
- ☐ Your Social Security card or Social Security number (used by some colleges as a primary student identification tool)
- ☐ A few sharpened No. 2 pencils, with erasers
- ☐ A few pens with dark blue or black ink
- ☐ A watch (optional)—not a smartwatch or a watch that beeps, makes noise, or has an alarm set to go off during the exam
- ☐ Your 6-digit school code
- ☐ Your SSD (Services for Students with Disabilities) Student Accommodation Letter, if you've requested a specific testing accommodation

What Not to Bring on Exam Day

Just as important as what you should bring on test day, here's a list of items that you should *not* bring to the test room, in order to avoid any issues or delays that could negatively impact your testing experience:

- A computer
- Books or reference materials of any kind
- Scratch paper or note paper
- Phones of any kind
- Portable listening devices or headphones
- Electronic equipment or recording devices of any kind
- Cameras or photographic equipment
- Any device that can access the Internet
- Food or drink of any kind (unless previously approved as an accommodation by the College Board Services for Students with Disabilities office prior to the exam)
- Smartwatches, or watches that beep or have alarms

NOTE

On exam day, be sure to complete your registration answer sheet completely and accurately to avoid any potential score reporting delays. If you'd like to get a jumpstart and read the exam procedures before test day, visit the official College Board website for AP® exams at *https://apstudent.collegeboard.org/home.*

- Clothing with subject-related information
- Office supplies, including compasses, protractors, mechanical pencils, correction fluid, highlighters, or colored pencils

BUILDING AN EFFECTIVE STUDY PLAN

We know you're aiming for your best possible score on exam day, and we're here to help you develop an effective study plan to make that goal a reality.

Being comfortable with critical thinking, drafting, and revision skills under a time crunch is essential—remember, the free-response essay section of the exam will count for 55% of your total exam score. Here are a few tips for making sure your writing skills are where they need to be:

- **Practice:** Make sure you practice writing persuasive essays on a wide variety of nonfiction topics. For most things in life—including writing—the best way to build your skills is through low-stakes practice and frequent repetition.
- **Remember the fundamentals:** Topics, focus, and points of view may vary, but some things that don't shift are the core tenets of essay writing—content, style, organization, and mechanics—which is what AP® Exam Readers will be grading. Make sure that your essay effectively delivers in all of these fundamental areas.
- **Get feedback:** It can be tough to judge the merits of your own writing. Your best approach as you practice for exam day is to have someone whose writing abilities you respect review and provide critical feedback on your work.
- **Target your weak areas:** As you practice for exam day, look critically at your writing and identify the areas that most need your attention in order to get your writing skills to the highest possible level. Then, make sure your subsequent writing attempts incorporate these weak areas to strengthen and polish them!

You've likely had your fair share of successes during your academic career. You know what study habits and writing tools work for you—and which don't—and you know the value of careful preparation. Make good use of this knowledge as you prepare for the exam.

Of course, your **critical reading and analysis** skills also need to be strong for test day; these skills are essential for success on both sections of the exam. Here are a few tips for making sure your reading skills are where they need to be:

- **Practice:** Be sure to make time between now and exam day to practice reading a variety of contemporary and historical texts thoughtfully and critically. You want to read nonfiction from all kinds of areas, so you're not thrown by more formal language, old-fashioned prose, or unfamiliar subject matter. Think about how to tackle a piece of prose: What do you need to do to break down a totally new text? What are the context clues or rhetorical devices you can learn to look for and analyze straight out of the gate?
- **Pace yourself:** Whether you're reading for pleasure or for a high-stakes exam, rushing through what you're reading only ensures that you increase your chances of missing critical information. Between now and exam day, practice building an effective reading pace—one that lets you read through more than once to assess and analyze passages similar to the

practice passages you'll encounter on exam day—so that you can complete the exam before time runs out.

- **Think it through:** When you read a practice passage, always keep the "5 *W*s and an *H*" in mind: *who*, *what*, *where*, *when*, *why*, and *how*. Think carefully about the intent and purpose of the piece, what the author is trying to convey, and how you can identify these things by reading the passage provided. These critical questions will help you discern the core elements of the writing and attack any question on exam day.

AP® English Language and Composition Test: Not a Cram Exam!

Doing well on this AP® Exam is *not* a race to memorize as many rhetorical terms or literary devices as possible between now and test day—especially since you won't know what passages and types of writing will appear until the day of the exam.

The exam is designed to test your ability to think critically, utilize your reading comprehension skills, and construct effective, targeted written responses.

Your *best* tools on exam day will be the knowledge and skills you've acquired throughout your academic career and during your AP® English Language and Composition course.

You may have a fully fleshed out study plan already devised. However, if you'd like some guidance or are open to advice for constructing a plan of attack, we suggest the following possible strategies for using this book and making the most of the time you have between now and test day.

The Full Review Strategy

This approach gives you an *equal* amount of time for each section of the exam, for comprehensive review, and skill building. It also factors in time for you to do some independent reading and writing; keeping your brain and skills sharp by practicing reading and writing on a variety of subjects is excellent preparation for this exam.

- **Step 1**: List the number of days you have until test day: ______ days.
- **Step 2**: Read this chapter completely to learn the AP® English Language and Composition Exam basics, including registration, scoring, and getting comfortable with the general format of each test section.
- **Step 3**: Build your study plan. Divide the number of days you have to prepare equally between each of the two test sections, splitting that time (days or hours) between *close-reading review* and *question/essay practice*, using the chapters and practice tests in this book.

Multiple-Choice Section

Close-reading review: __________

Question practice: __________

Free-Response Section

Close-reading review: __________

Essay practice: __________

- **Step 4**: Factor in some time each day to do some independent reading and/or writing. After all, this is a test of your ability to read critically and write effectively, so getting as much practice as possible can only prove helpful! Consider breaking up the days of the week so that you'll have a few days for independent reading practice and a few days for independent writing practice. These independent review sessions can be as short as a few minutes in length or as long as you like, depending on how much time you have available and how much skill-building and practice you need.
    - We suggest you practice with a variety of nonfiction sources—read newspapers, magazines, and long-form essays online. Make sure you seek out publications you're familiar with and some you've never encountered before!

    Independent Reading Practice Days/Hours: __________

    Independent Writing Practice Days/Hours: __________

- **Step 5**: Structure your study calendar. Now that you know the number of days you have to devote to topic review and question practice for each section of the exam, take some time to fill in a study calendar so you'll know exactly what prep you'll be tackling each day between now and test day. Structure your calendar to suit your study style—devote each day to a single test section or divide your days so you can work on one section for a set number of hours and switch things up with the other test section—whatever keeps you interested, focused, and on track. Make sure to include your independent reading and writing practice on your study schedule.
- **Step 6**: Adjust your study plan as needed. Remember, this is *your* study plan and no one knows what works best for you better than you do. Also, as you work through your study calendar, and your test strengths and weaknesses shift, adjust your study plan accordingly.

The Weakness Targeting Strategy

This approach lets you allocate the time you have between now and test day to target your weak areas and build your skills where you need to most.

- **Step 1**: List the number of days you have until test day: ______ days
- **Step 2**: Read this chapter completely to learn the AP® English Language and Composition Exam basics, including registration, scoring, and getting comfortable with the general format of each test section.
- **Step 3**: Assess your strengths and weaknesses. Rank each test section based on your strengths and weaknesses in each test section. We recommend you use your class grades as a guide. Are you great at answering questions but struggle with essay writing? Is the reverse true? Rank the test sections accordingly, giving a 1 to your strongest section and a 2 to your weakest section.

    Multiple-Choice Section: __________

    Free-Response Section: __________

- **Step 4**: Build your study plan. Divide the number of days/hours you have to prepare between the two test sections, splitting your time (days or hours) based on your rankings. You can divide your time however you see fit, as long as you're dedicating the majority of your time to improving your weak spots. One example for allocating your time is as follows:

- 75% of your time for the section you ranked 2
- 25% of your time for the section you ranked 1
- Once you're comfortable with your initial study plan percent allocations, fill in your initial number of study days for each test section.

Multiple-Choice Section: __________

Free-Response Section: __________

- If it's helpful, after you take a diagnostic practice exam, you can split the multiple-choice question types into those that fall under analysis and those that fall under rhetoric (see Chapter 2 for further explanation of those categories), to provide more time for the category you find most challenging. Now, decide how you want to divide your time for each section between analysis/rhetoric and topic review and question/essay practice. This should be based on your current skill set and needs.

Multiple-Choice Section

Analysis practice: __________

Rhetoric practice: __________

Free-Response Section

Topic review: __________

Essay practice: __________

- **Step 5**: Factor in some time each day to do some independent reading and/or writing. After all, this is a test of your ability to read critically and write effectively, so getting as much practice as possible is a winning strategy! We recommend that you devote your available time for independent reading and writing based on your current strengths and weaknesses. The majority—75% of your available independent skill-building time should be used for your weaker of the two areas and 25% of your available independent skill-building time should be used for the area in which you're strongest.
  - These independent review sessions can be as short as a few minutes or as long as you like, depending on how much time you have available and how much skill building and practice you need. We suggest you practice with a variety of language genres, from prose fiction to poetry and dramatic excerpts—and mix it up as much as possible to keep things interesting.

Independent Reading Practice Days/Hours: __________

Independent Writing Practice Days/Hours: __________

- **Step 5:** Structure your study calendar. Now that you know the amount of time you have to devote to topic review and question practice for each section of the exam, take some time to fill in a study calendar so you'll know exactly what prep you'll be tackling each day between now and test day. Feel free to structure your calendar to suit your style—devote each day to a single test section or divide your days so you can work on a section for a set number of hours and switch—whatever will keep you interested, focused, and on track!

- **Step 6**: Adjust your study plan as needed. Remember, this is *your* study plan and no one knows what works best for you better than you do. Also, keep in mind that as you work through your study calendar, your test strengths and weaknesses may shift; adjust your study plan accordingly.

The Quick Review Strategy

Perhaps you're short on time between now and test day—maybe you have just a few days, and need to make the most of them. This quick and efficient approach helps you make the most of the short amount of time you have left to earn your best possible exam score.

- **Step 1**: Quickly read this chapter to learn the AP® English Language and Composition Exam basics. Don't spend too much time on it—you have some serious test preparation to do and not much time in which to do it.
- **Step 2**: Take and score the first practice test in this book. Carefully review the answer explanations for the questions you got wrong, making sure that you understand *why* you answered them incorrectly. Use your results to help gauge your strengths and weaknesses.
- **Step 3**: Review the book chapter material that focuses on the areas in which you are weakest, based on the results you obtained on the first practice test. Make careful use of the time that you have, spending time on the areas in which you most urgently need to build your skills.
- **Step 4**: Take and score the second practice test in this book. Carefully review the answer explanations for the questions you got wrong, once more making sure that you understand why you answered them incorrectly. Once again, use your results to help gauge your strengths and weaknesses. Hopefully, your list of weak areas is shorter this time!
- **Step 5**: Review the book chapter material that focuses on the areas in which you are weakest, based on the results you obtained on the second practice test. Make careful use of the time that you have, spending time on the areas in which you most urgently need to build your skills.
- **Step 6**: Take and score the third practice test in this book. Carefully review the answer explanations for the questions you got wrong, making sure that you understand why you answered them incorrectly. Once again, use your results to help gauge your strengths and weaknesses. Hopefully, your list of weak areas is now even shorter!
- **Step 7**: If time permits, review the book chapter material that focuses on the areas in which you are still showing weakness, based on the results you obtained on the third practice test. Make careful use of the time that you have left, spending time on the areas in which you most urgently need to build your skills.
- **Step 8**: Once again, if time permits, factor in some time each day to do some independent reading and/or writing. It's a great way to build your skills and get your mind sharp for exam day.

A Note for Parents and Guardians

If you're the parent or guardian of a student who is planning to take the AP® English Language and Composition Exam, your support and encouragement can go a long way toward test-day success!

Help your child stick with a study plan between now and test day, and make sure that his or her needs for effective test preparation are well met.

The path to a great score on the AP® English Language and Composition Exam is not an easy one. The knowledge and skills you've obtained in your AP® course will be fully put to the test on exam day and you need to be practiced, polished, and ready. That's where this book comes in.

Consider this your indispensable guide for your test preparation journey. It includes a comprehensive review of the most-tested concepts on the exam, and helpful practice for all of the question types you can expect to encounter. Make the most of the resources in the following pages as you craft your study plan and move closer toward achieving your goal score.

Best of luck!

SUMMING IT UP

- The AP® English Language and Composition Exam tests your ability to read critically and apply rhetorical strategies, including analysis, argument, response to and incorporation of sources from various time periods and authors, and expository essay writing.
- Section I of the exam is composed of 52–55 multiple-choice questions that ask about published nonfiction excerpts, including essays, science, journalism, autobiography, and criticism. This section lasts 1 hour and makes up 45% of your exam score.
- Section II is composed of 3 free-response questions. Expect to face a prompt that asks you to craft a synthesis essay, a rhetorical analysis essay, and an argument essay. This section lasts 2 hours and 15 minutes and makes up 55% of your exam score.
- The complete AP® English Language and Composition Exam is 3 hours and 15 minutes long, with a break between Sections I and II.
- Take the practice tests in this book and online under simulated and timed test-like conditions to become comfortable with the pacing of the exam.
- Your score on Section I of the exam is based only on the number of correct answers you earn. Answer each question on exam day—you will not lose points for incorrect answers.
- Your written responses in Section II will be evaluated by expert AP® Exam Readers for content, style, organization, and mechanics. The highest-scoring essays offer well-constructed, persuasive analyses of the given prompt, with a clear point of view that offers a variety of perspectives.
- Your final AP® score will be a weighted combination of your scores on Section I and Section II, and will be based on a 5-point scale:
    - 1 = no recommendation
    - 2 = possibly qualified
    - 3 = qualified
    - 4 = well qualified
    - 5 = extremely well qualified
- Each college has its own set of criteria for granting course credit. Visit the official AP® website for complete details and a set of guidelines, options, and fees for score reporting and earning college credit.
- Your AP® Exam coordinator will collect all exam fees and order your AP® Exams. They will also help with scheduling if you are planning to take multiple AP® Exams that are scheduled for the same time period.
- Arrive early on test day. Make sure to complete your registration answer sheet completely and accurately in order to avoid any potential score reporting delays.
- Make sure you are feeling confident and well-prepared, with well-practiced writing, reading, and critical analysis skills on exam day. Practice writing persuasive essays on a broad range of nonfiction topics, incorporating outside sources and responding to specific essays. Make strengthening your weak areas the main focus of your study plan.

PART II

AP® ENGLISH LANGUAGE AND COMPOSITION EXAM STRATEGIES

Multiple-Choice Questions on the AP® English Language and Composition Exam

Chapter 2

OVERVIEW

- **What's the Point?**
- **What You Need to Know**
- **Key Terms and Concepts**
- **How to Approach a Passage**
- **Sample Question Types**
- **Sample Practice Passages**
- **Summing It Up**

Multiple-choice exams can be daunting—the right answer may seem too obvious, or the distractor choices may trip you up, or the question may get tricky by including "all of the following EXCEPT" or "Which of these is NOT an accurate summary." If you're not calm and collected on test day, you might stumble. But, if you've practiced quickly familiarizing yourself with a passage, marking up relevant phrases and important points, and decoding the question templates, you'll be well prepared and poised to succeed.

Unlike Section II—the free-response section of the exam that gives you 15 minutes to read the prompts and two whole hours to plan, compose, and revise—this section requires you to make quick assessments, fill in your answer sheet, and keep it moving. This means you don't have time to agonize over the finer points of the passage—you need to be able to determine in just a few minutes what the main idea is, how the passage is organized, what inferences you're able to make, and what evidence the author is providing. That all falls under the heading of **analysis**. You'll also be asked to answer questions about the **rhetoric** of a given passage—that means closely examining the tone, voice, diction, syntax, and vocabulary choices the author has made. Luckily for you, there are some strategies in this chapter that will teach you to quickly recognize and interpret what you're reading. And the good news is, you've likely been building these skills for a while—a key to test-taking success is learning to recognize these tools and become more efficient about using them.

Section I Essentials

You have 1 hour to complete this section.

- You will answer 52–55 multiple-choice questions about four passages of nonfiction prose.

Read on to get a head start on the whats, hows, and whys of the Language and Composition exam!

WHAT'S THE POINT?

When you are first given the signal to begin the exam, skim through all of the passages and questions without stopping. Doing so will help you manage your time by knowing what to expect. Put a star by any passages that look particularly dense or unfamiliar.

It may be easy for someone who already loves reading or spends his spare time scribbling in a journal to understand why we study rhetoric and analysis—it's more fun to be able to read deeply into things, and makes you a more persuasive, insightful communicator. But it's okay if that's not a compelling enough reason! The truth is, cultivating strong critical reading and writing skills can have a serious impact on your future.

The AP® English Language and Composition course is designed to help you become a better reader and writer—but just as importantly, to prepare you for the rigor and scope of the reading and writing you will do in college. Students who have taken and excelled in Advanced Placement courses in high school often find the transition to college easier—and not just in their required literacy courses. The STEM majors of today—future doctors, biologists, geneticists, chemists, engineers, and architects—need to know how to distill complex information into concise, manageable forms. Lives could depend on it! Lawyers, executives, directors, journalists and educators need to know how to communicate clearly and coherently too—they need to know how to assess a given text and understand its strengths and weaknesses in order to know how to interpret or enforce it. Publicists, marketing professionals, spokespeople, members of Congress—they must be persuasive and deliberate in everything they say or write. There is no educational path that is not made at least a little easier with more finely developed reading and writing skills.

That's why the AP® English Language and Composition course requirements include learning to compose in multiple forms—narrative, expository, analytical, and argument-based essays—and on a variety of subjects. In class, you've probably already been doing informal, or low-stakes, writing assignments designed to help you become self-aware as a writer. You'll read brilliant writers from across the spectrum of disciplines, from the historic thinkers who shaped our literary past to contemporary visionaries whose work carries us forward. Every writer is different, so every writer's process and toolkit are different—but it's important to explore all kinds of writing strategies to find out what suits you best.

WHAT YOU NEED TO KNOW

First and foremost, in order to succeed on Section I of this exam, you need to know how to read information closely and carefully. The passages you'll find in the multiple-choice section come from a range of nonfiction sources—essays, journalism, science writing, autobiographies, and criticism—that you will use to examine authors' use of rhetorical strategies and techniques in order to identify and explain their effectiveness. Part of your individual preparation for the AP® exam should involve seeking out all types of essays and getting used to their idiosyncrasies and scopes of inquiry. Read newspapers, check out science journals and magazines, read autobiographies, and get to know the conventions of literary criticism (that is, criticism that has literary merit itself—and keep in mind that a critic may review *any* medium, including visual art, literature, film, television, theater, etc.).

We can't stress this enough: In addition to all the prep you'll do in this guide, read as much as you can get your hands on—and don't just read passively on your computer screen or your phone. When possible, practice active reading strategies by marking up a hard copy with a highlighter or colorful pen, or download a PDF reader that will let you annotate documents digitally. Underline parts of an essay where you think an author makes a strong point. Keep track of words you don't know or writers you particularly enjoy. If you can team up with a friend who's also trying to fit in extra preparation, share what you're reading. You can practice making connections between multiple texts on the same topic and critiquing the way a writer invokes sources or sustains arguments.

You can't be expected to catch up on all the nonfiction writing published in the last 200 years in hopes that something you're familiar with will show up on the exam. Instead, study features of each form and genre, so that you can recognize them even when you aren't familiar with the writer or topic.

This next section is going to break down and explain each of the subsections within the categories of Analysis and Rhetoric. You may find that some of the information reiterates what's been covered in your coursework; feel free to skim through any information that's familiar, and to spend more time practicing the categories on which you've spent less time in class.

Here's the broad overview: to successfully navigate all these types of questions, you'll need a wide-ranging vocabulary and familiarity with appropriate word usage. You'll need to know how to recognize strategies for organizing short- and long-form writing, and be able to explain why and how they're useful. You'll need to identify strategies and tools like repetition and transitions, and understand how to distinguish generalized statements from details that illustrate a point or support an argument. You'll also need to understand all the moving parts that make up rhetoric, which involves knowing how to recognize and describe tone, voice, diction, and sentence structure. We'll look at each of those more closely now.

NOTE

Recent exams have included excerpted passages of nineteenth-century criticism of the work of Thomas Carlyle, an essay on the work of artist and actress Ellen Terry, a contemporary essay on Canadian book clubs, Theodore Roosevelt's memoir, and other representative samples from the history of written English.

KEY TERMS AND CONCEPTS

A crucial part of learning to decode the questions you're asked as part of the multiple-choice section is understanding the particular vocabulary that they use. As we've mentioned earlier, we can break the section down into categories and subcategories. We'll get into individual question templates and signal phrases later, but first let's look at the purpose of each type of question.

Analysis	Rhetoric
Main Idea	Vocabulary in Context
Organization	Tone
Evidence	Voice
Inference	Diction
	Syntax

Analysis

Analysis is the process of taking something apart, breaking it into its component pieces, or reducing it to a simpler form. All of the question types that fall within this category (main idea, organization, evidence, and inference) require either zooming out to take a big-picture look at a passage, boiling it down to its main idea or its structural elements, or zooming *in* to break it down into its evidence or identify its implications.

Main Idea

Detecting the main idea of an excerpted passage can be tricky; it can be tempting to make assumptions about the larger work from which the passage is excerpted, or to get distracted by what's most interesting or stands out the most. Questions that are asking about the main idea may not include actual sentences from the passage as answer choices—they may all be summaries, which simplify the passage's overarching message, or they may present a paraphrase, which involves taking a topic sentence or paragraph and rephrasing it to parse the meaning. To prepare for these types of questions, when you are skimming through the entire section at the beginning of the hour, jot down a few words that represent the main idea of the passage right after you read it. It may match one of the answer choices, or you may have to think more deeply about it when you return to the passage, but it will document what your first instinct was and help your brain get ready to revisit the passage in more detail.

Let's look at a sample excerpt from an essay by Montaigne, often considered the grandfather of the essay genre.

> The sages give us caution enough to beware the treachery of our desires, and to distinguish true and entire pleasures from such as are mixed and complicated with greater pain. For the most of our pleasures, say they, wheedle and caress only to strangle us, like those thieves the Egyptians called Philistae; if the headache should come before drunkenness, we should have a care of drinking too much; but pleasure, to deceive us, marches before and conceals her train.

> Books are pleasant, but if, by being over-studious, we impair our health and spoil our good humor, the best pieces we have, let us give it over; I, for my part, am one of those who think, that no fruit derived from them can recompense so great a loss. As men who have long felt themselves weakened by indisposition give themselves up at last to the mercy of medicine and submit to certain rules of living, which they are for the future never to transgress; so he who retires, weary of and disgusted with the common way of living, ought to model this new one he enters into by the rules of reason, and to institute and establish it by premeditation and reflection. He ought to have taken leave of all sorts of labour, what advantage soever it may promise, and generally to have shaken off all those passions which disturb the tranquillity of body and soul, and then choose the way that best suits with his own humor.
>
> In husbandry, study, hunting, and all other exercises, men are to proceed to the utmost limits of pleasure, but must take heed of engaging further, where trouble begins to mix with it. We are to reserve so much employment only as is necessary to keep us in breath and to defend us from the inconveniences that the other extreme of a dull and stupid laziness brings along with it. There are sterile knotty sciences, chiefly hammered out for the crowd; let such be left to them who are engaged in the world's service. I for my part care for no other books, but either such as are pleasant and easy, to amuse me, or those that comfort and instruct me how to regulate my life and death …

You may find the language a little formal, and it would be hard to infer much about the larger context from which this passage was taken. However, you can arrive at an interpretation of its main idea by summarizing each line, and distilling the whole down to its most essential concept.

Be careful though; determining "main idea" is not the same as summarizing or paraphrasing. In stating what the main idea is, you don't have to cover every topic from the excerpt—you have to choose which one is the passage's reason for being.

So if you saw this question about the passage from Montaigne, how would you answer it?

1. Which of the following best expresses the main idea of the passage?

A. The most virtuous way to live is to avoid pain and experience only positive, healthful things even if that means missing out on more rewarding opportunities we'd enjoy more.

B. The key to living well is to rationally consider what occupations make us happy without later making us unhappy, and spend our lives pursuing those.

C. People who are weak and sickly have only themselves and their lack of self-control to blame; everything that gives us pleasure is driven by passions we should master.

D. Pleasures are dangerous because they come with risks we can't see clearly enough to avoid, so drinking and education are not worth the potential consequences that follow.

E. The wisdom of the sages would tell us to avoid shallow pleasures and only do good work and virtuous leisure activities, but the author thinks pleasure is worth any amount of discomfort.

We'll talk more about how to parse questions later, but first, stop to note that the question is asking for which one "best" expresses—that should let you know it may not exactly reflect your interpretation, but that you should choose the one with the strongest evidence from the passage. Choice A seems to encapsulate the "sages" who give caution at the beginning of the excerpt, but is that the same as the author's perspective? How do you know? For this passage, the fact that Montaigne enters into the conversation as himself, with "I, for my part," suggests he is making distinctions between what beliefs belong to the "sages" and what he personally thinks. Choice B seems to incorporate the author's opinion pretty directly, even if the diction is different from his—you might mark that as a "maybe" while you review the other choices. Choice C seems to be referring to the part of the passage that discusses drinking or men who are "weakened by indisposition," but it reflects a tone of judgment that isn't present in the passage, and paraphrases the sages, who say passions can be deleterious, not the author, who says he'd rather have the pleasures than the pain any day. Choice D makes reference to two of the author's examples of pleasures that might have consequences, but overstates the conclusion the author reaches. He certainly doesn't suggest people should never drink or read! Choice E highlights the presence of both the author and sage attitudes in the passage, but it incorrectly paraphrases the author's attitude towards pleasure and discomfort.

That takes us back to revisit choice B! It captures not only what the passage is saying, but also what the author's intentions in having the discussion might be—how to determine what work to fill your life with, despite what the sages say. **The correct answer is B.**

Organization

Imagine taking your favorite story and condensing it to just the major plot points. If you took away the voice, the specific places or people in it, any details about how or why it happened, you'd be left with the basic events, which would probably proceed in chronological order. Learning to look past the detailed language of a passage to perceive the organizational principles underneath it is a skill that will save you loads of time. Eventually, you'll be able to glance at a passage and figure out if it's organized chronologically, or by cause and effect, or thematically, or in order of importance, or by examples that build for a desired effect, for example, to highlight contrast or similarity. Questions asking about organization may ask about the relationship between two paragraphs, or if the current order is the most logical. They may suggest alternate arrangements of sentences or even paragraphs. To prepare for these types of questions when you're initially skimming the passage, put an asterisk by moments of transition that you notice—those are a clue to how the author has organized his or her ideas. Be aware also that there may be overlap between these categories—a series of events that happened in order can still be interpreted through a cause-and-effect lens or an order-of-importance lens. The sequence may have been deliberate or it could have been accidental.

Chronology: This is the most basic, and for many nonfiction narratives, the most logical method of organization. You'll recognize it by transitions that have to do with time, such as: *first*, *secondly*, *afterwards*, *following*, *previously*, *finally*, and *lastly*. When the specific order in which something happened is important, chronology makes sense as an organizing principle.

Cause and Effect: A passage could be organized to show cause and effect in a number of ways. It might start with an accomplishment or outcome, and back up to explain how it came to be, or it could begin by describing a series of events and then move on to what happened as a result of those events. Look for transitions that indicate that kind of relationship:

because, *since*, and *for that reason* all show cause; *therefore*, *thus*, *consequently*, and *accordingly* all indicate effect.

Order of Importance: This method of organization is interesting because it sometimes tells you more about the author than about the content of the passage. If the author lists items recovered from a burning house in the following order, "First I got out my laptop and my wallet, then I went back for the cat and a family photo album, and only after that did I try to save the record collection," they're telling you something very revealing about their priorities and what they value. (The poor cat!) Order-of-importance narratives might also be about pragmatism—in an article about cleaning up the site of a natural disaster, such as a pipeline explosion, the environmental team might start by working to shut off the pipeline and flow of oil; then they could simultaneously organize crews to care for local wildlife, to remove large debris, and to physically clean up the terrain that had been contaminated. Writers of nonfiction are often very aware of building momentum, moving from least to most intense or most relevant to least relevant, depending on what they want the reader to focus on.

Thematically: Information that is organized thematically can be more loosely linked than the previous categories. If a writer were describing her childhood summers, she might group activities under headings like "at home," "at the beach," and "on road trips," to unite each paragraph by the place where events occurred. Or, she might take the same anecdote and organize it by mood: "Places I was bored," "Places I was excited," "Places I never wanted to go again." You can expect to see strong topic sentences—"The summers when we got to go to the family's lake house were full of the most vivid memories"—accompanied by transitions that indicate that you're about to hear some examples, perhaps words or phrases such as *to illustrate*, *for instance*, and *specifically*. You might also see transitions between paragraphs that highlight the comparison or contrast the author is hoping to achieve by putting different topics next to one another.

Let's look at another passage from Montaigne.

> A friend of mine the other day turning over my tablets, found therein a memorandum of something I would have done after my decease, whereupon I told him, as it was really true, that though I was no more than a league's distance only from my own house, and merry and well, yet when that thing came into my head, I made haste to write it down there, because I was not certain to live till I came home. As a man that am eternally brooding over my own thoughts, and confine them to my own particular concerns, I am at all hours as well prepared as I am ever like to be, and death, whenever he shall come, can bring nothing along with him I did not expect long before. We should always, as near as we can, be booted and spurred, and ready to go, and, above all things, take care, at that time, to have no business with any one but one's self:—
>
> "Why for so short a life tease ourselves with so many projects?" (Horace., Odes., ii. 16, 17.) for we shall there find work enough to do, without any need of addition. One man complains, more than of death, that he is thereby prevented of a glorious victory; another, that he must die before he has married his daughter, or educated his children; a third seems only troubled that he must

Underlining unknowns and even frustrating elements can often help you find patterns and context that you can either use to help you figure out the meaning of the word or to find repeated elements that you may find words for in the questions and answer choices.

lose the society of his wife; a fourth, the conversation of his son, as the principal comfort and concern of his being. For my part, I am, thanks be to God, at this instant in such a condition, that I am ready to dislodge, whenever it shall please Him, without regret for anything whatsoever. I disengage myself throughout from all worldly relations; my leave is soon taken of all but myself. Never did any one prepare to bid adieu to the world more absolutely and unreservedly, and to shake hands with all manner of interest in it, than I expect to do. The deadest deaths are the best.

2. How is this passage currently organized?

A. Chronologically

B. Cause and Effect

C. Order of Importance

D. Thematically

E. Disjointedly

Is there a strong sense of time, of beginning and end? Though the example Montaigne uses to show different men's attitudes toward death is using chronological transitions to link them (one man, another, a third, a fourth), remember the question is asking about the whole passage, not just that sentence, so we can rule out choice A. What about choice B? Does the action at the beginning of the passage have a significant effect on the rest of the passage? Maybe, in the sense that the friend who found Montaigne's memorandum caused him to ruminate on his expectations about preparing for death, but that also puts a lot of weight on an inciting incident. The passage isn't *about* understanding the connection between the friend's discovery and Montaigne's own thoughts, nor did Montaigne's thoughts change as a result of the memorandum being found. Choice C might appeal to you because of that sentence we discussed for choice A—Montaigne's hypothetical men might value their victory, their daughters' marriages or children's education, their wives', or their sons' conversations in that order, but we can't accurately infer that Montaigne agrees, since immediately afterward, he says he's ready to die with no regrets. Choice D is the most promising yet, because the first sentence raises the idea of preparing for life's impermanence, and each successive sentence adds to that idea or complicates it with a quote from Horace or some examples. He ends with a solid conclusion sentence that is related to the discussion found in the rest of the passage. Choice E wasn't one of the categories we discussed, and it also isn't supported by the passage, which may be written associatively, but is still cohesive. **The correct answer is D.**

Evidence

You've probably already worked with arguments and evidence in your English, science, or history courses. In order to persuade someone to agree with your claim, you have to convince them that your assumptions are correct and your interpretation is accurate. Evidence may include facts, statistics, personal experience, or textual connections. Questions asking about evidence may refer to connections between ideas or what lies behind an author's assertion. They may ask you to identify various points of support the author has introduced to support his claims. To prepare for these types of questions during your initial run-through, underline any arguments that you notice. Doing so will cue you to look for evidence that may back them up when you go through the passage again in more detail.

Here's another example from Montaigne:

> Men (says an ancient Greek sentence) are tormented with the opinions they have of things and not by the things themselves. It were a great victory obtained for the relief of our miserable human condition, could this proposition be established for certain and true throughout. For if evils have no admission into us but by the judgment we ourselves make of them, it should seem that it is, then, in our own power to despise them or to turn them to good. If things surrender themselves to our mercy, why do we not convert and accommodate them to our advantage? If what we call evil and torment is neither evil nor torment of itself, but only that our fancy gives it that quality, it is in us to change it, and it being in our own choice, if there be no constraint upon us, we must certainly be very strange fools to take arms for that side which is most offensive to us, and to give sickness, want, and contempt a bitter and nauseous taste, if it be in our power to give them a pleasant relish, and if, fortune simply providing the matter, 'tis for us to give it the form. Now, that what we call evil is not so of itself, or at least to that degree that we make it, and that it depends upon us to give it another taste and complexion (for all comes to one), let us examine how that can be maintained.
>
> If the original being of those things we fear had power to lodge itself in us by its own authority, it would then lodge itself alike, and in like manner, in all; for men are all of the same kind, and saving in greater and less proportions, are all provided with the same utensils and instruments to conceive and to judge; but the diversity of opinions we have of those things clearly evidences that they only enter us by composition; one person, peradventure, admits them in their true being, but a thousand others give them a new and contrary being in them. We hold death, poverty, and pain for our principal enemies; now, this death, which some repute the most dreadful of all dreadful things, who does not know that others call it the only secure harbor from the storms and tempests of life, the sovereign good of nature, the sole support of liberty, and the common and prompt remedy of all evils? And as the one expect it with fear and trembling, the others support it with greater ease than life.

Begin by using your main idea detecting skills to see if you can summarize the main idea of this passage. Put an asterisk in the margin by where it appears. Montaigne is investigating an assertion of ancient scholars—that human beings are bothered more by what they *think* about things they fear, rather than the things themselves. In his first paragraph he is laying out a central question—does "evil" depend on us to interpret it as bad in order to cause harm?

Now consider the following question:

3. Which of the following statements supports the author's argument that we have nothing to fear but fear itself?
   - A. "If the original being of those things we fear had power to lodge itself in us by its own authority, it would then lodge itself alike, and in like manner; for men are all of the same kind, and saving in greater and less proportions, are all provided with the same utensils and instruments to conceive and to judge."
   - B. "If what we call evil and torment is neither evil nor torment of itself, but only that our fancy gives it that quality, it is in us to change it."
   - C. "[N]ow, this death, which some repute the most dreadful of all dreadful things, who does not know that others call it the only secure harbor from the storms and tempests of life, the sovereign good of nature, the sole support of liberty, and the common and prompt remedy of all evils?"
   - D. "Now, that what we call evil is not so of itself, or at least to that degree that we make it, and that it depends upon us to give it another taste and complexion (for all comes to one), let us examine how that can be maintained."
   - E. "It were a great victory obtained for the relief of our miserable human condition, could this proposition be established for certain and true throughout."

Choices A and B might *sound* like they're supporting his argument, but they are actually evidence that supports his premise—the signal word that should convey this is the "If." This is a construction you may recognize from scientific hypothesis or mathematical theories. If ____, then ______. In the third sentence of the passage, Montaigne establishes the driving question that guides the passage "For if evils have no admission into us but by the judgment we ourselves make of them, it should seem that it is then, in our own power to despise them or turn them to good. If things surrender themselves to our mercy, why do we not concert and accommodate them to our advantage." He is asking, if it's true that we are fearful because of our imaginations, not because of actual "evil," why are we still bothered by something we could conceivably control?

Choices C and D have their opening transition in common as well—but which one is proffering evidence, and which one is just a statement of purpose? Read each choice closely. Choice C is choosing death as an example of an evil thing that some people fear, and juxtaposing that with the fact that some people look forward to death as a "secure harbor," "the sovereign good of nature," "the sole support of liberty," and a *remedy* to evil. Choice D is restating the premise (if evil is not evil, and it depends on us), and announcing the purpose of the rest of the essay: "Let us examine how that can be maintained." Choice E is describing the benefits of resolving this inquiry: it would be a relief of the human condition if we could determine the validity of this claim.

This close reading leaves us with choice C; it's an illustration of the theory being discussed, and thus helps to persuade the reader of the accuracy of the theory through their own capacity for logic. It is more specific than the questioning and theorizing prose around it. **The correct answer is C.**

Inference

An inference is a conclusion you reach on the basis of evidence and reason. If you heard a couple with whom you were acquainted say they were excited about their son Michael coming home that weekend, and later you saw them walking around with a young man you didn't recognize, it would be reasonable to infer—that is, to conclude, even absent further information about the young man—that the young man was Michael, their son. Sometimes inferences mean reading between the lines or reviewing what you know to be true and filling in the gaps. Questions asking you to make an inference may use signal words such as "which is most likely" or "the best explanation for this is…," or they may ask what a passage implies. During your first skimming of the passages, don't try to figure out what inferences to make, but do mark any lines that you're not sure of the significance of with a question mark in the margin.

Let's examine another Montaigne excerpt to get some practice on inferences:

> By this course a man shall never improve himself, nor arrive at any perfection in anything. He must, therefore, make it his business always to put the architect, the painter, the statuary, every mechanic artisan, upon discourse of their own capacities.
>
> And, to this purpose, in reading histories, which is everybody's subject, I use to consider what kind of men are the authors: if they be persons that profess nothing but mere letters, I, in and from them, principally observe and learn style and language; if physicians, I the[n] rather incline to credit what they report of the temperature of the air, of the health and complexions of princes, of wounds and diseases; if lawyers, we are from them to take notice of the controversies of rights and wrongs, the establishment of laws and civil government, and the like; if divines, the affairs of the Church, ecclesiastical censures, marriages, and dispensations; if courtiers, manners and ceremonies; if soldiers, the things that properly belong to their trade, and, principally, the accounts of the actions and enterprises wherein they were personally engaged; if ambassadors, we are to observe negotiations, intelligences, and practices, and the manner how they are to be carried on.

You may notice first that Montaigne is making a series of inferences—when he reads history, he considers the profession of each writer and bases his takeaway from the text on what he believes the writer's specialty to be. He's making assumptions about the author's areas of expertise—for scholars, he looks for style; for doctors, he gives their observations greater weight; for ambassadors, he'll give their state craft more credence.

4. Based on the passage, Montaigne would most likely agree with which of the following?
   - **A.** Any intellectual has the capacity to become an informed expert on any topic, as long as he or she puts in the diligent work to learn what they don't know.
   - **B.** Ability is innate—some professions are only suited to people with the natural capacity to do well in them.
   - **C.** Readers should make an effort to learn from experts in a given field, trusting that the people who've spent time in an area are best equipped to write about it.
   - **D.** Historians are the most likely to have general expertise in topics like law or religion; their accounts can be trusted over other types of professionals.
   - **E.** Every writer has unique strengths and weaknesses a reader must consider before deciding how seriously to take his or her work.

Inference questions can seem challenging because they ask you to infer—that is, to draw an informed conclusion from available evidence—an answer that is not explicitly spelled out by the author. For this question, choice C is the best answer because it is a logical application of what the author says he does in his own reading—letting the author's expertise guide his interpretation of his or her work. Choice A is incorrect because Montaigne is not suggesting everybody is capable of becoming any type of public intellectual. Choice B is also incorrect because it's suggesting the opposite of Montaigne's message: people are good at what they have learned to do. Choice D is incorrect because Montaigne doesn't regard historians as a class of scholars, but histories as a field of study in which many people have specific knowledge. Choice E is incorrect because Montaigne's main point isn't about writers as a whole, but about histories and the types of people who write them. **The correct answer is C.**

Close-Reading Strategies

Since you have only an hour for this section of the exam, expect that your mind will be racing. You can save time and energy by making a code for yourself, a visual shorthand that will save your brain the trouble of trying to remember what you thought when you read a passage for the first time. Suggestions for notation are included in this part of the chapter, but what matters most is that you develop a code of symbols, or underlining, or shorthand that you can recall instantly.

- Main idea: Summarize in 3–4 words
- Organization: Asterisks by transitions
- Evidence: Underline obvious opinions or assertions to look for evidence later
- Inference: Question mark in the margin

You can use any combination of underlining, letters, or symbols, but spend some time thinking it out ahead of time and practice using it during all your test-prep practice.

Rhetoric

Rhetoric is a big umbrella for a large field of study. Most simply, it is the study and practice of communication. Rhetoric may be intended to persuade, inspire, entertain or inform; it specifically targets its audience in order to change or reinforce their opinions or beliefs. The questions that fall within this category require you to close-read passages and assess their choice of words as well as the impact of those words.

Vocabulary in Context

This subtopic is straightforward—these types of questions will ask you things like "in context, [unfamiliar word] most nearly means …," and you will have to choose the answer you think is closest to that meaning.

Tone

It's easier to gauge someone's tone when he or she is speaking to us aloud, but the best writers can translate their spoken attitude into their written prose through word and syntax choices. Questions asking you to examine tone will often focus on what a given line or phrase of text "is meant to evoke" or what "note" the passage strikes.

Voice

In prose, voice is often indicated by point of view—you can determine whose "voice" you're "hearing" on the page by what they're saying and why. Whose perspective are you hearing? Is it the same as the author's, or is the author incorporating more views than his or her own? Questions about voice often involve determining audience or author intention, how the use of a particular voice develops the author's rhetorical purpose, or where you detect a shift in voice occurring.

Diction

Diction refers to what words you choose to bring your sentence to life. The primary distinction between "voice" and "diction" is that diction is visible on a smaller scale—a writer's diction comes down to word choice, cadence, phrasing, pacing, and the nuts and bolts of constructing a sentence, moreso than the overall perspective of the passage at hand. In poetry and fiction, diction is determined by quality of language—which is subjective, but you can close-read for consistency or changes. Many nonfiction writers also deliberately use literary techniques you'll recognize from other genres, such alliteration and imagery. Questions about diction may be very direct, as in "compared with X, the diction of Y is …" or they can be more subtle, perhaps asking about the effect of a particular word or phrase on your understanding of the text.

Syntax

Syntax is the blueprint for how words come together to form a sentence. Once again, creative writers, even in nonfiction, may adopt experimental or evocative structural choices for emphasis or effect. Syntax can be used to set the mood for a piece of prose, or to instill a specific pace for the reader—a long, complicated sentence will force you to be deliberate and thorough. Quick, breezy sentences may denote a less serious topic. Questions about syntax will ask about rhetorical techniques used in a given sentence, the function of a sentence or phrase, or even about a close-read of punctuation.

Close-Reading Strategies

Since questions about rhetoric are more targeted, it may make more sense just to make a small notation—like a checkmark or circle—by words or phrasing that stand out to you during your initial sweep. Do a more thorough read when you revisit the passage to actually answer the questions, and keep an eye out for especially striking literary devices, unusual sentences, or moments where the writer's tone or voice seems to shift.

This book not only gives you strategies for taking the test, it also gives you many examples of the exam's interpretive language and shorthand that you can learn to recognize. Make a note of key phrases that you notice appearing repeatedly in the sample questions in this chapter and the practice tests at the back of the book.

HOW TO APPROACH A PASSAGE

All of the passages you'll be tested on during the AP® English Language and Composition Exam will be nonfiction; that is, based on facts, real-life occurrences, and personal experience. They will come from one of the following categories within nonfiction: journalism, science, criticism, autobiography, and essays. The tricky part about these categories is that there is a good deal of overlap between them. An essay is simply a short (meaning less than book-length) piece of writing on a particular subject, intended for a public audience, so you can find essays on science topics, essayistic journalism, autobiographical essays, and critical essays. Still, each type of essay has some distinct characteristics that mark it, and if you learn what to expect, it can make the process of close-reading happen more quickly. For this section of the chapter, we've organized the types of writing from most to least distinctive. The types you'll be able to recognize most easily come first, followed by the categories that may be a little harder to classify at first glance. Sometimes the exam will just tell you "This passage is from a ninteenth-century essay," or "This excerpt comes from a contemporary work of criticism," but you may also have to make the determination for yourself.

Science Passages

Topics frequently covered in science writing include medicine, technology, bioethics, the environment, recent discoveries in biology, chemistry, physics or engineering, and the social implications of all of the above. Science writing is often done by journalists with technical expertise, but occasionally scientists with highly developed writing skills will discuss their own work in publications like *Scientific American*, *Discover*, or even *National Geographic*. If you like science but also enjoy spending time in the humanities, you may want to keep an eye out for potential careers that involve science writing—as distinct from scientific writing, which is the academic mode of writing that documents and analyzes research in the aforementioned fields.

A key distinguishing characteristic of science writing is how clearly and concisely its writers can break down and explain complicated concepts for a general audience, not just people who are already experts. You are likely to see more questions from the analytical category for these types of passages.

> **Genre flags:** Technical jargon that is clearly explained; citing sources for studies and statistics; commentary on that research from a variety of perspectives; emphasis on the implications and possible applications of a discovery or realization. Cites reputable publications or institutions known for research.

Example: Science Writing

NASA Confirms Evidence That Liquid Water Flows on Today's Mars

New findings from NASA's Mars Reconnaissance Orbiter (MRO) provide the strongest evidence yet that liquid water flows intermittently on present-day Mars.

Using an imaging spectrometer on MRO, researchers detected signatures of hydrated minerals on slopes where mysterious streaks are seen on the Red Planet. These darkish streaks appear to ebb and flow over time. They darken and appear to flow down steep slopes during warm seasons, and then fade in cooler seasons. They appear in several locations on Mars when temperatures are above minus 10 degrees Fahrenheit (minus 23 Celsius), and disappear at colder times.

"Our quest on Mars has been to 'follow the water,' in our search for life in the universe, and now we have convincing science that validates what we've long suspected," said John Grunsfeld, astronaut and associate administrator of NASA's Science Mission Directorate in Washington. "This is a significant development, as it appears to confirm that water—albeit briny—is flowing today on the surface of Mars."

Source: https://www.nasa.gov/press-releasenasa-confirms-evidence-that-liquid-water-flows-on-today-s-mars

Questions related to passages like this might ask about main idea, organization, evidence, and inferences. They could also ask about voice and diction, because science writers have to be very precise about what assertions they are making. What can you infer from the source of this text? Is it neutral? Trustworthy? Do you notice distinctions between the author's language and that of the person she is quoting in the third paragraph? Look at the function of each paragraph as well—you would need to be ready to answer questions that examine what the text *says* and what it *does* in presenting information about water on Mars.

5. Which of the following statements is best supported by the information given in the passage?

A. Scientists are confident there is life on Mars currently.

B. Scientists are hopeful they can now venture on to other planets.

C. Scientists believe there has been life on Mars in the past.

D. Scientists have potential confirmation of water on the surface of Mars.

E. Scientists secured samples of water from the planet Mars.

The correct answer is D. Choice D is correct because it is the only answer choice that accurately reflects the degree of certainty present in the passage—all of the evidence suggests the existence of water, but the writer was very careful about using "appear" and about using conditional language to announce the discovery without drawing firm conclusions about its implications. Choices A and C overstate the findings in the passage; choice B is not supported by the passage; choice E is not accurate according to the passage.

Journalism Writing

You likely encounter journalism every day—it's fact-driven and analytical writing done for newspapers, magazines, websites or other media outlets. Though today's media often combines reporting and commentary, journalism at its heart is intended to be as objective as possible. Journalists take nothing at face value—if they hear a rumor, they have to trace it to a source to verify it, and then get other sources to comment on it for context and accuracy. Reporting is the recounting of information acquired through research; commentary is the "spin" that interprets it according to the interests of the host news organization, the TV personality, or the industry being reported on. Historically the standards of journalism have evolved—at the turn of the century, it was still a highly editorialized form of media where writers felt free to embroider the facts or write in a tone designed to manipulate and instill fear or outrage in readers. Today, the most accomplished news sources avoid letting personal opinion color the story and instead let their editorial choices—what they cover and who they interview—speak for them.

> **Genre flags**: Journalism will reflect reporting from a variety of sources; while each source may have an opinion or distinct perspective, the recounting of the facts should be neutral, and even the conversation should unfold through the juxtaposition of the sources, not through the author's own opinion.

Example: Journalism Writing

From *Six Months in Mexico* by groundbreaking journalist
Nellie Bly (1864–1922)

A Mexican wedding is different from any other in the world. First a civil marriage is performed by a public official. This by law makes the children of that couple legitimate and lawful inheritors of their parents' property. This is recorded, and in a few days—the day following or a month after, just as desired—the marriage is consummated in the church. Before this ceremony the bride and groom are no more allowed alone together than when playing the bear. At a wedding the other day the church was decorated with five hundred dollars' worth of white roses. The amount can be estimated when it is stated roses cost but four reals (fifty cents) per thousand. Their delicate perfume filled the grand, gloomy old edifice, which was lighted by thousands of large and small wax candles. Carpet was laid from the gate into the church, and when the bridal party marched in, the pipe organ and band burst forth in one joyous strain.

The priest, clad entirely in white vestments, advanced to the door to meet them, followed by two men in black robes carrying different articles, a small boy in red skirt and lace overdress carrying a long pole topped off with a cross. The bride was clad in white silk, trimmed with beaded lace, with train about four yards long, dark hair and waist dressed with orange blossoms. Over this, falling down to her feet in front and reaching the end of the train back, was a point lace veil. Magnificent diamonds were the ornaments, and in the gloved hands was a pearl-bound prayer-book. She entered a pew near the door with

> her mother—who was dressed in black lace—on one side and her father on the other. After answering some questions they stepped out, and the groom stood beside the bride, with groomsman and bridesmaid on either side, the latter dressed in dark green velvet, lace, and bonnet. The priest read a long while, and then, addressing the girl first, asked her many questions, to which she replied, "Si, señor." Then he questioned the groom likewise. Afterward he handed the groom a diamond ring, which the latter placed on the little finger of the left hand of the bride. The priest put a similar ring on the ring-finger of the right hand of the groom, and a plain wedding ring on the ring-finger of the bride's right hand. Then, folding the two ringed hands together, he sprinkled them with holy water and crossed them repeatedly. The band played "Yankee Doodle," and the bride, holding on to an embroidered band on the priest's arm, the groom doing likewise on the other side, they proceeded up to the altar, where they knelt down. The priest blessed them, sprinkled them with holy water, and said mass for them, the band playing the variations of "Yankee Doodle." A man in black robes put a lace scarf over the head of the bride and around the shoulders of the groom; over this again he placed a silver chain, symbolic of the fact that they were bound together forever—nothing could separate them.

Notice how different the tone is from the scientific writing—where the science article was careful to use conditional words like "appears to confirm" and "strongest evidence yet," Bly's descriptions are more certain. You can tell by the author's birth and death dates that this is not modern journalism, and it features subjective word choices that are rooted in the author's observations. Still, despite the presence of adjectives like *magnificent* or *grand* and *gloomy*, it's a first-person account of something that the author witnessed. Consider its chronological organization, the way it incorporates not only what happened, but what it means, and the author's ability to document what she saw without judging it based on her own personal context—she isn't comparing the ceremony to how people do things where she is from, and she isn't present in the narrative as an active participant.

6. What is the relationship between the first and second paragraphs?

A. The first paragraph sets the scene and provides context; the second describes the actual ceremony.

B. The first paragraph explains the cultural symbolism of the objects in the ceremony; the second puts it in a physical context.

C. The first paragraph is judgmental and colored by the author's experience; the second is more neutral and descriptive.

D. The first paragraph addresses the reader's assumptions; the second recounts what actually happened.

E. The first paragraph is more descriptive and analytical, while the second is more thoughtful and appreciative of the culture.

The correct answer is A. Choice A accurately identifies the purpose of each paragraph. Choice B is incorrect because the only explanation of cultural symbolism is at the end of the second paragraph, and most of the context is provided in the first one. Choice C is incorrect because the first paragraph isn't particularly judgmental, and both paragraphs reflect the author's perspective. Choice D is incorrect because the author doesn't address the reader or present two versions of the event from different perspectives. Choice E is incorrect because the first paragraph isn't notably different from the second in terms of analysis or appreciation.

Autobiography Writing

If you ever have trouble distinguishing autobiography and biography, just remember an "autograph," which only a specific person can sign! From the Greek for *self, life,* and *write,* autobiography is an individual recounting his or her own experience. Anybody can life-write, but only *you* can self-life-write. Biography is written by someone else who seeks to uncover the story of someone's life through research, interviews, documents, and conjecture. Sometimes fiction writers have been known to get sneaky and dub their novel an autobiography because the protagonist speaks in the first person—but that's a problem for another exam day! Autobiography is also distinct from memoir, because it is presumed to adhere more closely to standards of chronology and accuracy. Often memoirs are understood to be rooted in memories, impressions, and subjectivity, but the expectation for autobiography is that it at least aspires to capture a more objective version of reality.

> **Genre flags:** Autobiography will contain the personal *I*, and should contain a narrative driven by the events in the writer's life. Where an essay may seek to capture a specific moment in time and make meaning by putting it in context, an autobiography will contain more exposition. It will make characters out of figures in the writer's life, which essays don't always do, and it may stay within the bounds of time and place more consistently.

Example: Autobiography Writing

From *The Autobiography of Benjamin Franklin* (1706–1790)

From a child I was fond of reading, and all the little money that came into my hands was ever laid out in books. Pleased with the Pilgrim's Progress, my first collection was of John Bunyan's works in separate little volumes. I afterward sold them to enable me to buy R. Burton's Historical Collections; they were small chapmen's books,[16] and cheap, 40 or 50 in all. My father's little library consisted chiefly of books in polemic divinity, most of which I read, and have since often regretted that, at a time when I had such a thirst for knowledge, more proper books had not fallen in my way, since it was now resolved I should not be a clergyman. Plutarch's Lives there was in which I read abundantly, and I still think that time spent to great advantage. There was also a book of DeFoe's, called an Essay on Projects, and another of Dr. Mather's, called Essays to do Good, which perhaps gave me a turn of thinking that had an influence on some of the principal future events of my life.

This bookish inclination at length determined my father to make me a printer, though he had already one son (James) of that profession. In 1717 my brother James returned from England with a press and letters to set up his

16. Small books, sold by chapmen or peddlers.

business in Boston. I liked it much better than that of my father, but still had a hankering for the sea. To prevent the apprehended effect of such an inclination, my father was impatient to have me bound to my brother. I stood out some time, but at last was persuaded, and signed the indentures when I was yet but twelve years old. I was to serve as an apprentice till I was twenty-one years of age, only I was to be allowed journeyman's wages during the last year. In a little time I made great proficiency in the business, and became a useful hand to my brother. I now had access to better books. An acquaintance with the apprentices of booksellers enabled me sometimes to borrow a small one, which I was careful to return soon and clean. Often I sat up in my room reading the greatest part of the night, when the book was borrowed in the evening and to be returned early in the morning, lest it should be missed or wanted.

And after some time an ingenious tradesman, Mr. Matthew Adams, who had a pretty collection of books, and who frequented our printing-house, took notice of me, invited me to his library, and very kindly lent me such books as I chose to read. I now took a fancy to poetry, and made some little pieces; my brother, thinking it might turn to account, encouraged me, and put me on composing occasional ballads. One was called *The Lighthouse Tragedy*, and contained an account of the drowning of Captain Worthilake, with his two daughters: the other was a sailor's song, on the taking of *Teach* (or Blackbeard) the pirate. They were wretched stuff, in the Grub-street-ballad style;[17] and when they were printed he sent me about the town to sell them. The first sold wonderfully, the event being recent, having made a great noise. This flattered my vanity; but my father discouraged me by ridiculing my performances, and telling me verse-makers were generally beggars. So I escaped being a poet, most probably a very bad one; but as prose writing has been of great use to me in the course of my life, and was a principal means of my advancement, I shall tell you how, in such a situation, I acquired what little ability I have in that way.

In contrast to the journalism and science writing, the author, venerable statesman Benjamin Franklin, is very much present in this passage. Without his achievements later in life, these details about what he read and what professions he considered as a young man would perhaps not be as interesting or relevant. With a passage like this, expect to be asked about the writer's tone and diction, the contributions of the footnotes, and how the author is overt about the purpose of details he decides to include—that is, how he signals what his main idea is.

17. Grub-street: famous in English literature as the home of poor writers.

7. Which rhetorical strategy does the author display in paragraph 2?
   A. Suggests reading was responsible for much of his later success
   B. Claims his skills as a statesman were developed as a result of hardship in his youth
   C. Gives examples of conditions related to indentured apprenticeship to provide context
   D. Acknowledges the privilege he experienced as a young man
   E. Cites facts to counter rumors related to his upbringing

The correct answer is C. Franklin was writing to an audience that might have been unfamiliar with the practice of indenturing family members, so he is building his authority as a narrator by explaining how that practice worked in real life. Choice A is not correct because it addresses what Franklin was doing in the *first* paragraph. Choice B is incorrect because Franklin is not making any claims about his future success in this paragraph. Choice D is incorrect because Franklin is not recounting a particularly privileged experience. Choice E is incorrect because Franklin has not mentioned any rumors that he's refuting so it's impossible to draw that conclusion just from the passage provided.

Criticism

Truly literary criticism—work that analyzes and judges the merits and faults of art in every form—goes above and beyond calling a work "good" or "bad." Writers of literary criticism use all the same rhetorical techniques to enliven and enrich their work that writers in every genre do: their language can be lyrical, abrasive, stirring, or engaging. The goals of criticism go all the way back to Johann Wolfgang von Goethe, who first declared that criticism should 1) assess what the artist was attempting to do, 2) assess how well the writer has done it, and 3) assess to what extent it was worth doing. Framing criticism this way frees writers from just writing about whether they "liked" a given work of art, literature, film, theater, etc. Instead they have to examine the creator's ambitions, articulate what he or she did well or poorly, and then evaluate why it was worth doing, all of which leads to more sophisticated analysis. Again, criticism can live within an essay, so if you come across a passage that you're not sure about, look for evidence of Goethe's three-part criterion to help you determine whether it's criticism or just a response to a work of art.

> **Genre flags**: Goethe's criterion, a critical review will also have a summary or description of the work it's reviewing, background of the work and its creator, comparisons to similar or contrasting works, and an evaluation of the work's significance in some other context—the larger "so what" of the writer's review. The writer will be interpreting the work in some new or unexpected way.

Example: Criticism

Leo Tolstoy (1828–1910) on Shakespeare

I remember the astonishment I felt when I first read Shakespeare. I expected to receive a powerful esthetic pleasure, but having read, one after the other, works regarded as his best: "King Lear," "Romeo and Juliet," "Hamlet" and "Macbeth," not only did I feel no delight, but I felt an irresistible repulsion and tedium, and doubted as to whether I was senseless in feeling works regarded as the summit of perfection by the whole of the civilized world to be trivial and positively bad, or whether the significance which this civilized world attributes to the works of Shakespeare was itself senseless. My consternation was increased by the fact that I always keenly felt the beauties of poetry in every form; then why should artistic works recognized by the whole world as those of a genius,—the works of Shakespeare,—not only fail to please me, but be disagreeable to me? For a long time I could not believe in myself, and during fifty years, in order to test myself, I several times recommenced reading Shakespeare in every possible form, in Russian, in English, in German and in Schlegel's translation, as I was advised. Several times I read the dramas and the comedies and historical plays, and I invariably underwent the same feelings: repulsion, weariness, and bewilderment. At the present time, before writing this preface, being desirous once more to test myself, I have, as an old man of seventy-five, again read the whole of Shakespeare, including the historical plays, the "Henrys," "Troilus and Cressida," "The Tempest," "Cymbeline," and I have felt, with even greater force, the same feelings,—this time, however, not of bewilderment, but of firm, indubitable conviction that the unquestionable glory of a great genius which Shakespeare enjoys, and which compels writers of our time to imitate him and readers and spectators to discover in him non-existent merits,—thereby distorting their esthetic and ethical understanding,—is a great evil, as is every untruth.

Altho I know that the majority of people so firmly believe in the greatness of Shakespeare that in reading this judgment of mine they will not admit even the possibility of its justice, and will not give it the slightest attention, nevertheless I will endeavor, as well as I can, to show why I believe that Shakespeare can not be recognized either as a great genius, or even as an average author.

For illustration of my purpose I will take one of Shakespeare's most extolled dramas, "King Lear," in the enthusiastic praise of which, the majority of critics agree.

"The tragedy of Lear is deservedly celebrated among the dramas of Shakespeare," says Dr. Johnson. "There is perhaps no play which keeps the attention so strongly fixed, which so much agitates our passions, and interests our curiosity."

...

Such are the judgments of the critics about this drama, and therefore I believe I am not wrong in selecting it as a type of Shakespeare's best.

As impartially as possible, I will endeavor to describe the contents of the drama, and then to show why it is not that acme of perfection it is represented to be by critics, but is something quite different.

This is an excerpt from a longer work, so you could expect to see questions about main idea, inferences about audience and the author's authority, and how he introduces other sources in order to engage with their views. Look for clear signals that tell you how the author intends to interpret the work he's reviewing, and examine the structure of his critique. How much time does he spend summarizing the plot? How does his tone differ from the other critics he quotes? You might find questions about individual sources appearing within the excerpt as well.

8. On the basis of the passage, the author's tone is best characterized as

A. brusque and dismissive.

B. offended but ostentatious.

C. outraged and indignant.

D. disdainful but deliberate.

E. critical and boastful.

The correct answer is D. Tolstoy has a clearly negative opinion of Shakespeare, but is stating his intended purpose of convincing the reader, not just announcing his interpretation or reveling in using excessively negative language to do it. Choice A is incorrect because, while Tolstoy is frank about his negative feelings, he is not brusque or egotistical about it. Choice B is incorrect because Tolstoy is not personally offended by his distaste for Shakespeare, nor is he seeking to suggest his opinion is better than everyone else's. He is hoping to persuade us. Choices C and E are also incorrect because they overstate the author's attitude in undertaking this academic project.

Essay Writing

A versatile and time-honored form, essays are the biggest umbrella in nonfiction. Practically everything fits within its boundaries, as long as it's no longer than 30 pages on average. All of your excerpts will of course be shorter, so one way to identify an essay is to consider its goal. Is it trying to inform you? Persuade you? Dissuade you? Warn you? Encourage you? Even without using a first person *I* pronoun, everything in an essay is filtered through an author's personal lens. Like journalists, essayists do incorporate facts and concrete information, but what really makes essays unique is the voice of the writer. Expect to see more questions about rhetoric in essay passages, where you're looking at the writer's craft and not just the writer's message or meaning.

> **Genre flags**: Look at the scope of the passage—it is probably trying to get one main idea across and supporting it with evidence; it is probably also putting that idea in context or even in conversation with other public thinkers. An essay can be on any topic, and can be structured in a variety of ways. It reflects primarily the voice of the individual who wrote it, unlike in fiction where you have to distinguish between the "author" and the "narrator."

Example: Essay Writing

From *The Essays of George Eliot* by George Eliot (1819–1880)

In proportion as the literature of a country is enriched and culture becomes more generally diffused, personal influence is less effective in the formation of taste and in the furtherance of social advancement. It is no longer the coterie which acts on literature, but literature which acts on the coterie; the circle represented by the word *public* is ever widening, and ambition, poising itself in order

> to hit a more distant mark, neglects the successes of the salon. What was once lavished prodigally in conversation is reserved for the volume or the "article," and the effort is not to betray originality rather than to communicate it. As the old coach-roads have sunk into disuse through the creation of railways, so journalism tends more and more to divert information from the channel of conversation into the channel of the Press; no one is satisfied with a more circumscribed audience than that very indeterminate abstraction "the public," and men find a vent for their opinions not in talk, but in "copy." We read the *Athenæum* askance at the tea-table, and take notes from the *Philosophical Journal* at a soirée; we invite our friends that we may thrust a book into their hands, and presuppose an exclusive desire in the "ladies" to discuss their own matters, "that we may crackle the *Times*" at our ease. In fact, the evident tendency of things to contract personal communication within the narrowest limits makes us tremble lest some further development of the electric telegraph should reduce us to a society of mutes, or to a sort of insects communicating by ingenious antenna of our own invention. Things were far from having reached this pass in the last century; but even then literature and society had outgrown the nursing of coteries, and although many *salons* of that period were worthy successors of the Hôtel de Rambouillet, they were simply a recreation, not an influence. Enviable evenings, no doubt, were passed in them; and if we could be carried back to any of them at will, we should hardly know whether to choose the Wednesday dinner at Madame Geoffrin's, with d'Alembert, Mademoiselle de l'Espinasse, Grimm, and the rest, or the graver society which, thirty years later, gathered round Condorcet and his lovely young wife. The *salon* retained its attractions, but its power was gone: the stream of life had become too broad and deep for such small rills to affect it.

You'll notice this excerpt has a formal tone, and the author is present more through the tone and voice than a personal engagement with the content as she comments on a larger societal issue. You could expect questions on rhetorical strategies, voice and diction, and inferences about the society in which the author was living at the time. Note also that there are elements of many of the other types of nonfiction prose we've looked at in this section present in this extract, just more proof that essays can be anything!

9. The passage makes use of all of the following EXCEPT:

A. Simile

B. Metaphor

C. Citing examples

D. Personal narrative

E. Abstract generalizations

The correct answer is D—Eliot uses simile (As the old coach-roads have sunk…so journalism tends …"), metaphor ("the stream of life had become too broad"), cites examples ("We read the *Athenaeum askance…")* and generalizes abstractly, "as the literature of a country is enriched…personal influence is less effective." She does not, however, include any personal narrative of her own experience, speaking instead in the collective "We."

SAMPLE QUESTION TYPES

One of the great benefits to doing this type of dedicated test preparation is learning to recognize the particular quirks of phrasing and structure in multiple-choice questions. As you learn to detect the architecture that underlies test-question writing, be on the lookout for signal words and phrases like *NOT* and *EXCEPT*, or "best matches" or "most nearly," or "least likely," or "primarily", as these are all telling you how to evaluate the question choices.

You should approach "not/except" questions as a process of elimination, since the "correct" answer will be the one that *doesn't* appear in the passage or *doesn't* accurately reflect the content of the passage. Questions asking you which answer choice "best" or "most nearly" interprets the passage are acknowledging that none of the answer choices may be precisely what you were thinking. Compare the answer choices for these types of questions to the passage and see what evidence there is for each one; when in doubt, make your best guess!

Here are some question formats that you can expect to see on the exam; you may not see these exact constructions, but look closely at how they seek to elicit information. Sometimes they are asking you to detect language or ideas present in the passage or evaluate the effect of those elements. Other times they are asking you to make a leap of logic or reason, to infer something from the text that is not actually present. Being able to easily "decode" the question construction can help you focus on choosing the correct answer and cut down on any second-guessing and overthinking that may slow you down.

Take a look at this sample passage, and then the sample questions for each question type that follow.

Historical notes: *Andrew Johnson was Abraham Lincoln's vice president, and became president upon Lincoln's assassination. He served as president with no vice president, was known for his opposition to policies designed to protect and advance the interests of former enslaved people and freedmen, and was impeached for attempting to fire Secretary of War, Edwin Stanton, who he disagreed with politically. He was impeached by the House of Representatives but avoided being removed from office by one vote in the Senate.*

From *History of the Impeachment of Andrew Johnson, President of the United States*, by Edmund G. Ross.

Chapter XIII—The Constitutional Power of Impeachment

The power conferred by the Constitution upon Congress to impeach and remove the President for cause, is unquestionably a wise provision. The natural tendency of the most patriotic of men, in the exercise of power in great public emergencies, is to overstep the line of absolute safety, in the conscientious conviction that a departure from strict constitutional or legal limitations is demanded by the public welfare.

The danger in such departures, even upon apparent necessity, if condoned or permitted by public judgment is in the establishment of precedents whereby greater and more dangerous infractions of organic law may be invited, tolerated, and justified, till government takes on a form of absolutism in one form or another, fatal to free institutions, fatal to a government of law, and fatal to popular liberty.

On the other hand, a too ready resort to the power of impeachment as a remedial agent—the deposition of a public officer in the absence of proof of the most positive and convincing character of the impeachability of the offense alleged, naturally tends to the other extreme, till public officers may become by common consent removable by impeachment upon insufficient though popular charges—even upon partisan differences and on sharply contested questions of public administration.

The power of impeachment and removal becomes, therefore, a two-edged sword, which must be handled with consummate judgment and skill, and resort thereto had only in the gravest emergencies and for causes so clearly manifest as to preclude the possibility of partisan divisions or partisan judgments thereon. Otherwise, too ready resort to impeachment must inevitably establish and bring into common use a new and dangerous remedy for the cure of assumed political ills which have their origin only in partisan differences as to methods of administration. It would become an engine of partisan intolerance for the punishment and ostracism of political opponents, under the operation of which the great office of Chief Magistrate must inevitably lose its dignity, and decline from its Constitutional rank as a co-ordinate department of the Government, and its occupant no longer the political head and Chief Executive of the Nation, except in name.

It was in that sense, and to a pointed degree, that in the impeachment and trial of Andrew Johnson the quality of coordination of the three great Departments of Government—the Executive, Legislative, and Judicial—was directly involved—the House of Representatives as prosecutor—the President as defendant—the Senate sitting as the trial court in which the Chief Justice represented the judicial department as presiding officer.

The anomaly of the situation was increased and its gravity intensified, by the fact that the President pro tempore of the Senate, who stood first in the line of succession to the Presidency in case of conviction, was permitted, in a measure, indeed, forced by his pro-impeachment colleagues, on a partisan division of the Senate, to sit and vote as such President pro tempore for the impeachment and removal of the President whom he was to succeed.

These facts of condition attending and characterizing the trial of President Johnson, pointedly accentuate the danger to our composite form of government which the country then faced. That danger, as it had found frequent illustration in the debates in the House of Representatives on the several propositions for the President's impeachment preceding the bringing of the indictment, lay in the claim of superiority of political function for the Legislative branch over the Executive. The quality of co-ordination of these departments was repeatedly and emphatically denied by conspicuous and influential members of that body during the initial proceedings of the impeachment movement, and even on the floor of the Senate by the managers of the impeachment. To illustrate:

Mr. Bingham, in the House, Feb. 22nd, 1868, announced the extraordinary doctrine that "there is no power to review the action of Congress." Again, speaking of the action of the Senate on the 21st of February, on the President's message announcing the removal of Mr. Stanton, he said: "Neither the Supreme Court nor any other Court can question or review this judgment of the Senate."

The declaration was made by Messrs. Stevens and Boutwell in the House, that the Senate was its own judge of the validity of its own acts. Mr. Butler, in his opening speech to the Senate, at the beginning of the trial, used this language:

A Constitutional tribunal solely, you are bound by no law, either Statute or Common, which may limit your constitutional prerogative. You consult no precedents save those of the law and custom of parliamentary bodies. You are a law unto yourselves, bound only by the natural principles of equity and justice, and salus populi suprema est lex.

Feb. 24, 1868, Mr. Stevens said in the House:

Neither the Executive nor the Judiciary had any right to interfere with it (Reconstruction) except so far as was necessary to control it by military rule until the sovereign power of the Nation had provided for its civil administration. NO POWER BUT CONGRESS HAD ANY RIGHT TO SAY WHETHER EVER, OR WHEN, they (the rebel States), should be admitted to the Union as States and entitled to the privileges of the Constitution of the United States. * * * I trust that when we come to vote upon this question we shall remember that although it is the duty of the President to see that the laws be executed, THE SOVEREIGN POWER OF THE NATION RESTS IN CONGRESS.

Main Idea:

10. What is the primary purpose of this passage?

A. To defend the decision to impeach President Andrew Johnson

B. To explain why the Supreme Court has no jurisdiction over Congress

C. To imply President Johnson did not deserve to be impeached

D. To argue only Congress has the right to interpret the Constitution

E. To examine the political circumstance surrounding the practice of impeachment

The correct answer is E. Choice E it best captures the broad scope of the passage; choices A and C aren't supported by the passage because they suggest the author was taking a side on this specific impeachment, rather than considering the practice as a whole. Choices B and D are incorrect because they are specific ideas being advanced by speakers quoted in the passage, not the main intention of the writer himself.

Other Questions Asking About Main Idea

- Which of the following is true of the comparison being made throughout the passage?
- Which statement does NOT describe [character or place]?
- The passage can best be described as which of the following types of writing?
- What does the author intend readers should take away from this essay?
- What is the primary purpose of this passage?

Organization:

11. The author develops the passage by moving from

A. overview to illustration.

B. analysis to argumentation.

C. narration to analysis.

D. assertion to definition.

E. specific evidence to broad generalization.

The correct answer is A. The passage begins with a big-picture overview of the process and its potential interpretations, and then ends with specific quotes from individuals demonstrating those interpretations in action. Choice B is incorrect because the author is not arguing for or against impeachment as a practice, or as it specifically relates to President Johnson. Choice C is incorrect because the passage doesn't conclude with analysis, but with examples of rhetoric from the period. Choice D is incorrect because the author doesn't end by introducing definitions. Choice E is incorrect because it inverts the progress of the passage.

Other Questions Asking About Organization

- The organization of the passage can be best described as
- What is the relationship between the two paragraphs in the passage?
- What purpose do *lines #–#* serve?
- What is the relationship of the second and third sentences (*lines #–#*) to the first sentence (*lines #–#*)?
- The first paragraph (*lines #–#*) serves to
- The function of *lines #–#* (" ") is to
- The final sentence (*lines #–#*) serves to
- One function of sentence " " (*lines #–#*) is to
- The author develops the passage primarily through
- When the passage moves from the first paragraph to the second, it also moves from
- The information below would fit most logically in which part of the passage?

Evidence:

12. Which of the following statements is best supported by information given in the passage?

A. Congress was unanimous about impeaching Andrew Johnson.

B. Nobody in Congress could agree whether to impeach.

C. The author doesn't believe in the practice of impeachment.

D. The balance of powers is a key question in understanding the implications of impeachment.

E. The position of vice president is most essential to avoiding a conflict of interest during the proceedings.

The correct answer is D. In paragraph 7, the author observes the circumstances surrounding the impeachment "pointedly accentuate the danger to our composite form of government," and goes on to analyze the conflicts between the legislative, judicial, and executive branches. Choices A and B are incorrect because the author describes a vociferous debate over the issue. Choice C is incorrect because it is not supported by the passage. Choice E is incorrect because the lack of a vice president is only one factor that contributed to a conflict of interest.

Other Questions Asking About Evidence

- The author uses the phrase " " (*lines #–#*) to set up a comparison between …
- Which of the following statements is best supported by information given in the passage?
- According to *lines #–#* [X's primary criticism of Y] is that they
- A function of [text] is to
- The statement " …" (*lines #–#*) is an admission that
- The information in footnote 2 is different from that in footnote 3 in that

Inference:

13. Which of the following best represents the author's intended audience?

A. Individuals who are well acquainted with this period of history

B. Readers who are unfamiliar with the dynamics of this political era

C. Writers who hope to produce books like this history of impeachment

D. Teachers looking to introduce the topic to their students

E. Scholars seeking information about Andrew Johnson's emotional state

The correct answer is B. The text is too basic for readers in choice A, insufficiently detailed for choice C, too detailed for choice D, and too unrelated for choice E. This passage is intended for readers who weren't alive or didn't understand the implications of the impeachment proceedings for Andrew Johnson.

Other Questions Asking About Inference

- Which of the following best represents the author's intended audience?
- On the basis of the first paragraph, [author] is best characterized as
- The author mentions [text] (*lines #–#*) primarily to
- The author's attitude toward [Character] can be best described as
- The passage implies that the primary enemy of " " and " " (*lines #* and *#–#*) is the
- The author suggests [text] (*line #*) chiefly because
- It can be inferred from [text] that [key term] is
- The author is best described as
- The passage implies that unlike [ ], [ ] because
- Which of the following best describes the images in the last sentences of the passage (*lines #–#*)?
- What does the author mean by [text]?

Vocabulary in Context:

14. The phrase "anomaly of the situation" suggests that this was a(n)

A. common occurrence.

B. unprecedented occurrence.

C. welcome occurrence.

D. frightening occurrence.

E. unnecessary occurrence.

The correct answer is B. An anomaly is something that is not standard, normal, or expected. For context clues that can help you determine the right answer, if *anomaly* is unfamiliar, read the preceding paragraphs and the rest of the sentence carefully. You'll notice the opening of the passage discusses dangerous infractions and compares impeachment to a sword. Then, the sentence where "anomaly of the situation" appears goes on to emphasize its gravity as well, which should suggest that choices C and E are incorrect. Choice A is incorrect because an anomaly is anything but common. Choice D is incorrect because it overstates the degree of emotional response the reader is intended to have during the passage—nothing in the prose suggests that actual fear is warranted.

Other Questions Asking About Vocabulary in Context

- The words "[word]" (*line #*) and "[word]" (*line #*) are used to describe/emphasize
- The "[symbolic object]" (*line #*) represents
- The phrase "[word]" (*line #*) suggests that
- The [ ] (*line #*) is most probably
- In context, the image of [ ] is meant to evoke

Tone:

15. Which of the following best describes the author's tone or mood in this passage?

A. Informal

B. Technical

C. Hysterical

D. Speculative

E. Measured

The correct answer is E. The author's tone is formal (so choice A is incorrect), explanatory and meant for a general audience (so choice B is incorrect), calm (so choice C is incorrect) and matter of fact (so choice D is incorrect). *Measured* is the most accurate description of his tone as expressed through the even-handed discussion of the issues at stake.

Other Questions Asking About Tone

- Lines 14–16 ("[insert quote]") contrast
- The last paragraph (*lines #–#*) marks a shift from
- The second paragraph of the passage relies especially on
- The passage ends on a note of
- What is ironic about the last sentence of the paragraph?
- Which of the following best describes the author's tone or mood in this passage?

Voice:

16. The author quotes specific political speakers in the final paragraphs of the passage in order to

- **A.** argue in favor of impeachment.
- **B.** demonstrate the extremity of political perspectives.
- **C.** convince the reader of his point of view.
- **D.** discredit the speakers as radicals or acting in bad faith.
- **E.** fill the reader with concern.

The correct answer is B. The three speakers directly quoted in the excerpt are expressing heightened attitudes toward the relationship between the branches of government, which illustrates how intense the stakes were (and are) when interpreting the Constitution. Choice A is incorrect because the speakers aren't directly commenting on whether Johnson should be impeached. Choice C is incorrect because the speakers almost cancel each other out and none of them seem to align precisely with the writer's view. Choice D is incorrect because he doesn't comment on the speakers to interpret them, much less attempt to discredit them. Choice E is incorrect because the language is direct and procedural; there is no appeal to the emotion of the reader.

Other Questions Asking About Voice

- The [text referred to] (*lines #–#*) tend to emphasize
- The [object] referred to in *line #* is discussed to suggest to the reader that
- The author uses the description of " " in order to
- The perspective in paragraph 3 shifts from

Diction:

17. In paragraphs 2 and 3, the author develops his rhetorical purpose by

- **A.** giving examples of impeachable offenses.
- **B.** contrasting two potential interpretations.
- **C.** citing facts to counter his critics.
- **D.** acknowledges the historical significance of the events.
- **E.** claiming his expertise of the events in question.

The correct answer is B. The contrast is indicated by the transition phrase, "On the other hand." Choice A is incorrect because there are no specific details about grounds for impeachment in these paragraphs. Choice C is incorrect because they have not yet introduced any critical perspectives to be countered. Choice D is incorrect because, although there is some discussion of the implications of each point of view, the actual discussion of significance takes place in paragraph 4. Choice E is incorrect because the author is not seeking to build his credibility in this section.

Other Questions Asking About Diction

- Compared with the rest of the passage, the diction of (_____) is
- Which rhetorical strategy does the author adopt in *lines #–#* (_______)?
- In *lines #–#*, the author develops her rhetorical purpose by
- In *line #*, " " function as a metaphor for the
- The effect of italicizing the words _____ (*line #*) is to
- The effect of mentioning _____ (*line #*) is to
- In context, the author [places the term " " in quotation marks in *line #*] in order to
- The first sentence of the passage (*lines #–#*) employs all of the following EXCEPT
- The phrase _______ (*line #*) does all of the following EXCEPT

Questions about Syntax:

18. The passage uses all of the following stylistic features EXCEPT:

A. Compound sentences

B. Parallel construction

C. Understatement

D. Metaphor

E. Repetition for emphasis

The correct answer is C. Examples of each of the other stylistic features can be found in the passage, but the author is trying to convince the reader of the extreme danger of underestimating the conflict over impeachment, and so is not using understatement as a technique.

Other Questions Asking About Syntax

- The pronoun "[word]" (*line #*) refers to which of the following?
- Which of the following stylistic features is used most extensively in *lines #–#*?

SAMPLE PRACTICE PASSAGES

To try out even more examples of these question types, let's revisit some sample passages, questions, and answer explanations. Here is another excerpt from *Personal Memoirs of U. S. Grant.* First you'll see the passage as you'd find it on the exam—a sample annotated passage follows.

Excerpt from *Personal Memoirs of U. S. Grant*

Although frequently urged by friends to write my memoirs I had determined never to do so, nor to write anything for publication. At the age of nearly sixty-two I received an injury from a fall, which confined me closely to the house while it did not apparently affect my general health. This made study a pleasant pastime. Shortly after, the rascality of a business partner developed itself by the announcement of a failure. This was followed soon after by universal depression of all securities, which seemed to threaten the extinction of a good part of the income still retained, and for which I am indebted to the kindly act of friends. At this juncture the editor of the *Century Magazine* asked me to write a few articles for him. I consented for the money it gave me; for at that moment I was living upon borrowed money. The work I found congenial, and I determined to continue it. The event is an important one for me, for good or evil; I hope for the former.

In preparing these volumes for the public, I have entered upon the task with the sincere desire to avoid doing injustice to any one, whether on the National or Confederate side, other than the unavoidable injustice of not making mention often where special mention is due. There must be many errors of omission in this work, because the subject is too large to be treated of in two volumes in such way as to do justice to all the officers and men engaged. There were thousands of instances, during the rebellion, of individual, company, regimental and brigade deeds of heroism which deserve special mention and are not here alluded to. The troops engaged in them will have to look to the detailed reports of their individual commanders for the full history of those deeds.

The first volume, as well as a portion of the second, was written before I had reason to suppose I was in a critical condition of health. Later I was reduced almost to the point of death, and it became impossible for me to attend to anything for weeks. I have, however, somewhat regained my strength, and am able, often, to devote as many hours a day as a person should devote to such work. I would have more hope of satisfying the expectation of the public if I could have allowed myself more time. I have used my best efforts, with the aid of my eldest son, F. D. Grant, assisted by his brothers, to verify from the records every statement of fact given. The comments are my own, and show how I saw the matters treated of whether others saw them in the same light or not.

With these remarks I present these volumes to the public, asking no favor but hoping they will meet the approval of the reader.

Now let's look at a version of the passage that has been annotated through close reading.

Excerpt from *Personal Memoirs of U. S. Grant (Annotated)*

Explaining why he didn't write before

Larger context

Vocab?

Reason for writing now/motivation

Although frequently urged by friends to write my memoirs I had determined never to do so, nor to write anything for publication. At the age of nearly sixty-two I received an injury from a fall, which confined me closely to the house while it did not apparently affect my general health. This made study a pleasant pastime. Shortly after, the rascality of a business partner developed itself by the announcement of a failure. This was followed soon after by universal depression of all securities, which seemed to threaten the extinction of a good part of the income still retained, and for which I am indebted to the kindly act of friends. At this juncture the editor of the *Century Magazine* asked me to write a few articles for him. I consented for the money it gave me; for at that moment I was living upon borrowed money. The work I found congenial, and I determined to continue it. The event is an important one for me, for good or evil; I hope for the former.

Statement of Project

Acknowledging limitations/building authority

Indicates primary audience—other soldiers?

In preparing these volumes for the public, I have entered upon the task with the sincere desire to avoid doing injustice to any one, whether on the National or Confederate side, other than the unavoidable injustice of not making mention often where special mention is due. There must be many errors of omission in this work, because the subject is too large to be treated of in two volumes in such way as to do justice to all the officers and men engaged. There were thousands of instances, during the rebellion, of individual, company, regimental and brigade deeds of heroism which deserve special mention and are not here alluded to. The troops engaged in them will have to look to the detailed reports of their individual commanders for the full history of those deeds.

Suggests differences between the two?

Higher expectation of truthfulness?

Suggests there may be controversy?

The first volume, as well as a portion of the second, was written before I had reason to suppose I was in a critical condition of health. Later I was reduced almost to the point of death, and it became impossible for me to attend to anything for weeks. I have, however, somewhat regained my strength, and am able, often, to devote as many hours a day as a person should devote to such work. I would have more hope of satisfying the expectation of the public if I could have allowed myself more time. I have used my best efforts, with the aid of my eldest son, F. D. Grant, assisted by his brothers, to verify from the records every statement of fact given. The comments are my own, and show how I saw the matters treated of whether others saw them in the same light or not.

With these remarks I present these volumes to the public, asking no favor but hoping they will meet the approval of the reader.

1. Which of the following best describes the purpose of the passage?
    - **A.** To articulate the historical significance of the work readers are beginning
    - **B.** To dispel any rumors of ghostwriting and make clear it's all the author's own work
    - **C.** To cover the publisher in terms of liability by blaming inaccuracies on the author
    - **D.** To caution the reader that they shouldn't believe everything they hear
    - **E.** To present the author's reasons for writing and expectations for the work

Let's look at this together—first, what kind of question is it? If you said Main Idea, you are correct! The phrase that should signal "main idea" is "the purpose of the passage." Now, which of these answer choices has the most evidence to support it in the passage? Choice A might look promising because the passage does touch on Grant's accomplishments, which points to the historical significance of his memoir. However, Grant's tone is fairly self-deprecating throughout, which might undercut the idea that he's trying to impress readers with how important his experience is. If you found this on a test you could perhaps consider this choice a "maybe" until you'd finished reading the other options, but we can assume this is not going to be the *best* description of the passage. Choice B is incorrect—it's reading way too much into the author's description of his health problems and his enthusiasm for the project. Choice C is incorrect because the author doesn't mention the publisher, and does describe his sons helping to verify the contents (though he does somewhat cover himself by acknowledging that no one person's account could capture everything that occurred). Choice D is incorrect—it is not supported by the passage. That leaves us with choice E, which accurately sums up the purpose of an introduction like this, in which the author explains how he came to write the work and sets the tone for his readers. **The correct answer is E.**

2. The relationship between the first and second paragraphs is
    - **A.** a segue from a broad overview to a specific discussion of events in the author's life.
    - **B.** moving from why the author decided to write into an explanation that seeks to manage audience expectations.
    - **C.** the first is an apology to readers for the quality of the writing, while the second is a defense of his methodology.
    - **D.** the first establishes the author's qualifications, while the second continues on to assert the importance of his narrative.
    - **E.** an opening that's *in medias res*, but broadening to become an interpretive look at key events in the narrative.

Which answer did you choose? This question is under the subcategory of organization—the focus on structural relationship should tip you off—but which answer is correct? The key terms in choice A are "broad overview" and "specific discussion of events"—do you see either of those in the first two paragraphs? The first paragraph actually has a more specific breakdown of the events leading to his writing, while the second seems to cover the big picture—so this choice isn't correct because it has the relationship backward. Now for choice B: If you look at the annotated version of the passage, you'll see a note commenting on the way the very first sentence reflects the author's explanation for what prompted him to write; the second paragraph then explains his project—"to avoid doing injustice"—while acknowledging that he couldn't have captured "the full history." This is an excellent rhetorical tool to help calibrate your audience's expectations by owning up to what you could not do and describing what you hoped to accomplish. **The correct answer is B.** Choice C is incorrect because there's no apology in the first paragraph, nor any specific discussion of how the author set about writing (that actually comes in the third paragraph). Choice D is incorrect because the first paragraph is almost comically devoid of an explanation of the author's credentials or experience that might justify a memoir, and as in the last question, he is not given to bragging about his narrative's significance to other people. Choice E is incorrect—*in medias res* might be a phrase that you aren't familiar with (it means "in the middle of things," for example, if Grant had chosen to open with dialogue or a specific recollection of an event from his Civil War campaign), but the fact that there are no key events mentioned in the second paragraph confirms it.

Be precise when going back and forth between a question and a specific line or paragraph number; it's easy to get flustered or distracted and miss the fact that a question is deliberately asking about a phrase or device that doesn't occur in the paragraph under discussion.

3. What explanation does the author offer for not writing his memoirs sooner?

A. He was injured.

B. He was impoverished.

C. He didn't have a good reason to write.

D. He was traveling.

E. He couldn't think of anything to say.

This question is providing several interpretations of the opening paragraph and asking you to choose the one that is supported by evidence in the passage. As you'll note the first paragraph indicates Grant didn't undertake his memoirs until *after* he was injured and impoverished, choices A and B are incorrect. As he was injured and homebound, and therefore unable to travel, you can conclude choice D is incorrect; while Grant is humble, he mentions in the very first sentence that friends were urging him to write his memoirs. It's reasonable to conclude that his refusal to write didn't come from not knowing what to say. That leaves us with choice C, which is supported by the evidence that the author didn't begin writing until he had several very good reasons to write—not only that friends urged him to, not only that he was injured and had the time, not only that he needed the money, but that he found the work "congenial" and realized it was important to him. **The correct answer is C.**

4. Which of the following best represents the author's intended audience?

A. Presidential and Civil War historians

B. Friends and family

C. Fellow statesmen and opponents

D. The general public, but especially soldiers

E. Readers conducting in-depth research

The correct answer is D. Grant refers to the public multiple times in this passage, but also gives a particular mention to soldiers, whom he knows are most likely to find things missing or undervalued. He acknowledges repeatedly the limitations of his perspective, which might compromise its value to historians, fellow politicians, or researchers, so the other choices are incorrect. This is an inference question, so although each of these groups is likely part of his intended audience, you have to determine that based on Grant's stated purpose, and his concern for soldiers, choice D is the best option.

5. The use of "whether others saw them the same way or not" in this context suggests what?
   - **A.** Grant believes the Civil War was an illegitimate conflict and won't consider other perspectives.
   - **B.** Grant doesn't respect those who fought for the Confederacy and diminishes their contributions.
   - **C.** Grant knows there are two sides to every story and hopes to account for both.
   - **D.** Grant doesn't care what anyone else thinks and wants to craft his own narrative.
   - **E.** Grant was already aware there would be disputed accounts of the war.

This is another inference question, because it requires you to read between the lines and detect what Grant is *not* actually saying about the broader context in which he is writing. When writing an autobiography, as we've discussed already, authors can either strive for objectivity or embrace their particular experience. In this part of the passage, Grant is acknowledging that there are multiple perspectives but that he has chosen to recount and verify his own, even though others may disagree. Choice C is incorrect because Grant is specifically saying that he *can't* account for things he didn't experience. Choice E is therefore the best answer. Choice A disregards the fact that Grant refers to all the acts of heroism he won't have time to get into. Choice B is incorrect because Grant has explicitly said he seeks to do no harm to either Union or Confederate soldiers. Choice D is incorrect because Grant has been thoughtful throughout the passage of how others will react, demonstrating that he knows many individual narratives can coexist. **The correct answer is E.**

From "Magmas to Metals" (from the United States Geological Survey, USGS.gov)

No one wants to have an active volcano in their backyard (just ask Dionisio Pulido*), but ancient eroded volcanoes can sometimes be literal goldmines for mineral ores.

Here at USGS, one way we're studying how molten earth cools into mineable ores is by looking at something called melt inclusions. Although it may sound like a particularly fancy hot sandwich, melt inclusions are actually tiny pockets of magma that get trapped in the crystals of growing igneous rocks.

Traditionally, volcano scientists study melt inclusions because they give us a snapshot of the conditions which drove explosive eruptions. Today, USGS scientists are looking at melt inclusions when studying mineral deposits. Thus, the study of how we get from magma to metal, as the saying goes, is an important one for learning where large mineral deposits might be found. So how do tiny hot pockets of melted rock help us learn about how and where mineral deposits might form? Just like insects getting trapped in amber, these melt inclusions give us a snapshot of what conditions were like when the rock was first forming.

Igneous rocks, which are where many hardrock mineral ores are found, take thousands, even millions, of years to form. So when they're studied, they only show the final product of all those years of development. Melt inclusions, on the other hand, remain mostly unchanged. By giving us an idea of what the original melt composition looked like, melt inclusions help us understand why that particular set of minerals formed as the magma cooled.

For instance, the hot mess of molten rock and magma can be thought of as a box of Legos. The box of legos (like the molten mix) contains the different colors and shapes of blocks to build structures (the mineral ores). As we use up legos from the box (melted rock cools and minerals begin to form) there are fewer legos remaining to choose from to build new structures. Similarly, when magma crystallizes underground, elements are removed from the mix to form some minerals, and they are not available to form others.

Melt inclusions can lead us to a better understanding of how and where metals like gold, copper, tin, zinc, and tungsten form.

*A Mexican farmer in whose field the volcano Parícutin suddenly erupted in 1943

Source: https://www.usgs.gov/news/magmas-metals

6. Which of the following best describes the author's tone in this excerpt?

A. Humorous and irreverent

B. Technical and dense

C. Informative and accessible

D. Analytical and practical

E. Assertive and brisk

Although the author is comparing geological features to sandwiches and LEGO®, the writer of the passage is still taking his job of explaining melt inclusions seriously, so choice A is not the right answer. The passage is also not overly technical, and the time the writer takes to unpack the LEGO comparison should be enough to prove the author wasn't going for density. Choice D reflects the passage's seriousness but is overstating the intensity of its analysis, though the passage does end on a practical note. Choice E is incorrect because it misreads the confident energy of the writer's words. Choice C is the best answer because it best reflects the content and quality of the passage—what it says is informative, what it does is provide access to these concepts for the average reader, the number one job of a science writer. **The correct answer is C.**

7. All of the following are examples of "voice" EXCEPT:

A. "No one wants to have an active volcano in their backyard (just ask Dionisio Pulido), but ancient eroded volcanoes can sometimes be literal goldmines for mineral ores."

B. "Although it may sound like a particularly fancy hot sandwich, melt inclusions are actually tiny pockets of magma that get trapped in the crystals of growing igneous rocks."

C. "Just like insects getting trapped in amber, these melt inclusions give us a snapshot of what conditions were like when the rock was first forming."

D. "For instance, the hot mess of molten rock and magma can be thought of as a box of Legos."

E. "Melt inclusions can lead us to a better understanding of how and where metals like gold, copper, tin, zinc, and tungsten form."

To answer questions about "voice," think about which sentences indicate the thoughts and opinions of a specific writer were behind them. In choice A, the writer makes a connection with another geologic event in a casual, offhand manner and invites the reader to imagine being part of the experience. In choice B, the writer brings a bit of levity to the passage in comparing melt inclusions to a patty melt (or possibly a hot pocket). Choice C features the introduction of a comparison to a very different kind of scientific concept that might be more widely recognized, which requires some creativity to observe, as does choice D, where the writer compares geological features to common children's toys to set up an extended metaphor. Choice E is the best answer because it is straightforward and simply explains the practical application of understanding melt inclusions. **The correct answer is E.**

8. Which of the following elements does the writer NOT use to help the reader understand the concept of melt inclusions?

A. Extended comparisons

B. Rhetorical questions

C. Etymological explanations

D. Parenthetical asides

E. Colloquial expressions

The correct answer is C. You should be able to identify each of the other answer choices in the passage. Extended comparisons (choice A) and parenthetical asides (choice D) join forces with colloquial expressions in paragraph 4, and you can find a rhetorical question and answer structure in paragraph 3. The article does not get into the etymology, or word origins, of any of the key terms or concepts.

9. In paragraph 3, the writer of this passage makes use of each of the following types of transition, EXCEPT:

A. Addition

B. Comparison

C. Consequence

D. Contrast

E. Sequence

Let's take a moment to identify each of the transitions that appears in paragraph 3:

Traditionally, volcano scientists study melt inclusions because they give us a snapshot of the conditions which drove explosive eruptions. **Today**, USGS scientists are looking at melt inclusions when studying mineral deposits. **Thus**, the study of how we get from magma to metal, as the saying goes, is an important one for learning where large mineral deposits might be found. So how do tiny hot pockets of melted rock help us learn about how and where mineral deposits might form? **Just like insects getting trapped in amber**, these melt inclusions give us a snapshot of what conditions were like when the rock was first forming.

1. There are actually ten types of transitions at your writerly disposal—addition, comparison, concession, contrast, consequence, emphasis, example, sequence, space, and summary. This particular passage uses contrast (see *Traditionally*, indicating it has previously been done

differently), sequence (*Today*, as opposed to yesterday), consequence (*Thus*, i.e., as a result of …), and comparison ("Just like insects …") to move from one idea to the next. The only one of the answer choices not accounted for is choice A, addition (which you would typically see with signal words like *Also* or *besides*).

10. The world "molten" (*line 4*) most nearly means

A. having lost all its feathers.

B. liquefied by intense heat.

C. congealed mineral fragments.

D. glowing with brilliance.

E. eroded by pressure.

The correct answer is B. You might be more familiar with the word *molten* in a dessert context, but here it's used to refer to rock that has been liquefied by extreme heat. The context clues to point you to choice B are the repeated references to cooling, melted rock.

Now that you've had a chance to review question types in order, separated into the categories Analysis and Rhetoric, let's try a passage in which they're all mixed together and see if you can still check off each kind of question you should expect to see.

Leo Tolstoy on Shakespeare, continued

1) But it is not enough that Shakespeare's characters are placed in tragic positions which are impossible, do not flow from the course of events, are inappropriate to time and space—these personages, besides this, act in a way which is out of keeping with their definite character, and is quite arbitrary. It is generally asserted that in Shakespeare's dramas the characters are specially well expressed, that, notwithstanding their vividness, they are many-sided, like those of living people; that, while exhibiting the characteristics of a given individual, they at the same time wear the features of man in general; it is usual to say that the delineation of character in Shakespeare is the height of perfection.

2) This is asserted with such confidence and repeated by all as indisputable truth; but however much I endeavored to find confirmation of this in Shakespeare's dramas, I always found the opposite. In reading any of Shakespeare's dramas whatever, I was, from the very first, instantly convinced that he was lacking in the most important, if not the only, means of portraying characters: individuality of language, *i.e.*, the style of speech of every person being natural to his character. This is absent from Shakespeare. All his characters speak, not their own, but always one and the same Shakespearian, pretentious, and unnatural language, in which not only they could not speak, but in which no living man ever has spoken or does speak.

3) No living men could or can say, as Lear says, that he would divorce his wife in the grave should Regan not receive him, or that the heavens would crack with shouting, or that the winds would burst, or that the wind wishes to blow the land into the sea, or that the curled waters wish to flood the shore, as the

gentleman describes the storm, or that it is easier to bear one's grief and the soul leaps over many sufferings when grief finds fellowship, or that Lear has become childless while I am fatherless, as Edgar says, or use similar unnatural expressions with which the speeches of all the characters in all Shakespeare's dramas overflow.

4) …In Shakespeare there is no language of living individuals—that language which in the drama is the chief means of setting forth character. If gesticulation be also a means of expressing character, as in ballets, this is only a secondary means. Moreover, if the characters speak at random and in a random way, and all in one and the same diction, as is the case in Shakespeare's work, then even the action of gesticulation is wasted. Therefore, whatever the blind panegyrists of Shakespeare may say, in Shakespeare there is no expression of character. Those personages who, in his dramas, stand out as characters, are characters borrowed by him from former works which have served as the foundation of his dramas, and they are mostly depicted, not by the dramatic method which consists in making each person speak with his own diction, but in the epic method of one person describing the features of another.

5) The perfection with which Shakespeare expresses character is asserted chiefly on the ground of the characters of Lear, Cordelia, Othello, Desdemona, Falstaff, and Hamlet. But all these characters, as well as all the others, instead of belonging to Shakespeare, are taken by him from dramas, chronicles, and romances anterior to him. All these characters not only are not rendered more powerful by him, but, in most cases, they are weakened and spoilt. This is very striking in this drama of "King Lear," which we are examining, taken by him from the drama "King Leir," by an unknown author. The characters of this drama, that of King Lear, and especially of Cordelia, not only were not created by Shakespeare, but have been strikingly weakened and deprived of force by him, as compared with their appearance in the older drama.

11. In context, the word "anterior" most nearly means

A. inside of.

B. presaging.

C. preceding.

D. outliving.

E. overshadowing.

The correct answer is C. Choice A might have tripped you up if you thought of *interior*, and choice B if you knew it had something to do with "pre" but thought the earlier works might have hinted at the eventual arrival of Shakespeare. Choice D is incorrect because it refers to something lasting longer than Shakespeare's work, rather than existing ahead of his time. Choice E is incorrect because even though Tolstoy may prefer these earlier works, it is not reasonable to say Shakespeare is overshadowed by his source material. If you find vocabulary-in-context questions challenging, spend some time learning prefixes and suffixes—that would have helped you recognize *ant–* as in *anticipate* or *antechamber* (not to be confused with *anti*—meaning "against").

12. According to the passage, what is Tolstoy's primary complaint about Shakespeare's work?

A. His characters' unrealistic speaking style

B. His anti-Semitic characterizations

C. His lack of believable female characters

D. The violence of his histories

E. The bleakness of his tragedies

The correct answer is A. While the passage opens with Tolstoy's list of grievances against Shakespeare, *King Lear* in particular, the aspect that gets the most attention in this passage is the unnatural, inhuman way that Shakespeare writes dialogue for his characters. According to Tolstoy, that style of Shakespearean speech that many scholars do close-read for nuance and individual character development leaves his portrayals hollow. Choice B is incorrect because Tolstoy doesn't get into the moral or social implications of Shakespeare's characters, nor his representation of women (choice C). He does touch on the violence (choice D), as well as the unrelenting sadness (choice E) of Shakespeare's tragedies, but these are secondary to Tolstoy's objections to the diction Shakespeare employs for his characters.

13. Paragraph 4 marks a shift from a(n)

A. general overview of Shakespeare's flaws to a targeted attack on his artistry.

B. discussion of the flaws of Shakespeare's dialogue to his lack of originality.

C. assessment of Shakespeare's relevance to a take-down of his cult of personality.

D. acknowledgment of his historical significance to a denial of his continued relevance.

E. speculation on what else he might have written to a survey of his legitimate achievements.

The correct answer is B. This is the point at which Tolstoy moves toward critiquing the way Shakespeare adapted characters from other stories rather than dismissing his voice as a writer of dialogue. Choice A is incorrect because this section was already fairly focused; it was never a general overview. Choices C and D are incorrect because this section is not examining Shakespeare's legacy or his historical significance, it is specifically analyzing his approach to individual characters. Choice E is incorrect because it is not supported by the passage.

14. In the passage, Tolstoy avoids invoking specific critics or scholars by use of which of the following?

A. Rhetorical questioning

B. Passive voice

C. Parenthetical asides

D. Allegorical comparisons

E. Errors of omission

The correct answer is B. Rather than engaging with the work of individuals, Tolstoy refers to a general disembodied common wisdom with phrases like "It is generally asserted" and "It is usual to say." Choice A is incorrect because Tolstoy does not seem much interested in anyone else's opinion.

Choice C is incorrect because he speaks directly, without meandering or digressing from his main point. Choice D is incorrect because he does not compare Shakespeare via narratives that involve symbolic figures. Choice E is incorrect because his approach, while passive, is not omitting crucial information that could compromise the efficacy of his argument.

15. What does the author mean by "blind panegyrists"?

A. Patrons of Shakespearean theater

B. Eager Shakespeare actors

C. Dismissive Shakespeare critics

D. Effusive Shakespeare scholars

E. Shakespeare's collaborators

The correct answer is D. The key context clue here is "blind"—since Tolstoy has been making observations that run counter to the high praise and veneration Shakespeare receives from "all," it's logical to infer that these unnamed enthusiasts are likely to be scholars. Choice A doesn't tell us if these are particularly talkative or appreciative patrons, merely that they attend the theater. Choice B is incorrect because there is no discussion of actors in the section. Choice C is incorrect because you don't get much more dismissive than Tolstoy on this topic. Choice E is incorrect because it is not supported by the passage; Tolstoy discusses Shakespeare's influences (or thefts) but not people he worked with. Choice D is therefore correct—even if you weren't entirely sure about the meaning of *effusive*, you could conclude by the process of elimination that panegyrists has to do with people who speak about something with great enthusiasm.

16. What other choice could Tolstoy have made in this section to moderate his tone from one of sharp criticism to one of more even-handed assessment?

A. Discussed other playwrights he enjoys and provided examples of their individually expressive dialogue or characters, to give the reader a spectrum of "voice" to consider

B. Acknowledged that in his own time, Shakespeare was more daring than most writers at the time gave him credit for, so the reader could have a sense of context

C. Provided examples of the text that most critics hold up as perfection, as well as the lines that Tolstoy finds unnatural, so the reader could decide for himself

D. Described specific performances that he disliked in order to show how actors bring a play to life, rather than speak to the reader about the literature on the page

E. Spoken at length about his own work and how much more distinctive his characterizations are, so the reader could trust his authority

The correct answer is C. This choice would have been most likely to illustrate Tolstoy's point in a way that seemed more like an observation than a harsh denunciation. By not providing evidence of what scholars think is eloquent or artful about Shakespeare, we as readers can't determine for ourselves if we agree with the supporters or with Tolstoy, who is quoting the verse out of context in paragraph 3. Choice A is incorrect because it would likely have involved equally harsh denunciations of Shakespeare compared to these other writers. Choice B is incorrect because this does not appear to be an opinion that Tolstoy espouses. Choice D is incorrect because Tolstoy is not seeking to critique performance but writing in this section. Choice E is incorrect because this would not moderate his tone, but add a layer of self-aggrandizement that wouldn't be any likelier to accomplish this goal.

17. Compared with the rest of the passage, the diction of paragraph 2 is

A. more insightful and restrained.

B. less abrasive and unfounded.

C. less technically analytical.

D. more personally indignant.

E. more literary and eloquent.

The correct answer is D. The first few lines of paragraph 2 are the only place where Tolstoy permits himself to be present in his review as an observer—the rest of the passage certainly reflects his opinions, even in tension with other leading critics, but this is the section of the passage in which his ire directly relates to a personal pronoun.

18. What is the relationship between paragraphs 2 and 3?

A. In paragraph 2, Tolstoy summarizes his points thus far in his review; in paragraph 3, he develops one particular theme to focus this section.

B. In paragraph 2, Tolstoy establishes reader expectations for Shakespearean verse; in paragraph 3, he introduces counter examples that might dissuade the reader.

C. In paragraph 2, Tolstoy acknowledges the strengths of Shakespeare's characterizations; in paragraph 3, he revisits his particular favorites.

D. In paragraph 2, Tolstoy speaks generally of the flaws in Shakespearean dialogue; in paragraph 3, he presents individual lines that he finds unrealistic.

E. In paragraph 2, Tolstoy shows off his own lyrical prowess; in paragraph 3, he juxtaposes his approach to character with Shakespeare's.

The correct answer is D. Following his move from summary to argument, Tolstoy follows paragraph 2's description with specific evidence of language from *King Lear* that he finds underwhelming. Choice A more accurately describes the relationship between paragraphs 1 and 2; choice B is incorrect because Tolstoy begins with the counterargument at the end of paragraph 1, and then responds to it in paragraph 2. Choice C is incorrect because Tolstoy doesn't seem to think Shakespeare *has* many strengths. Choice E is incorrect because Tolstoy is not holding up his characterizations next to Shakespeare's. He wisely leaves that to future critics.

19. This passage can best be described as which of the following types of writing?

A. Critical close-reading

B. Theatrical review

C. Scholarly analysis

D. Descriptive overview

E. Dramaturgical preview

The correct answer is A. It reflects both the tone and the project of the passage (what it says and what it does). While Tolstoy is commenting on a work of drama, he is not discussing a specific production, which means choice B is out. Choice C is also incorrect because Tolstoy isn't engaging with specific critics or citing any sources. Choice D is incorrect because we don't get a sense of the play's narrative arc from this section (though he does devote a section to it elsewhere in the full version of this piece). Choice E is incorrect—Dramaturgy is the study of drama, but a preview would be a piece of writing intended to prepare an audience for what they were about to see. Since Tolstoy is discussing *King Lear* as a work of literature, and not as it was interpreted by a particular performance, choice E can't be the answer.

20. Based on the very first sentence of the excerpt, you can infer that the previous sections of the essay have already covered all of the following EXCEPT:

A. The unlikeliness of Lear's tragedy

B. The faulty geography of the play's setting

C. The anachronistic references that Lear's fool makes

D. The inconsistent passage of time in Acts 3 and 4

E. Underdeveloped characterization of Lear's daughters

The correct answer is E. Even if you haven't read the play, the question is specifically asking you to infer what types of plot points Tolstoy could have used as examples earlier in his essay, which he would be summarizing when he says, "But it is not enough that Shakespeare's characters are placed in tragic positions which are impossible, do not flow from the course of events, are inappropriate to time and space …" Since this excerpt contains more specific discussion of characterization, you know it wasn't covered already, and the other answer choices must be incorrect.

How did you do?

Don't worry if you're still building up your close-reading and question-decoding skills. We're going to spend some time getting to know the Free Response section of the exam, and then there'll be three practice tests waiting for you in the back of this book, plus two more online! By test day, you'll feel like Analysis and Rhetoric are the most familiar tools in your toolbox.

SUMMING IT UP

- You will answer 52–55 multiple-choice questions in Section 1 of the AP® English Language and Composition Exam.
- This section is worth 45% of your score; it is weighted slightly less heavily than the free-response essays.
- You will have one hour to answer as many questions as you can.
- You will receive a point for every correct answer. You do not lose points for incorrect answers or unanswered questions.
- As a general guideline, read all the way through the passages and questions once before you begin.
- The passages will be taken from one of the following subcategories of nonfiction—essays, autobiography, science, journalism, or criticism.
- Analysis is the process of taking something apart to examine it, or reducing it to a simpler form. Question types that fall within this category include main idea, organization, evidence, and inference.
- Rhetoric questions ask you about tone, voice, diction, syntax, and vocabulary choices the author has made.
- When you read each passage, annotate as you read, marking the main idea, key terms or phrases, and rhetorical strategies that you notice.
- When you're initially skimming the passage, put an asterisk by moments of transition that you notice and underline any arguments.
- Keep an eye out for especially striking literary devices, unusual sentences, or moments where the writer's tone or voice seems to shift.
- If you are unsure about the significance of a particular line (or lines), mark it with a question mark in the margin.
- Learn to recognize questions asking you about the main idea, organization, or evidence, or to make an inference, identify vocabulary, assess the tone, voice, or diction, or to analyze the syntax of a given passage.

Chapter 3

Free-Response Questions on the AP® English Language and Composition Exam

OVERVIEW

- What is Your Ideal Writing Process?
- How to Approach a Prompt
- Pre-Writing Strategies
- The Three Essay Types
- Timeline for Test-Day Writing
- Guidelines for Writing a Good AP® Essay
- Sample Prompts and Passages
- Summing It Up

Picture yourself on test day—you've made it through the multiple-choice exam and you're confident in your close-reading and analytical skills. Then, you turn the page and see three free-response essay prompts awaiting your attention. How are you feeling? Eager? Nervous? Increasingly aware of the clock ticking? Even experienced writers may be daunted by the demands of the rigorous and multifaceted essay exam—that's okay! We're going to explore the ins and outs of the exam and prepare you with strategies and techniques so you will arrive at the free-response section ready to write your way to a top score.

As a reminder, the three kinds of free-response questions you'll face fall under the categories of synthesis, analysis, and argument. In this chapter we'll talk about how to prepare for each one, how to manage your time on test day, and what types of rhetorical strategies you'll need to do your best work on this section of the exam.

WHAT IS YOUR IDEAL WRITING PROCESS?

Many of the same skills you've been cultivating for the multiple-choice section will stand you in good stead here—identifying the main idea; analyzing the organization of the passages; detecting the difference between argument and the evidence that supports it; making connections and inferences between texts; interpreting vocabulary; and assessing tone, voice, diction, and syntax. But writing an essay in response to a text, or synthesizing multiple texts, requires you to go further—you'll have to move from analysis of other people's ideas to generating ideas of your own.

Take a moment to think about your typical writing process. Do you like to free-write after you read a prompt, just keep your pencil moving on the paper (or fingers moving on your keyboard) and record your initial thoughts? Do you like to brainstorm in an open-ended way, mapping your thoughts out as they arise and connecting them to one another other without worrying about the order in which they appear? Or maybe your approach is more structured—you don't begin writing until you have a clear idea of your thesis or argument, and then you create an outline of supporting points on which to base your essay.

Pause for some reflection here—grab a sheet of paper and a pen, or open up a document on your computer. Think about the most recent writing experiences you've had. If it was for a test, how did you prepare? What went well? What did you struggle with? If it was for a longer assignment, what information did you need in order to complete it? Was there research involved? How did you handle the pressure of a deadline? What kind of revision did you do? How did it turn out? What do you wish you had done differently?

TIP

Maybe your teacher likes you to prepare for and craft your essays in a specific way, but on test day it's just you and your exam booklet, so to thine own self be true.

No matter what your approach is, get to know yourself as a writer while you're practicing in class and on homework assignments. Every writer's process is different, and while it's good to be open to trying out different techniques, you can waste a lot of time and energy fighting your natural process!

Don't force yourself to just start writing if you know you need to organize your thoughts first; don't commit to a main idea initially if you need to scrawl some associative thoughts before you begin drafting. If your brain only works by sketching out fragmentary ideas in words or even images, then let it! That said, you only have about 40 minutes per essay, so a little later we'll talk about how to compress a typical writing timeline so you don't run out of time.

HOW TO APPROACH A PROMPT

The following passage is one you could see in a variety of contexts—maybe given with the initial prompt, maybe as one of the sources you can use when writing your essay. We'll look at possible related prompts after we read it closely. First, let's practice the same kind of close-reading techniques we introduced during our analysis of the best way to examine multiple-choice sections in Chapter 2.

Some important context—this is an excerpt from a biography of suffragist Susan B. Anthony, written in 1899 by Ida Husted Harper. It takes place while women's rights advocates were fighting for temperance legislation (the kind that would eventually lead to the passage of Prohibition in 1920) and women's access to decision-making in the halls of education, law, and government.

> ... The State Teachers' Convention was held in Corinthian Hall, Rochester, August 3, 1853, and true to Susan B. Anthony's resolve made the year previous she put aside everything else in order to attend. According to the rules any one paying a dollar was entitled to all the rights and privileges of the convention; so she paid her dollar and took her seat. There were over 500 teachers in attendance, two-thirds at least being women. For two entire days Miss Anthony sat there, and during that time not a woman spoke; in all the deliberations there

was not the slightest recognition of their presence, and they did not vote on any question, though all had paid the fee and were members of the association. In a letter describing the occasion Miss Anthony said: "My heart was filled with grief and indignation thus to see the minority, simply because they were men, presuming that in them was vested all wisdom and knowledge; that they needed no aid, no counsel from the majority. And what was most humiliating of all was to look into the faces of those women and see that by far the larger proportion were perfectly satisfied with the position assigned them."

Toward the close of the second day's session the subject under discussion was, "Why the profession of teacher is not as much respected as that of lawyer, doctor or minister?" After listening for several hours, Miss Anthony felt that the decisive moment had come and, rising in her seat, she said, "Mr. President." A bombshell would not have created greater commotion. For the first time in all history a woman's voice was heard in a teachers' convention. Every neck was craned and a profound hush fell upon the assembly. Charles Davies, LL. D., author of Davies' text books and professor of mathematics at West Point, was president. In full-dress costume with buff vest, blue coat and brass buttons, he was the Great Mogul. At length recovering from the shock of being thus addressed by a woman, he leaned forward and asked with satirical politeness, "What will the lady have?" "I wish to speak to the question under discussion," said Miss Anthony calmly, although her heart was beating a tattoo. Turning to the few rows of men in front of him, for the women occupied the back seats, he inquired, "What is the pleasure of the convention?" "I move she shall be heard," said one man; this was seconded by another, and thus was precipitated a debate which lasted half an hour, although she had precisely the same right to speak as any man who was taking part in the discussion.

She stood during all this time, fearing to lose the floor if she sat down. At last a vote was taken, men only voting, and it was carried in the affirmative by a small majority. Miss Anthony then said: "It seems to me you fail to comprehend the cause of the disrespect of which you complain. Do you not see that so long as society says woman has not brains enough to be a doctor, lawyer or minister, but has plenty to be a teacher, every man of you who condescends to teach, tacitly admits before all Israel and the sun that he has no more brains than a woman?"—and sat down. She had intended to draw the conclusion that the only way to place teaching upon a level with other professions was either to admit woman to them or exclude her from teaching, but her trembling limbs would sustain her no longer.

The convention soon adjourned for the day and, as Miss Anthony went out of the hall, many of the women drew away from her and said audibly: "Did you ever see such a disgraceful performance?" "I never was so ashamed of my sex." But a few of them gathered about her and said: "You have taught us our lesson and hereafter we propose to make ourselves heard."

…

The women had no desire to pull down the building, entablature and all, about the head of the magnificent President Davies, but some of them were aroused to the injustice with which they had so long been treated. To the astonishment of the professor and his following, these resolutions were presented by Mrs. Northrop, a teacher in the Rochester schools:

Resolved, That this association recognizes the right of female teachers to share in all the privileges and deliberations of this body.

Resolved, That female teachers do not receive an adequate and sufficient compensation, and that, as salaries should be regulated only according to the amount of labor performed, this association will endeavor by judicious and efficient action to remove this existing evil.

An attempt was made to smother them, and when Mrs. Northrop asked why they had not been read, the president blandly replied that he regretted they could not be reached but other order of business preceded them. Mrs. Northrop, having found her voice, proceeded to speak strongly on the discrimination made against women in the matter of salaries, and was ably supported by her sister, Mrs. J.R. Vosburg. J. D. Fanning, of New York, recording secretary, asked that the resolutions be read, which was done. Miss Anthony then made a forcible speech in their favor and they were passed unanimously, to the utter amazement and discomfiture of President Davies.

Close-Reading Your Given Passages/Sources

Now, take a look at some sample notes you could write while making your way through this passage for a close-read. Of course your notes will be different from the ones presented here, but these examples will give you a good idea of the types of passage highlights you should be making.

Locating us in time—this took place before the Civil War, and well before women received the right to vote

Establishing the status quo—the types of exclusion and injustice Anthony was fighting

… The State Teachers' Convention was held in Corinthian Hall, Rochester, August 3, 1853, and true to Susan B. Anthony's resolve made the year previous she put aside everything else in order to attend. According to the rules any one paying a dollar was entitled to all the rights and privileges of the convention; so she paid her dollar and took her seat. There were over 500 teachers in attendance, two-thirds at least being women. For two entire days Miss Anthony sat there, and during that time not a woman spoke; in all the deliberations there was not the slightest recognition of their presence, and they did not vote on any question, though all had paid the fee and were members of the association. In a letter describing the occasion Miss Anthony said: "My heart was filled with grief and indignation thus to see the minority, simply because they were men, presuming that in them was vested all wisdom and knowledge; that they needed no aid, no counsel from the majority. And what was most humiliating of all was to look into the faces of those women and see that by far the larger proportion were perfectly satisfied with the position assigned them."

Toward the close of the second day's session the subject under discussion was, "Why the profession of teacher is not as much respected as that of lawyer, doctor or minister?" After listening for several hours, Miss Anthony felt that the decisive moment had come and, rising in her seat, she said, "Mr. President." A bombshell would not have created greater commotion. For the first time in all history a woman's voice was heard in a teachers' convention. Every neck was craned and a profound hush fell upon the assembly. Charles Davies, LL. D., author of Davies' text books and professor of mathematics at West Point, was president. In full-dress costume with buff vest, blue coat and brass buttons, he was the Great Mogul. At length recovering from the shock of being thus addressed by a woman, he leaned forward and asked with satirical politeness, "What will the lady have?" "I wish to speak to the question under discussion," said Miss Anthony calmly, although her heart was beating a tattoo. Turning to the few rows of men in front of him, for the women occupied the back seats, he inquired, "What is the pleasure of the convention?" "I move she shall be heard," said one man; this was seconded by another, and thus was precipitated a debate which lasted half an hour, although she had precisely the same right to speak as any man who was taking part in the discussion.

Communicates the stakes of the conversation!

Depicted as a buffoon

Highlighting the depth of the problem—the men were allowed to debate whether she could speak, while a man trying to speak was given an opportunity immediately

She stood during all this time, fearing to lose the floor if she sat down. At last a vote was taken, men only voting, and it was carried in the affirmative by a small majority. Miss Anthony then said: "It seems to me you fail to comprehend the cause of the disrespect of which you complain. Do you not see that so long as society says woman has not brains enough to be a doctor, lawyer or minister, but has plenty to be a teacher, every man of you who condescends to teach, tacitly admits before all Israel and the sun that he has no more brains than a woman?"—and sat down. She had intended to draw the conclusion that the only way to place teaching upon a level with other professions was either to admit woman to them or exclude her from teaching, but her trembling limbs would sustain her no longer.

The convention soon adjourned for the day and, as Miss Anthony went out of the hall, many of the women drew away from her and said audibly: "Did you ever see such a disgraceful performance?" "I never was so ashamed of my sex." But a few of them gathered about her and said: "You have taught us our lesson and hereafter we propose to make ourselves heard."

…

The women had no desire to pull down the building, entablature and all, about the head of the magnificent President Davies, but some of them were aroused to the injustice with which they had so long been treated. To the astonishment of the professor and his following, these resolutions were presented by Mrs. Northrop, a teacher in the Rochester schools:

Resolved, That this association recognizes the right of female teachers to share in all the privileges and deliberations of this body.

Resolved, That female teachers do not receive an adequate and sufficient compensation, and that, as salaries should be regulated only according to the amount of labor performed, this association will endeavor by judicious and efficient action to remove this existing evil.

Showing the influence of Anthony, and the many-voiced nature of women's fight for equality

An attempt was made to smother them, and when Mrs. Northrop asked why they had not been read, the president blandly replied that he regretted they could not be reached but other order of business preceded them. Mrs. Northrop, having found her voice, proceeded to speak strongly on the discrimination made against women in the matter of salaries, and was ably supported by her sister, Mrs. J.R. Vosburg. J. D. Fanning, of New York, recording secretary, asked that the resolutions be read, which was done. Miss Anthony then made a forcible speech in their favor and they were passed unanimously, to the utter amazement and discomfiture of President Davies.

Sample Prompts

You might see a passage like this as one of several sources on closely related topics around a single theme (for example women's rights or the exclusion of women from seats of power), with a prompt that looks something like the following, for a **synthesis** question:

> The fight for equality in this country has existed along multiple fronts—women seeking the right to vote; African-Americans seeking equality in education, housing, and civil rights; LGBTQ Americans seeking equal protections under the law. These struggles have been led by individuals who helped inspire the movements that eventually enabled these groups to lobby for their rights with demonstrations of of collective strength. But many groups are still fighting for equality—equal pay, equal employment protections, equal representation—or lobbying for a significant change to the status quo.
>
> Read the selected sources carefully, including the introductory information for each source. Then, write a well-organized essay that synthesizes at least three of the sources to produce an argument in favor of a cause that is important to you. Drawing on the legacies of leaders such as Susan B. Anthony, Martin Luther King, Jr., Malcolm X, Ida B. Wells, Harvey Milk, and other voices from these sources, describe the status quo against which you are fighting, and use some of the rhetorical tactics demonstrated by these leaders to persuade your reader that your cause is just and that change must come.

Notice that the prompt is asking you to write a "well-organized" essay—be sure you take the time to figure out what your argument is, what your evidence will be, and where you want to conclude.

Close-reading the prompt: Note that in this case, the given passage is just one of several sources the prompt references. Your final essay response must include an original argument (one that you create and sustain yourself), and it must also incorporate explicit references to a minimum of *three sources*—whether as summary, paraphrase, or direct quotation. You might choose an issue from your everyday life, such as school uniforms, and select some rhetorical techniques or tactics of resistance mentioned in the sources. Or you might talk about a larger issue, such as the lack of pay equity that women, particularly women of color, still face in the United States.

Here's another example of a prompt, this time for an **analysis** question:

> When Susan B. Anthony attended this teacher's convention in Rochester, NY, she and the rest of America's women were still many years from succeeding in their battles for suffrage, temperance, or equal treatment, but this passage presents a snapshot of the tactics necessary for the success of the women's movement. Read the excerpt from her biography carefully, and then in a well-written essay, analyze the rhetorical choices made by Anthony, her biographer, and other women quoted in the extract.

Close-reading the prompt: This free-response prompt isn't asking you to bring any outside context to your examination of the provided text. It is asking you to read the text closely, take note of the rhetorical techniques at work, and then develop your own argument about what the effect those techniques have. You might examine the biographer's use of quotes from the convention attendees, or the biographer's more opinionated comments, or you might focus on what Susan B. Anthony actually said and did at the convention. Notice as many strategies as you can in your close-read, and then decide which ones are worth exploring in your essay response.

Finally, let's take a look at a sample **argument** prompt that asks you to write an essay on the same topic, but in a different style.

> Of a Teacher's Convention that admitted women but did not permit them to vote or speak, Susan B. Anthony once wrote: "My heart was filled with grief and indignation thus to see the minority, simply because they were men, presuming that in them was vested all wisdom and knowledge; that they needed no aid, no counsel from the majority. And what was most humiliating of all was to look into the faces of those women and see that by far the larger proportion were perfectly satisfied with the position assigned them."
>
> In a well-written essay, develop your position on the value or merit of minority representation, of equipping members of minority groups to advocate for themselves and determine their own welfare, or when it might be appropriate to turn authority over to a majority rule. Use evidence from your reading, experience, or observations to support your argument appropriately.

Close-reading the prompt: The big difference between this prompt and the other two types is that this one requires the most input from you, personally. Rather than responding specifically to this source text, or even to Susan B. Anthony's fight for suffrage, you have the opportunity to reframe the conversation around equal rights, and balancing majority and minority interests. You can use contemporary news events, literature, and your own personal experience here. You could talk about a situation in which equal representation ensured a more just outcome than what Susan B. Anthony was facing, or the impact on the minority representatives when their perspective was dismissed the way Anthony's was.

We'll practice each kind of prompt later in the chapter, but for now, just consider this sample passage. What in your close-reading approach might change depending on the kind of prompt it is?

PRE-WRITING STRATEGIES

We already talked about close-reading in the multiple-choice chapter, but let's run through some other common pre-writing tools you may find useful during the free-response essay.

Close-Reading

Make sure you're marking up the passage as you go with your own personal shorthand. Identify main ideas, all evidence presented, and any queries you have after finishing the passage. Close-read the prompt too, not just the texts you've been given to respond to.

Outlining

This is a structured approach that allows you to boil down even complicated ideas to just a couple of words. Outlines are helpful if you tend to start off your essays with a bang and then run out of steam in the second or third paragraph. An outline will jog your memory so you keep your end point in mind, and can even keep you from straying off-topic midway through your essay. You may find this one most useful for the analysis prompt, so you know that you're presenting your point of view in an organized, effective way.

Freewriting

This is an open-ended approach that lets you talk in your own voice, using the personal *I*. If you're someone who struggles to get started, freewriting is great low-stakes practice that just gets your pencil moving and your mind warmed up. One potential pitfall is going over time—unless you've found that your instructive organizational skills are exceptional, try to think of the freewrite as a springboard to start your essay, rather than your opening paragraph. Keep an eye on the clock and stop yourself when 5 minutes have passed. You may find this one most useful for the argument prompt.

Brainstorming

This is the least structured approach—start by putting the main idea of the text in the center of a bubble, then draw lines branching out from the bubble that contain supporting ideas—they may be summaries of evidence from the text, or they may be your responses to the text. You can start with a round of textual references, then branch off of *those* bubbles with your own interpretation. Again, don't let this take up too much time, and be sure you review your answers thoughtfully to curate just the best ones and put them in the most logical order when you start your draft. You may find this one most useful for the synthesis prompt.

THE THREE ESSAY TYPES

Now let's examine each specific prompt type in more detail, with sample prompts and sources, so you get a sense of what you'll see on test day.

Synthesis

The synthesis question is designed to assess your written argumentation skills; it will provide you with multiple written and visual sources that you must read, analyze, and use to develop your own argument. It will be important to cite the sources appropriately, and to go beyond merely summarizing the content of the provided passages.

Here are some sample prompts and source sets to give you a sense of what you might encounter—some are excerpts rather than full articles as published.

#1 Sample Synthesis Prompt

City planning requires balancing the needs and contributions of a whole range of communities and voices. The issue of whether to install bike lanes in a heavily traveled avenue in New York City's borough of Brooklyn requires negotiating complicating factors such as cost, efficiency, community needs and outcomes, and environmental impact.

Assignment: Read the following sources (including any introductory information) carefully. Then, write an essay that evaluates what a city or government agency would need to consider before deciding to move forward to scrap a proposal such as this one. Synthesize at least three of the sources in your answer.

Refer to the sources as Source A, Source B, etc.; titles/authors are included for your convenience.

Source A (news article)

Source B (Terry Mitchell interview)

Source C (NYC Department of Transportation)

Source D (Andi Lenox)

Source E (safety chart)

Source F (Paula Greenberry)

Source A

City planners from the Department of Transportation in Brooklyn, New York, are proposing the addition of eight miles of protected bike lanes—indicated by painted concrete and white hazard lines on the pavement—to a stretch of Fourth Avenue between Boerum Hill and Bay Ridge. Residents are invited to weigh in on the proposal at the next community council meeting in August. Proponents of the new installation suggest it will be safer, encourage environmentally friendly cyclists, take some of the pressure off the beleaguered subway and bus lines in the neighborhood, and will even be good for local businesses. People resistant to the suggested addition argue that business owners will actually lose out on business from drivers who can't see their businesses or find a place to park, it cuts off access to the curb for loading and unloading, and that it encourages cyclists who scoff at stoplights and street signs to ride even more recklessly through automotive traffic. Unveiled as part of the city's Vision Zero initiative, the additional lanes' primary purpose is to reduce pedestrian deaths.

Source B

Interview with Local Bike Lanes Advocate, Terry Mitchell (excerpted)

Q: What are the important factors for residents to know about the Brooklyn bike lane expansion?

A: If Mayor de Blasio really wants to cut down on bike related fatalities and make good on his "Vision Zero" initiative, he *must* follow through and install bike lanes on Fourth Avenue in Brooklyn. Pedestrians need this level of protection if we hope to make any kind of difference on the most dangerous stretch of Fourth Avenue in Brooklyn.

Q: Do you have any concerns about how the roads would be implemented?

A: I think what we've seen in some other neighborhoods was promises that they would be thoroughly installed, but then it's not sufficiently accomplished. The paths are shorter, or they're not installed with high quality materials. We need to keep people and cars apart and bike lanes are the best way to do that.

Q: What's the best design, in your opinion?

A: The most promising is the one that raises the original painted median above street level, using poured concrete and some kind of physical barrier—it's like an elaborate orange cone but it's still something. The fanciest ones have a wider median that can sustain plantings like trees, or even seating. The raised median allows for the biker to ride higher than traffic and be more visible, where the current painted lines leave them at the mercy of drivers who may not always stay in their lanes.

Source C

Since 2007, the New York City Department of Transportation has installed over 30 miles of protected bicycle lanes throughout the city, including several parking-protected bicycle lanes on various avenues in Manhattan. The following report contains an analysis of how some of these Manhattan routes have impacted safety, mobility, and economic vitality. Routes were chosen for inclusion if they had at least three years of "after" safety data available.

Mobility

- Travel speeds in the Central Business District have remained steady as protected bicycle lanes are added to the roadway network
- Travel times on Columbus Avenue have improved while vehicle volumes are maintained
- First Avenue travel speeds remained level through project area
- Travel times on 8th Avenue improved by an average of 14%

Economic Vitality & Quality of Life

- When compared to similar corridors, streets that received a protected bicycle lane saw a greater increase in retail sales
- 110 trees have been added to projects within this study area, enhancing the neighborhood through which they run
- Crossing distances along corridors have been shortened anywhere between 17' and 30'

Design of each protected bicycle lane looks similar but there are important distinctions:

- Lane Removal (y/n)
- Lane Narrowing (y/n)
- Pre-Existing Basic or Buffered Bike Lane
- Remove or Curbside Rush Hour Vehicle Lane
- Major Network Change (y/n)

Differences in final designs:

- Bus Lane Present
- Concrete vs.Painted Pedestrian Islands

Source D

My Fourth Avenue Nightmare
Andi Lenox

Last week I was riding back to my apartment on the corner of Union and 4th Avenue in Brooklyn after dropping my son off at his daycare center. Usually he rides in a seat on the back of my bike but thank goodness he was already safe at school. I was riding on the right side of the road, in the furthest lane to the right that's not actually a parking lane. There are no bike lanes there, and cars drive really fast on that stretch of the avenue so I was trying to be extra vigilant about watching behind and beside me. I have side mirrors on my handles and a little mirror lens on my helmet, so my visibility is usually pretty good. Suddenly a car parked on the right flung its door open without looking, and I crashed directly into it, skidding sideway out into the road where I slammed into the side of an MTA bus that was changing lanes without signaling. I sustained a minor concussion and serious contusions on my forearms and shins. My knee was dislocated and required an ambulance trip to the hospital; the driver whose car I hit had insurance to cover some of it, but I never saw a dime from the MTA. Something in the street configuration needs to change because I had no safe option to get home that day. I propose a driver education campaign to remind automotive owners to always check their mirrors before they open their doors when parked on an active roadway.

Source E

Project Corridor	Miles	Cyclist Risk Range
9th Avenue (16th–23rd)	0.33	–64.9%
Broadway (59th–47th)	0.60	–36.4%
1st Avenue (1st–34th)	1.62	–53.9%
2nd Avenue (2nd –14th)	0.59	–43.8%
2nd Avenue (23rd –34th)	0.54	–54.1%
8th Avenue (23rd–34th)	0.54	–2.4%
Broadway (23rd–18th)	0.25	11.2%
Columbus Avenue (96th–77th)	0.96	–37.6%

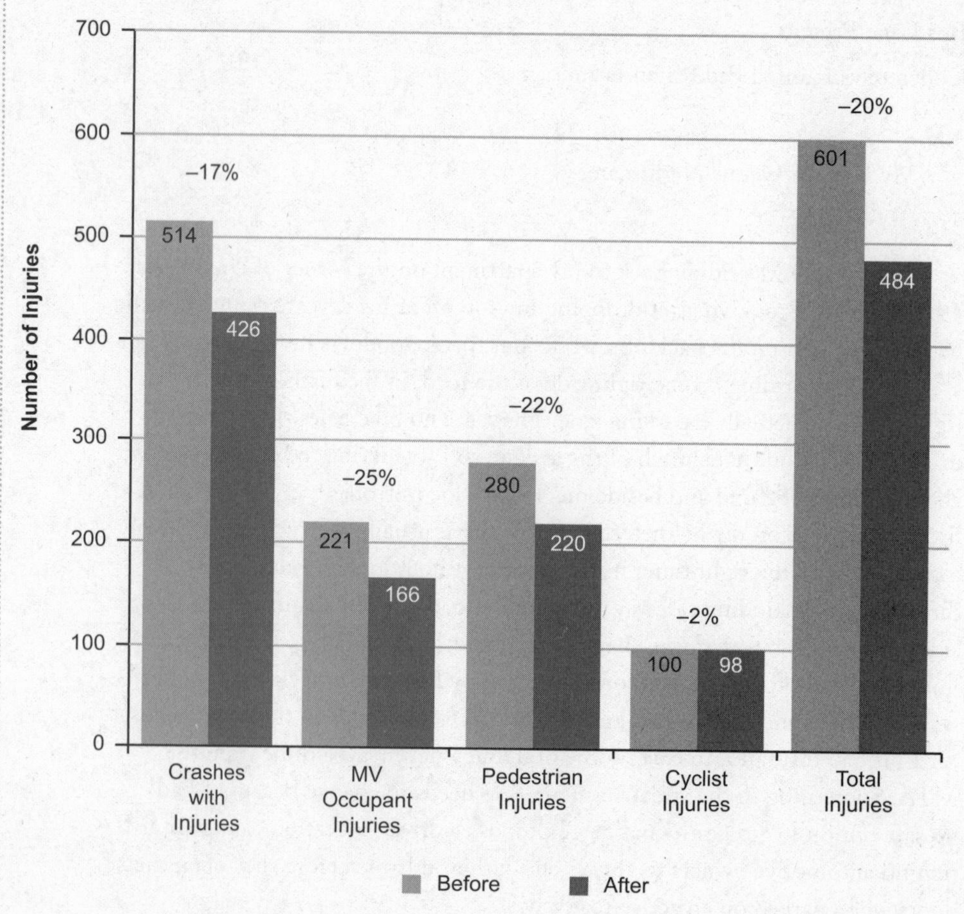

Source F

Local Businesses Protest Stagnation of Bike Lanes
Paula Greenberry

We the undersigned businesses of Park Slope and Gowanus, Brooklyn would like to hereby lodge a formal complaint against the proposal for 4th Avenue bike lanes as proposed by the sponsors of the project. As seen in other parts of the city, the addition of bike lanes puts an undue burden on businesses who can't receive deliveries without serious inconvenience. Trucks have to block a lane of active traffic—or block bike lanes in the process—to stop and deliver cargo or receive deliverables from a store. As the council knows, 4th Avenue is unlike other Brooklyn avenues in the vicinity because it gets a significant amount of car traffic, as well as foot traffic. The undersigned businesses also posit that pedestrians will be less able to see signage and advertisements for street-facing stores. It is also less safe for cyclists to have cars parking next to their lane instead of being able to ride on opposite sides of the street when the need arises. The proposed lane configuration that creates two active lanes, then a lane of parked cars, and then a cement median actually traps cyclists unsafely. Alternatively, we propose elevated crossing bridges cyclists could ride over, to prevent having to ride along 4th Avenue. Instead they could have the less busy 3rd Avenue and use these elevated bridges to get to 5th Avenue, and cars and pedestrians, not to mention business owners, would have easier access to storefronts.

TIP

Jot down a note or two by the title of each given source—where it's from, and the audience for whom you think it's written.

Here are some techniques for synthesizing multiple sources.

First, assess the purpose of each text. In addition to the text itself, you'll be given information about the excerpt's publication or origin source—read through it closely. Is it from a newspaper? A magazine? A government website? Another type of media? Can you determine anything about the writer's choice of audience from this information? Consider the difference in intention that could exist between a newspaper like *The Washington Post* and a company's public relations department—who would you trust more to be objective? Is the author's intent to persuade? Inform? Reveal? Argue against something? Does the author cite other sources? Do you think you're getting the various writers' personal perspectives, or are they achieving synthesis themselves?

In example #1 above, regarding the neighborhood bike lanes, first consider whose interests are being represented in each source. Source A seems pretty neutral—it's designed to garner attention to the upcoming city council proceedings and equip people with relevant information. Source B is from an advocate who still has concerns about how the project will actually be implemented, so he could potentially provide positive or negative evidence in your argument. Source C comes from the Department of Transportation, so while it's not neutral, since it's their proposal, it is concrete and specific, telling you exactly what they plan to do and how they evaluate plans to build bike lanes. Source D is a personal account that might help you argue for bike lanes or against bikes altogether! Source E provides statistics that could help bolster the specificity of your argument about bike lane effectiveness, if that's what you choose to support. Source F provides a counterargument; do you notice any tensions between it and other texts, though?

Then, read each text quickly and use your own close-reading shorthand (see the previous chapter for examples, or come up with a unique system that makes sense to you) to identify the main idea and the evidence the author is using. Be able to summarize it in just a few words.

Here's one example:

- Source A: There is a proposal to install bike lanes
- Source B: If we get these lanes, they need to be done well
- Source C: Biking lanes have been successful in New York City
- Source D: Biking without lanes is very dangerous
- Source E: Injuries have gone down between 2 and 22% since lanes were installed
- Source F: Bike lanes will harm my business

Next, put the source texts in relation to one another. Is there a text that you think provides a basic overview or just the facts? Is there a source that seems to be interpreting these facts with some kind of bias or agenda? Do any of the sources comment directly on one another?

If you have time, you can even map out the relationships, like so:

Source A, C, E (facts) → Pro: Source D→ Mixed: Source A → Anti: Source F

In our ongoing example, one source is arguing that Brooklyn absolutely must have bike lanes because it will save lives, and another source is just as vehemently insisting there cannot be bike lanes because it will cost too much and ruin too many people's commutes. This is a conflict you can present and examine for your reader.

Speaking of your reader, once you've distilled the sources down to manageable summaries and figured out how they correspond to one another, it's time to determine your own argument. Do you want to agree with the pro-bike-lane lobby, and help augment their case by addressing the concerns of the anti-bike-laners? Are you anti-bike lanes, because you see a flaw in the proponent's argument that you can draw the reader's attention to? How might you use the data provided in Sources C and E to support your argument?

Time to start your draft! Using whatever pre-writing strategy you feel most at home with, sketch out some quick notes for what you want to cover first, second, and third. Remember the organizational techniques we talked about for the multiple-choice section?

Organizational Strategies:

Chronologically

Cause and Effect

Order of Importance

Thematically

If you wanted to organize your synthesis essay chronologically, you might take a close look at the dates on the bike lane sources and determine the order in which they were published. This would reflect the evolution of thought on the topic. If you cite Department of Transportation statistics, bike lanes have been successful for years; however, you could rebut that source by providing your own context, and observing that these statistics hold true only if the amount of traffic is consistent, which may not be the case if the source's data is all from 2007. Source B seems to suggest that these lanes have not been implemented perfectly throughout that time, also.

If you thought cause and effect was your best bet, you might approach your argument by examining either the reasons why bike lanes are needed (what causes us to need special lanes instead of just sharing the road?) or the effects bike lanes have been shown to have (what will happen if we implement these lanes city-wide?).

To structure your argument in order of importance, you might decide first to consider cost, then environmental factors, then the impact on human life that bike lines could have, moving from least to most compelling reasons. Thematically, it could also make sense to group your evidence into categories like safety risks, health risks, and logistical risks. If you were interested in developing a policy argument, you might also cite Sources D or F as an example of alternative proposals, such as the driver awareness campaign, or elevated street-crossing bridges, suggesting that perhaps these lanes are not the only (or even the best) option.

TIP

Because you're using multiple sources, you may find an outline is a particularly helpful strategy for making sure you've structured your argument logically and are being mindful of transitions.

The great thing about free-response essays is that as long as you make your point thoughtfully and logically and use sources appropriately, you can argue whatever you want!

Take a look at two more sample prompts, followed by short explanations of how to apply different strategies.

#2 Sample Synthesis Prompt

Vaccines, once hailed as revolutionary advances of modern medicine, have become controversial in recent decades, as advocates for parental control have sought to reduce the influence of the social normalization of vaccinations against common diseases and childhood illnesses. But what evidence is there that vaccinations cause more illnesses than they prevent? Has it made public education healthier or more dangerous? Do parents have a right to withhold vaccinations or a responsibility to contribute to a collective immunity?

Assignment: Read the following sources (including any introductory information) carefully. Then, in an essay that synthesizes at least three of the sources for support, take a position that defends, challenges, or qualifies the claim that vaccinations are vital for the survival of children around the world.

Refer to the sources as Source A, Source B, etc; titles/authors are included for your convenience.

Source A (National Institute of Health)

Source B (Greenhow)

Source C (Miller interview)

Source D (NIH table)

Source E (Douglass)

Source A

Testing of Investigational Inactivated Zika Vaccine in Humans Begins

The first of five early stage clinical trials to test the safety and ability of an investigational Zika vaccine candidate called the Zika Purified Inactivated Virus (ZPIV) vaccine to generate an immune system response has begun at the Walter Reed Army Institute of Research (WRAIR) Clinical Trial Center in Silver Spring, Maryland. Scientists with WRAIR, part of the U.S. Department of Defense (DoD), developed the vaccine. The National Institute of Allergy and Infectious Diseases (NIAID), part of the National Institutes of Health (NIH), is co-funding the Phase 1 clinical trial with WRAIR, serving as the regulatory sponsor and providing other support.

The experimental ZPIV vaccine is based on the same technology WRAIR used in 2009 to successfully develop a vaccine for another flavivirus called Japanese encephalitis. The ZPIV vaccine contains whole Zika virus particles that have been inactivated, meaning that the virus cannot replicate and cause disease in humans. However, the protein shell of the inactivated virus remains intact so it can be recognized by the immune system and evoke an immune response. NIAID partially supported the preclinical development of the ZPIV vaccine candidate, including safety testing and non-human primate studies that found that the vaccine induced antibodies that neutralized the virus and protected the animals from disease when they were challenged with Zika virus. WRAIR, NIAID and the Biomedical Advanced Research and Development Authority (BARDA) part of the HHS Office of the Assistant Secretary for Preparedness and Response (ASPR) have established a joint Research Collaboration Agreement to support the development of this vaccine.

"We urgently need a safe and effective vaccine to protect people from Zika virus infection as the virus continues to spread and cause serious public health consequences, particularly for pregnant women and their babies," said NIAID Director Anthony S. Fauci, M.D. "We are pleased to be part of the collaborative effort to advance this promising candidate vaccine into clinical trials."

Source: National Institute of Health; https://www.nih.gov/news-events/news-releases testing-investigational-inactivated-zika-vaccine-humans-begins

Source B

An Estimate of the True Value of Vaccination as a Security Against Small Pox by T. M. Greenhow (1825)

INTRODUCTION

What reliance may safely be placed on Vaccination as a means of exemption from Small Pox?

It may be affirmed, without hazard of contradiction, that no question connected with the physical well being of mankind involves considerations of more serious interest, or consequences of more vital moment, than that which has just been proposed. During the last quarter of a century, it has engaged a degree of attention, both from medical practitioners and from society in general, proportionate to the great importance of the subject; and though among the former, with very few exceptions, one pretty uniform opinion may prevail respecting the true value of the Jennerian discovery, I have reason to know, that many doubts and apprehensions still linger in the minds of not a few of the latter. These have been cherished or revived by circumstances, of a nature, it must be admitted, well calculated to shake their confidence in Vaccination as an absolute preventive of Small Pox; which, unfortunately for the cause, on its first introduction into practice, it was generally believed and asserted to be; but which subsequent experience has proved can no longer be contended for. I trust, however, to be enabled to prove, to the satisfaction of every impartial enquirer, that the value of Vaccination is not essentially diminished on that account; that an imperfect knowledge of its effects can alone have given rise to the doubts and apprehensions referred to; and that nothing is required for their entire removal but a more intimate acquaintance with the subject. It is the purpose of the present Essay, then, to bring under review the principal facts connected with the history of Small Pox and of Vaccination which, in any way, bear upon the question proposed; to arrange them in such order, and to place them in such lights, as may best elucidate the subject, and enable those, who have children not yet protected in any way from the infection of Small Pox, to form a clear and satisfactory judgment; a judgment unbiassed by prejudice, matured by a serious and candid consideration of the evidence that will be laid before them, and on which may depend life itself, or much that renders life desirable.

Source C

Controversies and challenges of vaccination: An interview with Elizabeth Miller (excerpt), 2015

2) What are the controversies regarding vaccines?

Vaccines differ from other medications as they are given to millions of healthy individuals, usually children, to prevent diseases that may no longer pose an immediate threat. Concern about vaccine safety is therefore perfectly legitimate and, when potential safety signals arise, they must be investigated promptly and rigorously. Many of the concerns about vaccine side effects have arisen as a result of reports of a temporal association between administration of a vaccine and development of a rare disease for which the cause is currently unknown. Such case reports are still the way that most safety signals are generated; indeed, health professionals and parents are encouraged to report any side effects that they suspect may have been caused by a vaccine to authorities such as the Centers for Disease Control and Prevention (CDC) in the US or the Medicines and Healthcare products Regulatory Agency (MHRA) in the UK.

In other instances, signals are generated from ecological associations, where an increase in the incidence of a disease is noticed to coincide with introduction of a vaccine. Examples of vaccine safety concerns that have arisen in this way are the alleged association between the combined MMR vaccine and autism, which was based on both a reported temporal link for some cases and a suggested ecologic association. This developed into a "controversy", as despite sound epidemiological studies showing no excess of autism onsets after MMR vaccine, there remained a vocal lobby that did not accept the evidence.

Source: National Institute of Health, https://www.ncbi.nlm.nih.gov/pmc/articles/PMC4608187/#__ffn_sectitle

Source D

The Impact of Vaccines in the United States

Disease	Baseline 20th Century Pre-Vaccine Annual Cases	2009 Cases	Percent Decrease
Measles	503,282	71	99.9%
Diphtheria	175,885	0	100%
Mumps	152,209	1,991	98.7%
Pertussis	147,271	13,214	91.0%
Smallpox	48,164	0	100%
Rubella	47,745	3	99.9%
Haemophilus influenzae type b, invasive	20,000	35	99.8%
Polio	16,316	0	100%
Tetanus	1,314	18	98.6%

Source: https://www.niaid.nih.gov/research/vaccine-benefits

Source E

How Vaccines Change Lives
by Lucia Douglass

Back in the 1980s, my family and I lived in Little Rock, Arkansas. Our home was happy and slightly chaotic, with four kids under the age of eight running around and getting into what we thought were moderate amounts of trouble. Lindsey, our youngest, gave us the shock of our lives when she was barely six months old and caught a case of the measles. She was too young to be vaccinated, though our older kids had been. Not every child at her day care facility was—though she could have caught it at the grocery store or at the park, or anywhere that kids are, if it's not protected by herd immunity. She recovered from this infant illness and we thought everything was fine, but in

> early adolescence she began to have behavioral difficulties, seizures, and more serious health problems. She lost her short-term memory, her seizures became more frequent, and finally, to our shock and dismay, she was left in a vegetative state by something called Subacute Sclerosing Panencephalitis, which is a later stage of an early measles disease. Our family—my partner, our three other children, and I—face a future wildly different than we thought we'd be facing, and maybe back then, nobody understood the risks or had access to the measles vaccine. But today there's no excuse for being too caught up in rumor and misinformation to embrace the help of real science that could have protected our little girl's health.

An essay responding to this collection of sources could take several angles—it might track the progress of attitudes toward vaccinations, or put the new announcement of Zika research in context of historical progress toward effective vaccines. You'll need to first determine what your stance will be, and look for moments in the various sources that can help you support it.

For example, if you decided to advocate for mandatory vaccines in all public schools, you might sketch out an outline like this:

Main idea: Vaccines should be mandatory in public schools to create collective immunity.

Paragraph 1: Quote from Source C, Dr. Miller, about how the controversy over vaccines emerged; link to fears families may have

Paragraph 2: Quote from Source E, Douglass story of consequences from not having vaccines; explain why this should trump fears of other families

Paragraph 3: Quote from Source D, Statistics to support personal anecdote; answer concerns with facts, not just empathy

Paragraph 4: Conclusion: These three perspectives suggest that having vaccines mandatorily provided at schools would ensure student health, because the link between vaccine and autism was never proven, unlike the link between early childhood measles and later serious health issues like the Douglass family experienced.

#3 Sample Synthesis Prompt

Modern approaches to education often minimize or underrate the value of memorization in an academic curriculum, saying that the old tradition of learning particularly important speeches by heart has nothing to do with how young people learn today. Historians such as Ken Burns, however, are seeking to revive the practice by supporting projects that require students to memorize and perform famous speeches, including the Gettysburg Address.

Assignment: Read the following sources (including any introductory information) carefully. Then, in an essay that synthesizes at least three of the sources for support, take a position that defends, challenges, or qualifies the idea that the Gettysburg Address, and speeches like it, are irrelevant or impractical for students to learn.

Refer to the sources as Source A, Source B, etc.; titles/authors are included for your convenience.

Source A (Lincoln)

Source B (Hay)

Source C (Burns)

Source D (statistics)

Source E (Against Memorization)

Source A

Lincoln's Gettysburg Address, given November 19, 1863 on the battlefield near Gettysburg, Pennsylvania, USA

Four score and seven years ago, our fathers brought forth upon this continent a new nation: conceived in liberty, and dedicated to the proposition that all men are created equal.

Now we are engaged in a great civil war, testing whether that nation, or any nation so conceived and so dedicated, can long endure. We are met on a great battlefield of that war.

We have come to dedicate a portion of that field as a final resting place for those who here gave their lives that this nation might live. It is altogether fitting and proper that we should do this.

But, in a larger sense, we cannot dedicate, we cannot consecrate, we cannot hallow this ground. The brave men, living and dead, who struggled here have consecrated it, far above our poor power to add or detract. The world will little note, nor long remember, what we say here, but it can never forget what they did here.

It is for us the living, rather, to be dedicated here to the unfinished work which they who fought here have thus far so nobly advanced. It is rather for us to be here dedicated to the great task remaining before us, that from these honored dead we take increased devotion to that cause for which they gave the last full measure of devotion, that we here highly resolve that these dead shall not have died in vain, that this nation, under God, shall have a new birth of freedom, and that government of the people, by the people, for the people, shall not perish from this earth.

Source B

Account of John Hay, one of Lincoln's secretaries

"At Gettysburg, the President went to Mr. Wills who expected him, and our party broke like a drop of quicksilver spilled. MacVeagh [Chairman of the Pennsylvania Republican Party], young Stanton [Son of Lincoln's Secretary of War], and I foraged around for awhile - walked out to the college, got a chafing dish of oysters then some supper, and finally loafing around to the Court House where Lamon [Chief Marshall of the event and a close friend of Lincoln's] was holding a meeting of marshals, we found Forney [a reporter]and went around to his place, Mr. Fahnestock's, and drank a little whisky with him. He had been drinking a good deal during the day and was getting to feel a little ugly and dangerous. He was particularly bitter on Montgomery Blair [Lincoln's Postmaster General]. MacVeagh was telling him that he pitched into the Tycoon [Hay's nickname for Lincoln] coming up, and told him some truths. He said the President got a good deal of that from time to time and needed it …

We went out after a while following the music to hear the serenades. The President appeared at the door and said half a dozen words meaning nothing and went in. Seward [Lincoln's Secretary of State], who was staying around the corner at Harper's, was called out, and spoke so indistinctly that I did not hear a word of what he was saying.

We went back to Forney's room, having picked up Nicolay [another of Lincoln's private secretaries], and drank more whisky. Nicolay sang his little song of the 'Three Thieves,' and we then sang 'John Brown.' At last we proposed that Forney should make a speech and two or three started out, Shannon and Behan and Nicolay, to get a band to serenade him. I stayed with him. So did Stanton and MacVeagh … I walked downstairs with him.

The crowd was large and clamorous. The fuglers [military guards] stood by the door in an agony. The reporters squatted at a little stand in the entry. Forney stood on the threshold, John Young [a reporter] and I by him.

The crowd shouted as the door opened. Forney said, 'My friends, these are the first hearty cheers I have heard tonight. You gave no such cheers to your President down the street. Do you know what you owe to that great man? You owe your country - you owe your name as American citizens.'

In the morning I got a beast and rode out with the President's suite to the Cemetery in the procession. The procession formed itself in an orphanly sort of way and moved out with very little help from anybody, and after a little delay, Mr. Everett took his place on the stand - and Mr. Stockton made a prayer which thought it was an oration; and Mr. Everett spoke as he always does, perfectly - and the President, in a fine, free way, with more grace than is his wont, said his half dozen words of consecration, and the music wailed and we went home through crowded and cheering streets."

Source C

The documentarian Ken Burns has embarked upon a public art project in his latest documentary, *The Address*, which aired on PBS last week. In it, Burns works with students at The Greenwood School in Vermont who are tasked with memorizing and reciting the Gettysburg Address; his project is especially poignant because all of the students have some kind of learning difficulty that make it exceptionally difficult. According to Burns, it is not only the specific language of the Gettysburg Address that make it so memorable—but the effect of learning about this particular moment in time that renders the address so essential and relevant to learning and civic engagement today. Lincoln, in this address, is emphasizing the importance of the values espoused by America's founders in the Declaration of Independence. He is seizing the opportunity, as part of dedicating a cemetery to the dead and fallen at Gettysburg, to reiterate his support for the union and the future of this country the Union army was fighting for. He points out that when September 11 happened, we didn't develop an entirely new inspirational rhetoric, but people returned to the Gettysburg Address, because it reinforces the bedrock qualities that our nation was founded upon.

Source D

Location: Gettysburg, Pennsylvania in Adams County
Union General: George G. Meade
Confederate General: Robert E. Lee
Soldiers involved: Union Army 82,289; Confederate Army 75,000
Dates: July 1-3, 1863
Casualties: 23,049 Union; 28,063 Confederate

Source E

Against Memorization
Excerpted from an opinion piece in a college newspaper

Many students march through their academic careers without ever learning that knowledge is a journey, not a destination. They cram facts and figures, equations and quotations, without ever learning what Romeo and Juliet were all about, or what Pythagoras was up to before or after his famous realization. Even if supporters argue that it gives the brain good exercise or can give rise to important insights, memorization shouldn't replace skills-driven teaching. Students need to be learning transferable, versatile tools they can carry with them from subject to subject, class to class. Even if drills are fun, they're not the same as a process of discovery. They don't lead to the uncovering of unexpected things about yourself. You answer, but you don't understand. Isolated facts lead to insufficient knowledge, and students deserve better.

In preparing to write an essay for this prompt, you might begin by reflecting on your own experience with memorization, and taking a less structured approach to the essay. A five-minute freewrite might yield something like the following:

When I was a kid we had to learn a passage of Shakespeare, and sometimes I still think about the words I learned then. Part of the lesson was figuring out what Shakespeare was writing about in his time, and why people keep performing it today. Even so memorizing is really hard and makes me really nervous. Back then he was an expression of popular beliefs and ideas. So maybe it is like that with Lincoln. The ideals he was talking about were really important to him. I wonder if there is any value in learning his words as well as his ideology, if people reacted the same way, and if that might be something students still care about later.

That could translate into an essay that begins by establishing the counterargument, that speeches like the Gettysburg Address aren't useful because they reflect a negative attitude toward learning. Then, you might counter that with Ken Burns's attitude toward the Address, and the benefits it can have. You might then go on to demonstrate the value in learning more about the address in close-reading the address and Hay's description of the response to it. The details of the war provided might help you suggest something about the high stakes of the speech, the audience investment in it, or the lasting relevance of the issues under discussion. You could bring your own perspective in to explain how the speech inspires you in a contemporary moment.

Analysis

The analysis question will ask you to describe and assess the rhetoric of a single text—this is likely the prompt where your multiple-choice practice and experience will serve you the best. You'll want to be familiar with examining a writer's intended audience, purpose, argument, and evidence; rhetorical techniques such as allusion, imagery, irony, description, pacing, style; and appeal to ethos, logos or pathos, colloquialisms, example, comparison/contrast, transitions, etc.

Audience

You're obviously familiar with the concept of audience in other contexts—when you're reading a text, consider who the author is writing *to*, and how you can tell. Sometimes he or she will describe the audience—"people who support effort to perfect cloning," "students who object to standardized testing," "cyclists who are skeptical about bike lanes." Other times, you may have to make inferences based on word choice and level of detail. A writer who is explaining the basics is probably writing for a casual audience; a writer who is using a lot of technical language is writing for a more experienced reader.

Purpose

Can you tell from a piece of prose writing why the author set out to publish it? Is she trying to call readers to action? Expect words like *must* and *should*, paired with specific goals the writer hopes to accomplish. Is she hoping to persuade? Look for counterarguments and a logical structure of argument, followed by evidence. We'll talk more about appeals using particular types of rhetoric in a minute. Seek to answer the questions, "Why did the writer need to say this?" and "What did she hope to accomplish?"

Argument

Fix in your mind that whatever else it is, an argument must be a debatable statement. It cannot be an observation of fact or a statement of opinion like "I like tacos." To turn that statement into an argument, you have to be trying to convince someone of something—"Tacos are the best lunch," or "Everybody should have a taco a day." In order to be most persuasive for your reader, your assertion should be supported by evidence.

Evidence

Simply put, evidence is what comes after *because.* "Tacos are the best lunch because they provide you with a serving of protein, dairy, veggies, and they're portable!" "We need bike lanes because roads are dangerous for cyclists; there are 15 accidents on this corner every year, and bike lanes have been proven to reduce injuries and traffic fatalities."

Style

In writing, style is the accumulated effect of the techniques a writer uses; it can involve syntax, word choice, and tone. Four main categories of style include expository/argumentative writing, descriptive writing, persuasive writing, and narrative writing. You'll see a variety of the same techniques used in different ways to create an individual's "voice" on the page.

You have doubtless encountered the following rhetorical techniques and more in your AP coursework, but here's a selection of strategies you should learn to recognize and apply in your own work as well.

Allusion

> **Definition:** an indirect reference that serves to highlight something specific without explicitly mentioning it
>
> **Example:** "His name was Bluther, but what's in a name, anyway?"

"What's in a name" is an allusion to Romeo and Juliet—the speaker is comparing his or her feelings for someone with an unusual name to the way Juliet felt about Romeo, whose family was feuding with hers.

Imagery

> **Definition:** visually descriptive language
>
> **Example:** "The sun set dreamily, behind gold-drenched fields and beneath a darkening azure sky, with whispering trees around the horizon."

It's possible to go too far with imagery in literary works (the most extreme examples are called "purple prose"), but well-crafted descriptive language makes the scene come alive for your reader.

Irony

> **Definition:** the expression of meaning by using language that would usually indicate the opposite, for humor or emphasis
>
> **Example:** "Thank goodness you're not overreacting," Lisa said after Doug shrieked and dropped the vase he was holding.

Irony is sometimes hard to achieve in writing, but if you can detect and analyze its meaning within a given passage, you'll be operating on a higher level of perception.

Pacing

> **Definition:** the speed at which an idea is developed
>
> **Example:** "As the crowd watched, the tension built as the man on the bicycle slowly ventured out on to the tightrope stretched taut between the two buildings. His foot slipped on a pedal, the crowd gasped. His hands seemed to wobble on the handlebars, but then his grip tightened and his feet took another slow revolution, inching the bike forward into the gap."

Pacing is sometimes more visible through lack of attention. In this brief example, you'll notice the writer is taking his time to create a sense of feeling by describing actions deliberately. He could also have just said, "A man rode a bicycle on a tightrope while people watched," which would have communicated the same main idea but provided much less of an experience for the reader.

Colloquialisms

Definition: words or phrases that originate from a specific context, most often informal, and used in conversation

Example: "When he saw the glass broke on the ground, he was just fit to be tied."

Colloquial expressions, using language you might use every day, can serve an important purpose for readers. It can make them feel included—or excluded. It can increase your authority, as being in the "in-group" that knows a particular mode of slang, or it could decrease it, suggesting you are not someone to be taken seriously.

Juxtaposition

Definition: comparison of two things being placed together for contrasting effect

Example: "The judge's fury was fearful to behold in the courtroom, but afterward in his chambers he was gentle with the spaniel who often lay beneath his desk."

In this case, the contrast between the judge's public and private behavior perhaps gives you a greater appreciation for the one, or makes you less inclined to respect the other.

Transitions

Definition: signal words and phrases that indicate the relationship between moments or ideas in the text.

Examples:

- **Additive:** *Indeed, further, as well, also, moreover, in addition, on the other hand*
- **Introduction:** *To begin, such as, for instance, particularly, including, by way of example*
- **Reference:** *considering, regarding, concerning, speaking about*
- **Clarification:** *that is to say, in other words, I mean*
- **Conflict:** *but, however, when in fact, conversely, still*
- **Emphasis:** *even more, above all, indeed*
- **Effect/result:** *as a result, consequently, for the purpose of*

There are many more—look online for lists of transition words so you can learn to recognize them when you read and implement them in your own work.

Metaphors/Similes

Definition: a literary comparison. A metaphor describes one thing as being another thing; simile uses *like or as.*

Examples:

A metaphor: Love is a battlefield.

A simile: He roared like a lion.

You've acquired experience with these devices in the preparation for the multiple-choice section of the exam, but don't forget to take advantage of them in your free-response analysis as well. You can get a lot of mileage out of recognizing a meaningful comparison and close-reading it for significance. What does the comparison mean to the author? What does it mean to you as the reader?

Synecdoche

> **Definition:** A figure of speech in which a term for a part refers to the whole of something (or the whole refers to a part)
>
> **Examples:** "A hired hand," "The United States won another gold medal," a few police officers described as "the police"

Synecdoche is often used to make the specific feel universal, and vice versa.

Rhetorical Appeals

Ethos: an appeal to someone's ethics, convincing them of the writer's character or credibility. You'll see this often in moral arguments, or moral *reasons in support of policy arguments.*

> **Example:** "Implement bike lanes because it's the right thing to do."

Logos: using reason to persuade an audience

> **Example:** "Students who receive training in public speaking during middle school are 27% more likely to pursue leadership roles in high school and college."

Pathos: an appeal to emotion, requiring rhetoric that is designed to elicit an emotional reaction on the part of the reader. Think about the kinds of things that cause you to react emotionally—descriptions of strong emotional or physical experiences, perhaps?

> **Example:** "Make vaccines mandatory so more kids don't suffer like mine."

Let's get some practice on an analysis prompt.

Sample Analysis Prompt

The eulogy for Chief Justice of the Supreme Court, Joseph Story, delivered by Daniel Webster (1782–1852), a politician who served as a Congressional representative, Senator, and Secretary of State. Webster was known for his oratory skills, his political career, and his dedication to the Constitution. Read the eulogy he delivered for Justice Story, then, in a well-written essay, analyze the rhetorical choices Webster makes to develop his presentation of Story's legacy.

Joseph Story, one of the Associate Justices of the Supreme Court of the United States, and for many years the presiding judge of this Circuit, died on Wednesday evening last, at his house in Cambridge, wanting only a few days for the completion of the sixty-sixth year of his age.

...

Mr. Chief Justice, one sentiment pervades us all. It is that of the most profound and penetrating grief, mixed, nevertheless, with an assured conviction, that the great man whom we deplore is yet with us and in the midst of us. He hath not wholly died. He lives in the affections of friends and kindred, and in the high regard of the community. He lives in our remembrance of his social virtues, his warm and steady friendships, and the vivacity and richness of his conversation. He lives, and will live still more permanently, by his words of written wisdom, by the results of his vast researches and attainments, by his imperishable legal judgments, and by those juridical disquisitions which have stamped his name, all over the civilized world, with the character of a commanding authority. "Vivit, enim, vivetque semper; atque etiam latius in memoria hominum et sermone versabitur, postquam ab oculis recessit."

Mr. Chief Justice, there are consolations which arise to mitigate our loss, and shed the influence of resignation over unfeigned and heart-felt sorrow. We are all penetrated with gratitude to God that the deceased lived so long; that he did so much for himself, his friends, the country, and the world; that his lamp went out, at last, without unsteadiness or flickering. He continued to exercise every power of his mind without dimness or obscuration, and every affection of his heart with no abatement of energy or warmth, till death drew an impenetrable veil between us and him. Indeed, he seems to us now, as in truth he is, not extinguished or ceasing to be, but only withdrawn; as the clear sun goes down at its setting, not darkened, but only no longer seen.

This calamity, Mr. Chief Justice, is not confined to the bar or the courts of this Commonwealth. It will be felt by every bar throughout the land, by every court, and indeed by every intelligent and well informed man in or out of the profession. It will be felt still more widely, for his reputation had a still wider range. In the High Court of Parliament, in every tribunal in Westminster Hall, in the judicatories of Paris and Berlin, of Stockholm and St. Petersburg, in the learned universities of Germany, Italy, and Spain, by every eminent jurist in the civilized world, it will be acknowledged that a great luminary has fallen from the firmament of public jurisprudence.

Sir, there is no purer pride of country than that in which we may indulge when we see America paying back the great debt of civilization, learning, and science to Europe. In this high return of light for light and mind for mind, in this august reckoning and accounting between the intellects of nations, Joseph Story was destined by Providence to act, and did act, an important part. Acknowledging, as we all acknowledge, our obligations to the original sources of English law, as well as of civil liberty, we have seen in our generation copious and salutary streams turning and running backward, replenishing their original fountains, and giving a fresher and a brighter green to the fields of English jurisprudence. By a sort of reversed hereditary transmission, the mother, without envy or humiliation, acknowledges that she has received a valuable and cherished inheritance from the daughter. The profession in England admits with frankness and candor, and with no feeling but that of respect and admiration, that he whose voice we have so recently heard within these walls, but shall now hear no more, was of all men who have yet appeared, most fitted by the comprehensiveness of his mind, and the vast extent and accuracy of his attainments, to compare the codes of nations, to trace their differences to difference of origin, climate, or religious or political institutions, and to exhibit, nevertheless, their concurrence in those great principles upon which the system of human civilization rests.

Justice, Sir, is the great interest of man on earth. It is the ligament which holds civilized beings and civilized nations together. Wherever her temple stands, and so long as it is duly honored, there is a foundation for social security, general happiness, and the improvement and progress of our race. And whoever labors on this edifice with usefulness and distinction, whoever clears its foundations, strengthens its pillars, adorns its entablatures, or contributes to raise its august dome still higher in the skies, connects himself, in name, and fame, and character, with that which is and must be as durable as the frame of human society.

All know, Mr. Chief Justice, the pure love of country which animated the deceased, and the zeal, as well as the talent, with which he explained and defended her institutions. His work on the Constitution of the United States is one of his most eminently successful labors. But all his writings, and all his judgments, all his opinions, and the whole influence of his character, public and private, leaned strongly and always to the support of sound principles, to the restraint of illegal power, and to the discouragement and rebuke of licentious and disorganizing sentiments. "Ad rempublicam firmandam, et ad stabiliendas vires, et sanandum populum, omnis ejus pergebat institutio."

But this is not the occasion, Sir, nor is it for me to consider and discuss at length the character and merits of Mr. Justice Story, as a writer or a judge. The performance of that duty, with which this Bar will no doubt charge itself, must be deferred to another opportunity, and will be committed to abler hands. But in the homage paid to his memory, one part may come with peculiar propriety and emphasis from ourselves. We have known him in private life. We have seen him descend from the bench, and mingle in our friendly circles. We have known his manner of life, from his youth up. We can bear witness to the strict uprightness and purity of his character, his simplicity and unostentatious habits, the ease and affability of his intercourse, his remarkable vivacity amidst severe labors, the cheerful and animating tones of his conversation, and his fast fidelity to friends. Some of us, also, can testify to his large and liberal charities, not ostentatious or casual, but systematic and silent, --dispensed almost without showing the hand, and falling and distilling comfort and happiness, like the dews of heaven. But we can testify, also, that in all his pursuits and employments, in all his recreations, in all his commerce with the world, and in his intercourse with the circle of his friends, the predominance of his judicial character was manifest. He never forgot the ermine which he wore. The judge, the judge, the useful and distinguished judge, was the great picture which he kept constantly before his eyes, and to a resemblance of which all his efforts, all his thoughts, all his life, were devoted. We may go the world over, without finding a man who shall present a more striking realization of the beautiful conception of D'Aguesseau: "C'est en vain que l'on cherche a distinguer en lui la personne privée et la personne publique; un même esprit les anime, un même objet les réunit; l'homme, le père de famille, le citoyen, tout est en lui consacré à la gloire du magistrat."

Mr. Chief Justice, one may live as a conqueror, a king, or a magistrate; but he must die as a man. The bed of death brings every human being to his pure individuality; to the intense contemplation of that deepest and most solemn of all relations, the relation between the creature and his Creator. Here it is that fame and renown cannot assist us; that all external things must fail to aid us; that even friends, affection, and human love and devotedness, cannot succor us. This relation, the true foundation of all duty, a relation perceived and felt by conscience and confirmed by revelation, our illustrious friend, now deceased, always acknowledged.

He reverenced the Scriptures of truth, honored the pure morality which they teach, and clung to the hopes of future life which they impart. He beheld enough in nature, in himself, and in all that can be known of things seen, to feel assured that there is a Supreme Power, without whose providence not a sparrow falleth to the ground. To this gracious being he entrusted himself for time and for eternity; and the last words of his lips ever heard by mortal ears were a fervent supplication to his Maker to take him to himself.

Let's start by practicing a structured close-reading approach—you might be able to start with the main idea, or you might need to assess the body of the text for its component parts and then see what they add up to at the end. In this example, we start with the main idea.

What is the main idea?

- Justice Joseph Story, who has recently died, leaves behind a significant legacy that stretches around the world, which is especially important because of how he advanced America's reputation for justice and legal wisdom.

What is the evidence that Webster uses to support his claim?

- Details from the life of Justice Story—that he died at 65, that his words live on, that he lived a long life, that his work had an impact on many courts and lawyers.
- Justice Story's work on the Constitution and in the American legal profession helped contribute to jurisprudence abroad—"restraint of illegal power" and "discouragement and rebuke of licentious and disorganizing sentiments."
- In addition to his strengths as a writer and a judge, Justice Story was also a friendly person, morally upright, animated, generous.

How does he communicate about his main idea and evidence with the reader? What rhetorical strategies and techniques do you notice in the extract above? Since you have a list of what the text is saying, now you can start to consider what tools Webster uses to make his point and leave readers with the impression he wants to give them.

- **Mournful tone:** Webster makes it clear the judge will be missed personally and professionally.
- **Laudatory tone:** Webster praises Justice Story's professional accomplishments and the lasting, global value of his contributions.
- **Ostentatious language:** Webster uses French and Latin to enhance not only Justice Story's status, but his own; it also supports his legal qualifications and elevates the significance of Justice Story's contributions.
- **Metaphor:** Webster compares England and America to a mother and daughter, and Justice (as an abstract concept) to a ligament, a religion, and a building.
- **Context:** By addressing multiple facets of Justice Story's career, as a writer, a judge, and a person, Webster conveys a complete portrait of the departed judge.
- **Details:** Though Webster is not explicit about individual cases, he does make observations that illustrate Justice Story's ability to synthesize "codes of nations, to trace their differences … And to exhibit, nevertheless, their concurrence in those great principles upon which the system of human civilization rests."
- **Synecdoche:** According to Webster, by contributing to justice as an institution, Justice Story has made an indelible legacy for himself ("… connects himself in name, and fame and character, with that which is and must be as durable as the frame of human society.").

You are not only articulating what the author has done (which reflects your perspective), you're also evaluating its effectiveness.

If you didn't get all of these aspects out of this text on your first read-through, that's okay. You'll be able to get more practice in the sample exams in this book and online.

Here is how to turn that into your own argument and support it with meaningful evidence from the text.

It may seem obvious, but your reading of the text is actually already subjective. By summarizing the author's main idea, you've made a determination about what they were trying to do, and by citing individual moments of the text as evidence, you are arguing that they did it! But how do you take that to the next level and turn it into meaningful analysis?

You must interpret the *effect* of the writer's rhetorical strategies—was the writer successful? Ineffective? Hypocritical? Do you want to make a claim about the writer's intent? Did the writer overlook a crucial counterargument that could have strengthened or weakened his or her stance? Keep asking yourself, "so what?" as you identify evidence in support of what the main idea is, and be sure to consider what the argument might have lost if the writer *hadn't* included that particular rhetorical technique. Your analysis should not only document what the writer did, but also how he or she did it, and why it matters.

A focused freewrite may be a good way to generate ideas for this essay—only spend about 5 minutes on it, though, so that you can leave yourself 35 minutes for drafting and revision.

Sample Freewrite (5 min)

This eulogy sounds like one intelligent legal mind praising another, and maybe trying to make sure people don't panic and think the progress that was made will not last since people from this generation of lawmakers are dying. The element of this text I was most struck by was the use of other languages. Why would a speaker do that? Would they know their readers/listeners understood? What might they achieve by using that? Other devices included metaphors and broader context. I think I want to focus on the cues the speaker gives that tell us who his intended audience is because that's the most significant aspect of this kind of speech.

Sample Outline (5-7 min)

Introduction: Daniel Webster, one of the prominent politicians of his era, delivered a heartfelt and thoughtful eulogy after the death of a Supreme Court Justice, Joseph Story. His speech is notable for not only its depth of feeling, but the intensity of the writing itself. Webster clearly felt he was speaking to more people than just those who were in the room to observe the judge's passing.

Body paragraph 1: Rhetorical techniques used to support the main idea (references to political/global context, use of metaphor, including phrases in other languages)

Body paragraph 2: Discussion of a technique that seems most significant (use of other languages). Possible explanations—pretentious, reflection of law profession at the period, sign of respect

Body paragraph 3: Analysis of that technique. Use of other languages makes the departed Justice sound like part of a more elevated group, and elevates the listeners by association. Rather than mourning someone who is gone, tactics that link him to a larger ongoing context make the listeners feel less bereft and less worried about negative impact to the legal profession.

Conclusion: Considering the point of a eulogy, Webster uses what made the man great to discuss what makes the profession great, so the man's legacy can live on.

Argument

The third type of free-response prompt, the argument question, requires the least interaction with outside texts, which makes it harder for some writers and easier for others, You'll likely be provided with a quote from another famous writer for inspiration, and asked to argue a position in response to it. Your examples will come from your own reading, experience, or observations, but must still contribute to making your argument effective and well crafted.

Here's how to use a short quote as a jumping-off point:

Sample Argument Prompt

> *"No place is ever as bad as they tell you it's going to be."*
> —Chuck Thompson

> *"I am not the same, having seen the moon shine on the other side of the world."*
> —Mary Anne Radmacher

> *"Travel makes one modest. You see what a tiny place you occupy in the world."*
> —Gustave Flaubert

These writers each share a personal perspective on the benefits of traveling the world. Write an essay that argues your position on the value of travel for broadening horizons or shifting perspective. Use appropriate examples from your reading, experience, or own observations to support your argument.

Again, rely on your personal process to do a quick pre-write for this essay—you may find brainstorming is particularly helpful for this kind of question, because it will allow you to generate more ideas than you need. For this particular prompt, you might jot down notes about places you've traveled, books you've read that involved unfamiliar locations, the benefits of experience that make you uncomfortable and challenge your assumptions, or anything else that the idea of hopping on a plane sparks for you! Don't be afraid to think beyond the first idea that occurs to you—there are potentially successful essays to be drafted that argue for travel as life-changing, against travel as environmentally negligent, or on behalf of specific types of trips. You could support educational journeys but disagree with consumeristic cruises, for example, or take a stance on availing oneself of electronic distractions instead of being present for a long road trip. Think about particular writers whose work was irrevocably changed by exploring someplace new—Charlotte Brontë in Brussels, Ernest Hemingway in Spain, Chimamanda Ngozi Adichie coming to the United States, Mark Twain rafting down the Mississippi. Any of these anecdotes are fair game.

Types of Argument

There are several categories of argument that may be useful for you to understand and practice writing—once you've mastered them, you'll be a much more effective communicator because you'll know how to respond to each flavor of argument with the appropriate counter-evidence or interpretation. We'll try these out on our traveling prompt after we get to know each category a little better.

Fact: "My car was stolen." This may sound like a definitive statement—either it happened, or it didn't! But, it actually contains a lot of room for debate. Was it in fact this person's car? Is there proof that someone else took it unlawfully? Could it have been towed? Debates of fact often occur in legal proceedings, but they are also subordinate issues in larger cases, the things you have to establish in order to move on to other things.

Definition: "You stole my car." The person being accused of stealing the car could reply that *he* didn't steal it (challenging "you"). Or, he could deny that what he has is in fact the accuser's car (challenging "my"). He could even challenge "stole" by responding he had permission to take it, and it's your word against his.

Value/Morality: "I only stole it to take my sick mother to the hospital, so it wasn't morally wrong." Notice how the grounds for debate have shifted? The person making this argument isn't debating whether the car was stolen, or even whether he stole it. He has moved the goalposts and is now crafting an argument about what the theft *means*. He might even try to use this argument to avoid serious consequences.

Cause/Consequence: "Poverty made me steal the car." This argument is about why the incident happened; this angle could also involve an approach like, "If I hadn't stolen the car, my mother could have died," or "It's your fault I stole the car because you wouldn't give me a ride." At this point the person whose car was stolen might protest, "Stealing the car was *your choice*, not *my fault*!" But, then they've gone back to a definition argument and aren't engaging apples to apples, oranges to oranges!

Policy/Proposal: "We need better public transportation and financial assistance for sick people." This argument approach disregards what happened, what it meant, or why it happened in favor of preventing it from happening again. Political approaches to problem-solving often involve identifying underlying causes and coming up with suggestions—using the fact or definition that's being debated as evidence—for how to address the issue.

Choosing a Type of Argument

Let's look again at the travel prompt.

> *"No place is ever as bad as they tell you it's going to be."*
> —Chuck Thompson
>
> *"I am not the same, having seen the moon shine on the other side of the world."*
> —Mary Anne Radmacher
>
> *"Travel makes one modest. You see what a tiny place you occupy in the world."*
> —Gustave Flaubert

A prompt with these quotes might look something like this:

These writers each share a personal perspective on the benefits of traveling the world. Write an essay that argues your position on the value of travel for broadening horizons or shifting perspective. Use appropriate examples from your reading, experience, or own observations to support your argument.

Which of the three quotes are you most interested in responding to? Let's first label each with the type of argument implicit in its short statement.

> *"No place is ever as bad as they tell you it's going to be."*
> —Chuck Thompson

The judgment implied in "bad" tells you there's a value argument being made here, that many places are not that bad, or even good! Do you have any stories about going places you thought might be bad or difficult that turned out to be enjoyable or valuable experiences? That kind of experience might lend itself well to responding to this value argument in an additive way, saying "Yes and…" to contribute your own experience in support of Thompson's argument.

> *"I am not the same, having seen the moon shine on the other side of the world."*
> —Mary Anne Radmacher

You could read this as either a definition argument—"I am not the same" suggests the writer's assessment of who or what she is has changed—or potentially a cause/consequence argument because she's saying that "having seen the moon shine" is what made her change.

How would you respond to this one? Possible avenues might include recounting a story of a time when travel changed you, or an analysis of why seeing the moon in a new way leads to one feeling a sense of change.

> *"Travel makes one modest. You see what a tiny place you occupy in the world."*
> —Gustave Flaubert

This could also be interpreted as a cause/consequence argument; you could respond to it with a value argument (is it good to be modest?) or a policy argument (more people need to see what a tiny place they occupy in order to . . .). Consider your own experience, readings, and observations carefully to determine what kind of argument *you* want to make.

Let's say, for practice, you decide to focus on the Radmacher quote, "I am not the same, having seen the moon shine on the other side of the world." You might begin with a freewrite, or try some graphic organizing (aka "brainstorming"), as seen here:

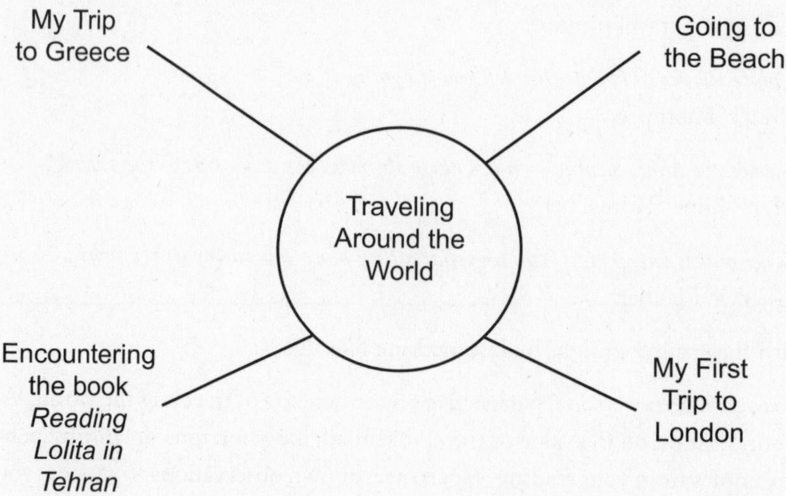

So you've generated some ideas related to this international travel prompt. The Greece trip may initially look the most promising, but imagine that after you've looked at them all written out, you realized you learned more about the experience of someone on the other side of the world from reading a book about Iranian women fighting for their education. Perhaps your London trip made you realize how similar other parts of the world are to where you already live, or maybe your trip to Greece just wasn't as transformative. That's okay! Because this is an argument essay, you can decide to expand on Mary Anne Radmacher's perspective, and even make use of the contrast between your Greece trip and your experience of reading Azar Nafisi's book. Your essay might look something like this, in outline form:

Introduction: Description of the quote, and the potential for transformation in travel—mention Greece and how you thought it would be transformational

Body paragraph 1: However, it's not only actual travel, but literature that has the power to make us imagine the moon shining on the other side of the world. A couple of examples from the book

Body paragraph 2: Compare/contrast of the Greek experience, where you were with a tour group, with *Reading Lolita in Tehran*, where you were immersed in the author's experience

Body paragraph 3: Compare/contrast with the London experience, where everything was similar in terms of language and culture, more or less, with *Reading Lolita in Tehran*, which brought all these cultural differences to life

Conclusion: Knowledge of the world is transformative, as Radmacher says, but luckily for those of us who can't always go see how the moon is shining, literature can transport us to these places, too. Conclude with a sentence about how reading that book meant you aren't the same.

TIMELINE FOR TEST-DAY WRITING

You have 2 hours and 15 minutes for the entire section. Plan on taking 15 minutes at the beginning to skim the entire exam—run over every text, circle key words in each prompt, and jot down any immediate thoughts you have upon reading the questions you'll be answering.

The suggested time for each question is 40 minutes. You may find that one type of exam comes to you much more easily than the other two, and you may be able to borrow some extra editing time by writing that one more quickly. As you take the practice exams in this book and online, make a note of your time for each type of prompt to see if you notice any patterns. The free-response questions are arranged from most intensive to least intensive already (synthesis requires the most close-reading and careful revision to check source use; analysis is anchored by only one text; argument is based on only your own experience), but you could be even more strategic by doing the one that takes you the least time first, to save any extra time in the exam period for the more difficult types of essays.

Let's say that you're equally challenged by each type.

Synthesis

Plan for a timeline that looks something like this:

- 10 minutes to read all 5-7 sources; use arrows to annotate their relationship, if they directly comment on or respond to one another
- 5 minutes to map out your outline or brainstorm using a graphic organizer—if you can, include transition signal phrases to help you remember how you're incorporating the sources (First, then, but, however, in conclusion, etc.)
- 20 minutes to write
- 5 minutes to read over/edit/proofread

You may be thinking, *a quarter of the exam time for just reading sources?!* But trust us—it is much easier to envision and craft an essay when you have actually processed the information you're trying to use. It's much less efficient to start writing while you're still analyzing the sources, starting sentences without being certain how you're going to finish them or how the next sentence is going to relate to the one you've just written!

Your priorities when you are rereading your work are to look out for missed words and obvious errors. You may find it helpful to do all your generating work—that is, drafting all three essays—and then save 15 minutes at the end to read over and proofread them all at once. Generating and editing are separate skills and demand different brain activity, so sometimes it's good to separate them. Alternatively, you may find it's more useful to reread when the essay and sources are fresh in your mind for this essay type.

Analysis

Plan for a timeline that looks something like this:

- 5-7 minutes to read the source, annotating as you go with close-reading strategies
- 5-7 minutes to make notes on main idea, evidence, and rhetorical techniques you notice
- 30 minutes to draft
- 5 minutes to read over/edit/proofread

Keep proportion firmly in mind for this essay. Try to limit your descriptive writing, just introducing the passage for an unfamiliar reader or recounting what happens in the excerpt, to a single paragraph. That should be enough time to summarize the main idea and a few points of evidence; then you can get straight to introducing your own rhetorical analysis. What are they saying, and how are they saying it? And why does it matter? If you are attempting a five-paragraph essay, the "What are they saying" gets one paragraph, "how are they saying it" gets three paragraphs, and the "so what" gets one paragraph. Don't get drawn into too much summary, or you'll run out of time or wind up cramming your analysis into your conclusion. Exam readers are going to be seeing a ton of essays that fall into the "play-by-play" trap, so do your best to avoid it!

Argument

Plan for a timeline that looks something like this:

- 2-3 minutes to read the prompt and circle key words
- 10 minutes to freewrite or brainstorm relevant personal experiences, observations, and readings
- 20 minutes to draft
- 5 minutes to read over/edit/proofread; make sure you have answered the prompt

The dangerous part about freewriting or writing associatively with a short prompt is sometimes you can drift away from what the prompt is actually asking you to do. Remember that even though your evidence includes personal experience, you are still required to craft an argument. An argument must be debatable. It must be supported by evidence.

GUIDELINES FOR WRITING A GOOD AP® ESSAY

You may be asking yourself, what are the AP® Exam Readers looking for? What do they expect from me in 2 hours and 15 minutes? The good news is, the readers know that you only have roughly 40 minutes per exam question, and aren't looking for a finished product or the same kind of work you're capable of in an out-of-class assignment. They want to reward you for what you do well. Let's break down what they're looking for on each score, for each type of exam.

Synthesis

8-9, Effective: At this level, the writer has effectively argued in favor of his or her position, used appropriate and convincing explanations, and showed evidence of an ability to use multiple techniques to craft compelling writing in a successful way. The distinction between an 8 and a 9 comes down to the sophistication of the argument or impressiveness of the language.

5-6-7, Adequate: A writer earning this score has successfully taken a stance on the prompt; he or she has developed an argument by synthesizing at least three sources, used appropriate and sufficient evidence, and has generally clear prose. The difference between a 6 and a 7 is related to how completely or thoroughly the writer has crafted the argument, or the maturity of his or her prose.

3-4, Inadequate: A response in this range fails to argue any kind of position; the writer may synthesize as many as two sources, but the evidence is inaccurate or unconvincing. The writer may have neglected the argument in favor of the sources, or oversimplified them. The prose may communicate the writer's meaning but be inconsistent or lack the elements of effective writing and editing. Examples may be limited or too simple. The difference between a 3 and a 4 is the maturity of the writing and the perceptiveness the writer demonstrates toward the sources.

1-2, Little Success: A response that gets this score wasn't able to do much more than reiterate information gained from the prompt, or may have mentioned information gained from those sources without actually citing them appropriately. The writer may end up in this range if he or she has misread the sources, failed to develop an argument, or responded with unrelated tangents.

0, Incomplete: A writer who receives a zero went off topic in the response, merely repeated the prompt, crossed out his or her response, or left the page blank.

Analysis

8-9, Effective: The most successful essays for this prompt will clearly articulate and analyze the rhetorical strategies present in the passage; their evidence and explanations are appropriate and persuasive and refer consistently to the passage. The prose is competent and controlled, and conveys meaning well.

5-6-7, Adequate: At this level, writers are appropriately analyzing rhetorical strategies at work in the passage; the writer's analysis is developed via sufficient explanations and evidence, and refers specifically to the passage throughout. The writing may have errors of diction or syntax, but is generally clear.

3-4, Inadequate: An essay at this level is insufficiently analytical of the rhetorical strategies present in the passage; the writer may have misunderstood those strategies, or the explanation may be inappropriate or unconvincing. The prose is generally comprehensible but inconsistent and lacking in control.

1-2, Little Success: Essays with this score demonstrate misunderstanding of the prompt, misreading of the passage, failure to identify or analyze any rhetorical strategies, or they answer the prompt with an unrelated, inaccurate, or inappropriate explanation. The prose shows weaknesses of thought, planning, organization, and execution (grammar).

0, Incomplete: A writer who receives a zero went off topic in the response, merely repeated the prompt, crossed out his or her response, or left the page blank.

Argument

8-9, Effective: Essays that earn this score have successfully argued for the author's perspective on the given issue. The evidence is well explained and convincing; the argument is coherent and developed appropriately. The prose is consistent, controlled, and informative.

5-6-7, Adequate: Prose at this level is making an argument that is sufficient and coherent. The development is appropriate and addresses the prompt directly and clearly. The writing may have errors but is generally clear.

3-4, Inadequate: Essays with this score struggle to argue a position in response to the prompt; the evidence or examples are insufficient, unconvincing or inappropriate, or may be incoherent or underdeveloped. The prose is communicative but inconsistent and uncontrolled, showing little mature ability.

1-2, Little Success: At this level, the writer has failed to argue a position about the prompt; he or she may have misunderstood the question or responded with an unrelated, inaccurate, or inappropriate narrative. The essay is underdeveloped and lacks coherence.

0, Incomplete: A writer who receives a zero went off topic in the response, merely repeated the prompt, crossed out his or her response, or left the page blank.

Notice anything about the specific language attached to each of these categories? Even the top score describes writing that is only "effective"! Not exceptional, not fantastic, not brilliant—just effective! Don't use that as an excuse to phone it in (there's a colloquialism for you), but keep it in mind if you tend to have grade anxiety. This doesn't mean you can't be inspired or write an eloquent, thoughtful essay, but it means you should manage your expectations by keeping the criteria for a top score in mind.

Across the board, effectiveness means that you accurately read the prompt, developed an argument of your own, and supported it with information from your sources or the passage or your own experience. Your prose was clear and thoughtful, and you didn't get so worried about occasional lapses in grammar or syntax that you derailed from your goal of clearly articulating your position. Calibrate your expectations, and it should help with some of the high-stakes feelings that exams like this tend to create in many test-takers.

Writing Under Pressure

The most important thing to do when you're writing under tight time constraints is to breathe. Decide what you want to say before you start writing, and then record your entire thought. Refer to your pre-writing documents as often as you need to in order to figure out what's next. Remember, the readers know you have only 40 minutes for each assignment, so the most important goal to accomplish is coming up with a clear idea and communicating it coherently and as thoughtfully as you can.

To practice, use timers on the sample exams and try to make the room where you practice as much like the testing conditions as possible. Take a few minutes to calm yourself before you start, and after you finish, take some time to jot down reflections about what went well, what was more challenging than you expected, and anything you might like to do differently next time.

Revision Techniques

If this were a regular class assignment, you'd have a few days—maybe even a week—to revise and polish your prose. But this is crunch time! On exam day, if you follow our suggestions, you'll be spending only 5 minutes or so rereading your free-response essays. How do you focus?

1. **Look for missing words.** One of the challenges of writing by hand is that your brain moves faster than your pencil can, so when you re-read, make sure you're "hearing" every word in your head. If you need to mouth the words, go for it—just make sure you're not audible or distracting anyone near you. When you're feeling stressed, it's really easy to just remember what a sentence is *supposed* to say and totally miss what it is *actually* saying. Read as carefully as you can while still moving quickly.
2. **Look for misspelled words or serious errors of grammar.** The test readers know that you're writing under duress, so they are not going to expect every turn of phrase to be perfect. That said, too many obvious errors will impact your score significantly.
3. **Check for punctuation**. Make sure there are periods at the end of every sentence, apostrophes where they belong, and commas that make reading as clear and easy as possible.

SAMPLE PROMPTS AND PASSAGES

Practice your new free-response test taking skills by trying out these sample passages and prompts. Set a timer, experiment with different prewriting strategies, and don't glance at the sample answers before you're done!

Synthesis

Since the very earliest days of the country's founding, the United States has had to grapple with multiple groups of people laying claim to the same areas of land. One way political leaders sought to balance these competing needs and interests was by establishing national parks, with certain protections and enforcement authorizations that allowed them to preserve areas of the country deemed of value to the nation as a whole.

Carefully read the following sources, then synthesize information from at least three of them into a coherent, well-developed argument for your own position on whether or not national parks deserve to be protected, maintained, established, or eliminated altogether. Your argument should be the focus of your essay. Use the sources to explain your reasoning, citing them clearly and appropriately through summary, paraphrase, and direct quotation.

Source A (news bulletin)

Source B (National Park System Advisory Board)

Source C (NPS)

Source D (A Visitor to the Grand Canyon)

Source E (Yard)

Source F (Native Perspective on National Parks)

Source A

House Moves to Encourage Drilling in National Parks

In the early months of 2017, Congressman Paul Gosar (R-Ariz) proposed a piece of legislation designed to dismantle and undermine legal safety, planning and administration guidelines for oil and gas drilling inside more than 40 national parks that have what's called "split estate" ownership, that is, the government claims the rights to the surface land, but not the mineral rights beneath it. The House has also voted on legislation that repeals restrictions on methane gas waste and planning regulations from the Bureau of Land Management, which attempt to balance the needs of multi-use lands where different organizations pursue energy development, conservation and recreation. Senior members of the national parks Conservation Association released statements urging Congress to reject these challenges to the autonomy and environmental health of the nation's national parks. The rules put in place by the Bureau of Land Management, called 9B rules, require the would-be developer to create a Plan of Operations, give the National Park Service an opportunity to enforce safety policies and technical specifications that protect the wildlife, air, and water of the parks. Should Congress succeed in repealing these rules, the National Park Service will lose the authority to reject proposed actions, hold developers accountable for any damage they do, or manage the relationship between drilling companies and park visitors, who would no longer have to be notified of any drilling work in the park.

Source B

Rethinking the National Parks for the 21st Century
A Report of the National Park System Advisory Board
July 2001

The creation of a national park is an expression of faith in the future. It is a pact between generations, a promise from the past to the future. In 1916, Congress established the National Park Service to conserve the parks "unimpaired for the enjoyment of future generations." This act and the many others that have created the National Park Service and related programs echoes the promise of the Constitution "to secure the Blessings of Liberty for ourselves and our Posterity." We are that future, and we too must act on behalf of our successors.

We must envision and ensure a system of parks and programs that benefits a new generation of citizens in a changing world.

National parks are greatly admired. Inspiring us, uplifting our spirits, they serve as powerful reminders of our national origins and destiny. Yet there are opportunities unfulfilled. The parks should reach broader segments of society in ways that make them more meaningful in the life of the nation.

As a nation, we are re-examining the effectiveness of our educational institutions. The Park Service should be viewed as such an institution. Parks are places to demonstrate the principles of biology, to illustrate the national experience as history, to engage formal and informal learners throughout their lifetime, and to do these things while challenging them in exciting and motivating settings. Parks are places to stimulate an understanding of history in its larger context, not just as human experience, but as the sum of the interconnection of all living things and forces that shape the earth.

When Yellowstone National Park was established in 1872, it signaled a new way the world would view its land and, eventually, its seas. A youthful, growing nation absorbed in westward expansion had set aside two million acres on which no one could lawfully settle, extract minerals or timber, and—after the turn of the 19th century—even hunt. This truly American idea later spread to other nations.

National parks in America succeeded beyond their originators' wildest dreams. By the mid-20th century, they were meccas for warm-weather vacationists. A summer pilgrimage to the great parks of the West was a rite of passage for the American family. For some it was a journey of hope to understand the American way of life; for others, to rediscover their place in the natural world. A third of all adults of this country have visited a unit of the National Park Service sometime within the past two years. Surveys show visitors give the parks an approval rating of 95 percent for their inspiring sights, useful information, and helpful personnel. The experience is often powerful and sometimes memorable over a lifetime.

In these days of concern about personal safety, national parks are considered safe places to take a family. In an era of glitz and technological wizardry, they awe people with natural wonders, authentic places, and dramatic stories. At a time of public cynicism about many matters on the national scene, opinion surveys indicate that the National Park Service enjoys one of the highest public approval ratings of all government agencies.

From the beginning the National Park Service has sought to be people-friendly. The leadership of the new organization realized that the best way to engender support for the parks was to ensure that the visitors "enjoyed" them. They set about providing facilities to promote a positive experience. They were successful.

Managing for people, however, had an effect on some areas the Service was supposed to protect. Villages sprang up in wild places. Fish populations were manipulated to enhance sportfishing. Popular species of ungulates such as bison, elk, moose, and bighorn sheep were protected, while predators such as wolves and mountain lions were trapped and shot. (Bears came into favor once tourists showed a fancy for feeding them and watching them scavenge at garbage dumps.) Forest fires were suppressed, despite warnings that the buildup of debris would fuel more destructive conflagrations.

It is time to re-examine the "enjoyment equals support" equation and to encourage public support of resource protection at a higher level of understanding. In giving priority to visitor services, the National Park Service has paid less attention to the resources it is obliged to protect for future generations. As a result, few parks have adequate inventories of flora and fauna. Most archaeological sites in the system have not been surveyed. These oversights must not continue. A sophisticated knowledge of resources and their condition is essential. The Service must gain this knowledge through extensive collaboration with other agencies and academia, and its findings must be communicated to the public. For it is the broader public that will decide the fate of these resources.

Source: https://www.nps.gov/policy/report.htm

Source C

PASSENGER STATISTICS BY ROUTE & COSTS - 1974 to Present

Visitor Transportation System - Grand Canyon National Park

National Park Service
U.S. Department of the Interior
Grand Canyon National Park
Grand Canyon, Arizona

YEAR	PARK VISITS	DAYS OF VTS OPN	VILLAGE ROUTE RIDES	HERMITS REST ROUTE RIDES	KAIBAB TRAIL ROUTE RIDES	CANYON VIEW/ MATHER POINT RIDES	SOUTH GATE RIDES	TOTAL RIDES	RIDES PER VISITOR	CONTRACT: DRIVERS + MECHS + PARTS	COST PER RIDE	MILES DRIVEN (Not incl Trailer)	COST PER MILE (Not Incl Fuel)	PASS PER MILE
1974	2,028,194		955,069	371,839	0	0	0	1,326,908	0.65					
1975	2,754,791		1,185,284	416,913	0	0	0	1,602,197	0.58					
1976	3,026,235		1,147,986	484,823	0	0	0	1,632,809	0.54					
1977	2,848,419		1,187,464	455,907	0	0	0	1,643,371	0.58					
1978	2,984,138		1,196,114	442,579	0	0	0	1,638,693	0.55					
1979	2,275,712		1,246,549	370,469	0	0	0	1,617,018	0.71					
1980	2,618,713		1,181,896	377,843	0	0	0	1,559,739	0.60					
1981	2,674,117		1,087,458	327,167	0	0	0	1,414,625	0.53					
1982	2,499,799		1,070,339	362,335	0	0	0	1,432,674	0.57					
1983	2,448,545		1,039,887	372,357	2,163	0	0	1,414,407	0.58					
1984	2,360,767		934,160	400,741	4,603	0	0	1,339,504	0.57					
1985	2,983,436		764,684	654,690	5,292	0	0	1,424,666	0.48					
1986	3,347,872		894,255	1,322,490	4,255	0	0	2,221,000	0.66					
1987	3,513,084		906,897	1,675,651	6,452	0	0	2,589,000	0.74					
1988	3,858,708		1,065,838	1,475,609	8,193	0	0	2,549,640	0.66					
1989	3,968,605		766,897	1,368,786	4,838	0	0	2,140,521	0.54		Average			
1990	3,752,901	129	725,813	1,385,654	4,754	0	0	2,116,221	0.56	Cumulative	Since			
1991	3,905,989	130	845,971	1,562,778	6,779	0	0	2,415,528	0.62	Since Start	Start			
1992	4,547,027	132	872,215	1,572,228	6,541	0	42,474	2,493,458	0.55	12,647,000	0.39			
1993	4,928,509	122	749,691	1,467,566	0	0	0	2,217,257	0.45	629,583	0.30			
1994	4,704,070	122	689,822	1,449,528	0	0	0	2,139,350	0.45	587,841	0.29			
1995	4,908,073	128	657,600	1,397,400	0	0	0	2,055,000	0.42	541,255	0.28			
1996	4,730,682	143	712,885	1,318,207	0	0	0	2,031,092	0.43	655,892	0.34			
1997	4,851,931	185	690,305	1,527,478	132,340	0	0	2,350,123	0.48	974,854	0.43	315,406	3.22	7.5
1998	4,578,089	220	848,829	2,113,436	225,493	0	0	3,187,758	0.70	1,114,206	0.36	348,797	3.31	9.1
1999	4,937,652	220	920,980	2,311,456	243,876	0	0	3,476,312	0.70	1,183,673	0.40	487,977	2.82	7.1
2000	4,816,559	297	1,254,052	2,573,318	427,142	0	0	4,254,512	0.88	2,114,811	0.54	561,610	4.10	7.6
2001	4,400,823	365	1,591,822	2,564,422	615,188	0	0	4,771,432	1.08	2,527,717	0.57	535,264	5.08	8.9
2002	4,339,139	365	1,631,929	2,280,003	350,238	0	0	4,262,170	0.98	2,668,275	0.67	661,320	4.32	6.4
2003	4,464,400	365	1,588,657	2,375,727	380,586	19,806	0	4,364,776	0.98	2,775,215	0.68	669,026	4.43	6.5
2004	4,672,910	366	1,656,236	2,418,496	403,987	20,705	0	4,499,424	0.96	2,728,457	0.65	684,005	4.27	6.6
2005		365					0							
TOTAL	114,729,889		32,067,584	39,197,896	2,832,720		42,474	74,181,185	0.65	31,148,779	0.42			

SUMMER 2003 SURVEY REPORTED THAT THE AVERAGE RIDER BOARDED 4.5 TIMES DURING THEIR VISIT

1995 statistics collected differently from other years; amounts estimated
On March 10, 2000, system began year-round operations.

January 13, 2005

Visitor stats

[Source: https://www.nps.gov/grca/learn/management/upload/VTS-Route-Stats.pdf]

Source D

Personal Account (2016)

They told us at the gate that 90% of visitors to the Grand Canyon never go below the rim. They come on buses and in cars and aboard helicopters from Las Vegas even and they assemble in varying degrees of disbelief and solemnity and ebullience at the edge of the world, looking out on a mile of depth and miles of width and length. They see rock formations that tell the story of Earth's adolescence. If they go even a quarter of a mile beneath the rim on the Bright Angel Trail, they'd see petroglyphs drawn by the Canyon's original inhabitants as they moved from their summer farming sites to their winter ones. If they went another mile, they'd find a rest house with water and bathrooms and outcroppings that seem to launch you out over the side canyons. If they braved the full descent down to the Indian Garden campground, one of the trails would take them out on Plateau Point and if they timed it just right, they would feel themselves the only person in the Grand Canyon, because not a soul would be visible way up on the rim or around a curve and bend of the angular trail. The people ahead of them would have vanished after the rising plateau dips down a little. The people behind would be hidden by a promontory uplifted rock. All they would experience is the whistle of the wind, and the glow of the sun, and the looming canyon walls all around for miles. And this is part of the magic. Looking down into the chalky green Colorado River from Plateau Point, or feeling its chill close around you if you boldly plunge in, these are not things you can experience from the relative safety of the rim. You will not see the colorful striations of rock—and not the rusty red and orange you've almost gotten used to, but pale greens and purples from when this was the bottom of a primordial sea. Go beneath the rim. Pack a bag and bring some water and go beneath it. Don't stand for a paltry 45 minutes when this Canyon has been waiting for your gaze for millions of years.

Source E

***The Book of the National Parks*, by Robert Sterling Yard**
"On the Appreciation of Scenery"

To the average educated American, scenery is a pleasing hodge-podge of mountains, valleys, plains, lakes, and rivers. To him, the glacier-hollowed valley of Yosemite, the stream-scooped abyss of the Grand Canyon, the volcanic gulf of Crater Lake, the bristling granite core of the Rockies, and the ancient ice-carved shales of Glacier National Park all are one—just scenery, magnificent, incomparable, meaningless. As a people we have been content to wonder, not to know; yet with scenery, as with all else, to know is to begin fully to enjoy. Appreciation measures enjoyment. And this brings me to my proposition, namely, that we shall not really enjoy our possession of the grandest scenery in the world until we realize that scenery is the written page of the History of Creation, and until we learn to read that page.

The national parks of America include areas of the noblest and most diversified scenic sublimity easily accessible in the world; nevertheless it is their chiefest glory that they are among the completest expressions of the earth's history. The American people is waking rapidly to the magnitude of its scenic possession; it has yet to learn to appreciate it.

…

Love of beauty is practically a universal passion. It is that which lures millions into the fields, valleys, woods, and mountains on every holiday, which crowds our ocean lanes and railroads. The fact that few of these rejoicing millions are aware of their own motive, and that, strangely enough, a few even would be ashamed to make the admission if they became aware of it, has nothing to do with the fact. It's a wise man that knows his own motives. The fact that still fewer, whether aware or not of the reason of their happiness, are capable of making the least expression of it, also has nothing to do with the fact. The tourist woman whom I met at the foot of Yosemite Falls may have felt secretly suffocated by the filmy grandeur of the incomparable spectacle, notwithstanding that she was conscious of no higher emotion than the cheap wonder of a superlative. The Grand Canyon's rim is the stillest crowded place I know. I've stood among a hundred people on a precipice and heard the whir of a bird's wings in the abyss. Probably the majority of those silent gazers were suffering something akin to pain at their inability to give vent to the emotions bursting within them.

I believe that the statement can not be successfully challenged that, as a people, our enjoyment of scenery is almost wholly emotional. Love of beauty spiced by wonder is the equipment for enjoyment of the average intelligent traveller of to-day. Now add to this a more or less equal part of the intellectual pleasure of comprehension and you have the equipment of the average intelligent traveller of to-morrow. To hasten this to-morrow is one of the several objects of this book.

Source F

A Native Perspective on Wilderness and Nostalgia (excerpt)

While the idea of establishing National Parks plays into a collective nostalgia for the past and a nationalistic yearning for wilderness, the conversation about preservation and "geographic destinies" often disregards the experience of Native tribes and their ongoing fight to retain their tribal lands and resources. Painter George Catlin once called for a "nation's park" where tourists could come gawk at Native Americans, because at the time of his writing (1833), the nation was prone to romanticizing a Native way of life as depicted through the work of artists and writers like Catlin, while also pursuing federal legislation that continually disenfranchised Native populations from coast to coast in service of an idea of "Americanness" that meant not sharing. Many tribes were coerced into signing treaty after treaty, which required them to move further west, displacing other tribes in the process, only to find those treaties vacated and their "sovereign lands" filled with settlers and homesteaders. So it's hard for some Natives to join the fight to save national parks when their own tribal land on which they are still living is being invaded by pipelines from oil companies and drilling from mining companies. Wouldn't it be better, instead of investing the National Park Service with more authority, if the government could restore autonomy to "Indian Country" across the nation? This would mean sacrificing some of America's tourism, yes, but if it means enfranchising a group of people historically prone to federal destruction with no recourse, wouldn't it be worth it?

Analysis

On the 71st anniversary of the destruction of Hiroshima and Nagasaki by American pilots dropping the atomic bomb, President Barack Obama was the first sitting U.S. President to visit Hiroshima, where he declared the memory of that act of warfare "must never fade," but didn't say Americans should be or were sorry for the action. Read the original statement issued by President Harry S. Truman following his decision to drop the atomic bomb; then in a well-written essay, analyze the rhetorical choices Truman makes to develop his argument in support of dropping the bomb.

August 6, 1945: Statement by the President Announcing the Use of the A-Bomb at Hiroshima
Transcript

Sixteen hours ago an American airplane dropped one bomb on Hiroshima, an important Japanese Army base. That bomb had more power than 20,000 tons of T.N.T. It had more than two thousand times the blast power of the British "Grand Slam" which is the largest bomb ever yet used in the history of warfare.

The Japanese began the war from the air at Pearl Harbor. They have been repaid many fold. And the end is not yet. With this bomb we have now added a new and revolutionary increase in destruction to supplement the growing power of our armed forces. In their present form these bombs are now in production and even more powerful forms are in development.

It is an atomic bomb. It is a harnessing of the basic power of the universe. The force from which the sun draws its power has been loosed against those who brought war to the Far East.

Before 1939, it was the accepted belief of scientists that it was theoretically possible to release atomic energy. But no one knew any practical method of doing it. By 1942, however, we knew that the Germans were working feverishly to find a way to add atomic energy to the other engines of war with which they hoped to enslave the world. But they failed. We may be grateful to Providence that the Germans got the V-1's and V-2's late and in limited quantities and even more grateful that they did not get the atomic bomb at all.

The battle of the laboratories held fateful risks for us as well as the battles of the air, land and sea, and we have now won the battle of the laboratories as we have won the other battles.

Beginning in 1940, before Pearl Harbor, scientific knowledge useful in war was pooled between the United States and Great Britain, and many priceless helps to our victories have come from that arrangement. Under that general policy the research on the atomic bomb was begun. With American and British scientists working together we entered the race of discovery against the Germans.

The United States had available the large number of scientists of distinction in the many needed areas of knowledge. It had the tremendous industrial and financial resources necessary for the project and they could be devoted to it without undue impairment of other vital war work. In the United States the laboratory work and the production plants, on which a substantial start had already been made, would be out of reach of enemy bombing, while at that time Britain was exposed to constant air attack and was still threatened with the possibility of invasion. For these reasons Prime Minister Churchill and President Roosevelt agreed that it was wise to carry on the project here. We now have two great plants and many lesser works devoted to the production of atomic power. Employment during peak construction numbered 125,000 and over 65,000 individuals are even now engaged in operating the plants. Many have worked there for two and a half years. Few know what they have been producing. They see great quantities of material going in and they see nothing coming out of these plants, for the physical size of the explosive charge is exceedingly small. We have spent two billion dollars on the greatest scientific gamble in history—and won.

But the greatest marvel is not the size of the enterprise, its secrecy, nor its cost, but the achievement of scientific brains in putting together infinitely complex pieces of knowledge held by many men in different fields of science into a workable plan. And hardly less marvelous has been the capacity of industry to design, and of labor to operate, the machines and methods to do things never done before so that the brain child of many minds came forth in physical shape and performed as it was supposed to do. Both science and industry worked under the direction of the United States Army, which achieved a unique success in managing so diverse a problem in the advancement of knowledge in an amazingly short time. It is doubtful if such another combination could be got together in the world. What has been done is the greatest achievement of organized science in history. It was done under high pressure and without failure.

We are now prepared to obliterate more rapidly and completely every productive enterprise the Japanese have above ground in any city. We shall destroy their docks, their factories, and their communications. Let there be no mistake; we shall completely destroy Japan's power to make war.

It was to spare the Japanese people from utter destruction that the ultimatum of July 26 was issued at Potsdam. Their leaders promptly rejected that ultimatum. If they do not now accept our terms they may expect a rain of ruin from the air, the like of which has never been seen on this earth. Behind this air attack will follow sea and land forces in such numbers and power as they have not yet seen and with the fighting skill of which they are already well aware.

The Secretary of War, who has kept in personal touch with all phases of the project, will immediately make public a statement giving further details.

His statement will give facts concerning the sites at Oak Ridge near Knoxville, Tennessee, and at Richland near Pasco, Washington, and an installation near Santa Fe, New Mexico. Although the workers at the sites have been making materials to be used in producing the greatest destructive force in history they have not themselves been in danger beyond that of many other occupations, for the utmost care has been taken of their safety.

The fact that we can release atomic energy ushers in a new era in man's understanding of nature's forces. Atomic energy may in the future supplement the power that now comes from coal, oil, and falling water, but at present it cannot be produced on a basis to compete with them commercially. Before that comes there must be a long period of intensive research.

It has never been the habit of the scientists of this country or the policy of this Government to withhold from the world scientific knowledge. Normally, therefore, everything about the work with atomic energy would be made public.

But under present circumstances it is not intended to divulge the technical processes of production or all the military applications, pending further examination of possible methods of protecting us and the rest of the world from the danger of sudden destruction.

I shall recommend that the Congress of the United States consider promptly the establishment of an appropriate commission to control the production and use of atomic power within the United States. I shall give further consideration and make further recommendations to the Congress as to how atomic power can become a powerful and forceful influence towards the maintenance of world peace.

Argument

"Bilingual educators say today that children lose a degree of "individuality" by becoming assimilated into public society . . . but the bilingualists oversimplify when they scorn the value and necessity of assimilation. They do not seem to realize that a person is individualized in two ways. So they do not realize that, while one suffers a diminished sense of *private* individuality by being assimilated into public society, such assimilation makes possible the achievement of *public* individuality."

—Richard Rodriguez, "Aria"

In a well-written essay, develop your position on the efficacy or necessity of assimilation in a culture or community with which you are familiar. Examples might include language, modes of dress, styles of communication, or any other aspect of difference for which you can find evidence in your reading, experience, or observations to support your argument.

Sample Responses: Synthesis

High-Scoring Response

The National Parks are an essential part of our national identity as Americans. All of the problems we have as a people, we see enacted in our national parks. For example, the mistreatment of Native populations that occurred just so we could *have* parks, by seizing Native lands and favoring our idea of what wilderness is over their claims to the land they live on (source F). Still we see some of our strengths as Americans in our parks too. Beginning in the early 1900s, Americans began seeking to preserve some of what one Parks enthusiast called "our possession of the grandest scenery in the world," because of our emotional attachment to the sights and scenes of this country. The same historian said, "Love of beauty spiced by wonder is the equipment for enjoyment of the average intelligent traveler of today" (Source E) which is backed up by the reminiscences of a visitor to the Grand Canyon who agreed with the author of Source E about the stillness at the rim of the Canyon—"they assemble in varying degrees of disbelief and solemnity and ebullience at the edge of the world," (Source D). So our emotional attachment is fairly undisputed and supported by the regularity of visitors to parks like Yellowstone and the Grand Canyon, which doubled from the mid-70s to the early 2000s (source C).

But it is not our emotional attachment to the national parks that needs tending, it is our willingness to fight for their preservation. In early 2017, the Congressional House of Representatives began considering legislation that would "dismantle and undermine legal safety, planning, and administration guidelines for oil and gas drilling" inside many of the nation's parks that have unreserved mineral rights (Source A). Essentially declaring war on the Bureau of Land Management, Congressman Paul Gossar put forth this legislation designed to protect the interests of drilling and oil companies over the survival of the people, animals, and plants who still live on National Park land. I put people first, because as Source F points out, Native interests should really supersede everyone else's.

The trouble is, the National Park Service seems unprepared for the fight. In 2001 when they were first beginning to rethink the parks system, they stated that "The creation of a national park is an expression of faith in the future" (Source B). They didn't say who that pact was really between, though, aside from "generations". They said their intention was to "envision and ensure a system of parks and programs that benefits a new generation of citizens in a changing world." But what if the new generation is entirely made up of miners and oil companies? Can we justify the survival of the Parks as an educational institution if livelihoods and jobs are also on the line? Of course this is not a moral argument, but we gave up on moral arguments when we reneged on the first treaties that sent Native tribes Westward under false pretenses. Even the Park Service commission came to a more defensible conclusion at the end of their policy report—they noted that in prioritizing the experiences of visitors, they neglected the mission of preservation for future generations that is their real higher calling. But they left an important gap in their vision for the future by saying "it is the broader public that will decide the fate of these resources" (Source B). Unfortunately the House of Representatives is part of that broader public, and it is the obligation of all who love the beauty of our National Parks to fight the efforts of those who lack the emotional capacity or the faith in the future to protect them.

Score explanation: This writer has effectively argued for his position, that the public must push back on efforts to undermine the Park Service and Bureau of Land Management, and has used multiple techniques to make his writing compelling, including entertaining multiple perspectives for and against the object of the writer's argument. The prose is clear and the organization is logical. Sources are cited appropriately.

Middle-Scoring-Response

Many Americans feel strongly about preserving National Parks. When they hear about legislation being considered by congress that would cause the Park Service to "lose the authority to reject proposed actions, hold developers accountable. Or manage the relationship between drilling companies and park visitors," (source A) they get upset and start talking about their love of scenery and landscape. I do agree that National Parks should be preserved, but my reasons are different from the people who just think the lands are beautiful. As the Park Service itself decided in an advisory board meeting in 2001, the parks must do more than ensure park visitors enjoy their surroundings (Source B).

The Park Service must survey the land, get to know its resources to make sure they're being protected appropriately (for example, allowing natural wildfires instead of suppressing them, and being cautious about introducing different flora or fauna even if it promotes sport fishing). I also think they have a greater duty to get visitors past the easily accessible parts of the park—as a personal visitor to the Grand Canyon National Park said in 2016, "90% of visitors … never go below the rim." (Source D) But there are lots of things you can only see if you travel down into new areas.

The flip side is, of course, that these visitors are often the ones destroying habitats. As a historian of parks wrote in 1919, "The American people is waking rapidly to the magnitude of its scenic possession; it has let to learn to appreciate it." Love of beauty may be a "universal passion" but it doesn't mean anybody knows how to take care of the park (Source E). According to a native scholar of the park service, native lands are still being invaded by pipelines and oil companies, which is not the right point of Parks legislation.

Score explanation: The writer of this essay did begin to develop an argument, by introducing the broader context and mentioning some of the competing interests around the national parks. However, the writer misread or inaccurately attributed some of his or her references to sources, and struggled to fully explain the argument with a thoughtful conclusion. The prose is capable but not particularly sophisticated or well crafted. The writer leaves a number of source quotations unattributed or insufficiently explained.

Low-Scoring Response

The trouble with National Parks is the lack of regulation—we need more laws and oversight organizations because one time I went to Yellowstone and it was closed because of tourists what messed with the animals there and that was disappointing because I was so mad, I really wanted to see a bear and a buffalo and none of these sources talks about how to make sure we get the most out of animals that we want to experience. Next time I'll just go to Disney World or the beach if parks are gone anyway.

Score explanation: This writer fails to respond appropriately to the prompt; his sentences are unpolished and rambling, he does not cite any sources directly or indirectly, and the essay fails to advance a meaningful argument on the topic provided.

Sample Responses: Analysis

High-Scoring Response

When the time came for President Truman to announce and explain his decision to drop an atomic bomb on two cities in Japan, he needed some very specific types of rhetoric to accomplish the task of informing the American public and continuing to appear aggressive to the people of Japan. He accomplishes his dual goal by using a cause/consequence argument to explain the events that led to the decision ("The Japanese began the war from the air at Pearl Harbor" and rejected an ultimatum at Potsdam) and to make it clear that if the Japanese do not surrender, there will be *more* consequences even though Truman himself acknowledges the score is settled. He makes a policy argument about both the process of creating the bomb—involving both American and British scientists, establishing the plants for the work in the United States—and keeping it secret. All of this makes sense as a justification for the act of war that the United States committed. He claims the workers at the sites have been safe, and cites the speed of the discovery as an achievement as momentous as the work itself, both of which sound a little like rationalization to the modern ear.

He also uses a methodical pacing to explain the process of discovery, though he also uses valorizing rhetoric, almost as if to absolve the scientists who worked to develop this deadly technology ("we have now won the battle of the laboratories as we have won the other battles). This also serves to make this kind of warfare seem legitimate just another kind of war long side tanks and torpedoes. He uses elaborate metaphors to make this point—"harnessing the basic power of the universe" like it's a horse; "the force from which the sun draws its power" and threatens the Japanese with "a rain of ruin" as though we have the ability to command the planets and the weather.

The most chilling technique however, is the brutal juxtaposition of war-talk and a pursuit of peace. The president taunts the Germans for failing to create a similar weapon of destruction, and seeks to intimidate the Japanese by naming all the "productive enterprises" America is now prepared to destroy, bragging on American might of "sea and land forces". But then he pivots to research, and the energy potential of this new technology, and finally ends with declaring he will enable Congress to pursue "how atomic power can become a powerful and forceful influence toward the maintenance of world peace." Even his gesture towards peace has to involve power and force! But more striking is the lack of transition between war and peace. He never interrogates the idea that this discovery is a method of "protecting us and the rest of the world from the danger of sudden destruction." How is creating a danger of sudden destruction a method of protecting us from it? How could this danger be worth it?

His reasons for this style of blustery, bellicose rhetoric are of course clear—he must appear strong to the Germans and Japanese. Any admission of remorse, any acknowledgement of the Japanese people he ordered American pilots to murder, would be out of place in a wartime victory speech. But the tone of this speech, so absent of conscience, has given rise to 70 years of insistently insensitive rhetoric from American politicians. We can be grateful that President Obama finally took a trip as a sitting president to offer a more thoughtful response, but even he didn't offer any apology.

Score explanation: This writer successfully articulates and analyzes the rhetorical strategies present in the passage, citing examples and discussing their significance. The writer's analytical approach is persuasive and incorporates a variety of techniques, and the prose is capable and insightful.

Middle-Scoring Response

The statement from President Truman on the occasion of dropping the atomic bomb is an inspirational one from a more straightforward time of warfare. Japan bombed us, we destroyed them, and everyone agreed not to let it happen again. We need a president to use this kind of strength. He's really intimidating, in the paragraph about obliterating Japan and destroying their power to make war, that's a hyperbolic description designed to make them think twice about mounting another attack. He praises the multiple minds and collaboration that created the bomb, which is sort of surprising because he's also making this about American supremacy in wartime.

He uses a lot of exultant rhetoric—"more power than 20,000 tons of TNT." "The end is not yet." "Harnessing of the basic power of the universe." The mention of German failure. Calling it "marvelous." "The greatest achievement of organized science in history."

Noticeably absent is any mention of casualties, any remorse for loss of life, or any indication that there was a downside of this aggressive act of destruction. The implication of this is possibly just that he's not sorry, but also that it is important in warfare of this period to show no weakness. This is an American problem around this event, as even when President Obama paid his anniversary visit, he still didn't apologize. What would happen if we took responsibility and expressed something more than victorious gloating over this traumatic event?

Score explanation: This writer successfully identifies and examines multiple rhetorical strategies in the source text—hyperbole, intimidation, and win-rhetoric. Strikingly, the writer also notices what is missing from the text, any sign of remorse or regret for having had to make such a monumental decision. The writer considers some possible explanations but stops short of further analysis or identification of other rhetorical strategies.

Low-Scoring Response

It was totally wrong that President Truman wanted to use the atomic bomb and I don't agree with it at all. He had no right to bomb the Japanese I don't care what they did to us, and it was gross that he bragged about it and insisted they were going to do it more. I think that's disgusting. I would never want a country to do that if I lived there. How does he not get it. People must have been so mad at the time. It's embarrassing. And it's bad that no presidents until Obama went over there to say sorry. This statement is wrong.

Score explanation: While this writer had a strong reaction to this text, the bigger problem with the essay, besides its brevity, was its lack of an analytical approach to the rhetoric of the statement. The writer appears caught up in his or her response and wasn't able to answer the prompt appropriately.

Sample Responses: Argument

High-Scoring Response

According to Richard Rodriguez, individualization happens in two ways—both publicly and privately. It's natural to think children who give up one language for another are losing something important, and advocates of bilingual education are smart to push for different modes of education. However as Rodriguez says, there is "value and necessity" in assimilating, in certain respects. There are times when assimilation is crucial for survival, when the cultivation of a public self is even more important than preserving one's private self.

One example of this is seen in a fantasy series by author Tamora Pierce; in it, a young magically gifted girl decides she wants to be a knight. While her "private self" is still female, externally she has to learn how to assimilate with all the boys who are also in training as pages. What I learned from reading this as a child was that you should always know who you are, but if your goal is important enough, it may be worth it to you to acquire a different public self. In Alanna's case, she was then able to fulfill her dream of becoming a night, and reclaim something of her private self once she had attained this status.

Another example would be during times of crisis when people are being persecuted for their beliefs, such as during the Holocaust or at American Indian Boarding Schools; you can make a moral argument about staying true to one's own language or culture, but if the consequences for being publicly known as a speaker of a persecuted language are death, then you're going to lose your opportunity to keep that language alive anyway, so you might as well assimilate and survive. My own ancestors faced this dilemma prior to the Trail of Tears, and now it's a big challenge to reconnect with a lost language. However, we have survived and pursued other opportunities available to us as Americans, so it's a mixed problem.

A poignant counter example, however, is depicted in Arthur Miller's *The Crucible.* In it, the teen girls of Salem give up their private individuality for public identities as witch-hunting trouble-makers, and John Proctor's stoic refusal to give up his private convictions (and just admit to witchcraft) are portrayed as necessary and essential to retaining his humanity. After seeing that play you might argue the girls should have retained their private selves and avoided getting drawn into the public hysteria, because Proctor's choice is shown as so important.

The aspect of this conversation that both Rodriguez and the bilingualists seem to miss is that it's not entirely necessary—or at least it shouldn't be—to entirely give up either aspect of individualization. You can be cross-culturally familiar without losing either language that you grew up with! It may be more difficult to occupy that middle space, but it's a reasonable option. In Alanna's story she found it by being open about being a girl with one or two select people in her life. In the case of persecuted people, many start secret societies or hope that if they survive long enough their story will be told. It's only impossible in scenarios like the Crucible where there is no escape. Fortunately we don't have to base educational policies on the worst case scenarios—we can adapt these ideas of public and private in more humane ways and make space for those who feel the need to assimilate and those who can't imagine it.

Score explanation: This writer is successfully able to adapt the concepts Rodriguez is discussing in the prompt and apply them to observations drawn from the writer's reading of literature and history. The writer's argument is clear—chart a middle ground between the public and private extremes—and while the evidence cited isn't perfectly applicable, it serves to illustrate the different conditions this idea might be applied to. The writer's language is cohesive and controlled, and the prose is descriptive and thoughtful.

Middle-Scoring Response

The problem with Rodriguez's argument is that it's not oversimplifying to say some kids don't want to assimilate. For some it is a very harmful experience and bilingualists are right to try to maintain that right for them.

I'm left-handed, and when I was a kid, my school would try to get me to use left-handed scissors. They thought they were being helpful, but the scissors were uncomfortable, and they didn't work well, and my left hand had never really learned to use scissors since all the ones I used at home were right-handed! This is a little bit of a silly example, because my identity isn't wrapped up in which kind of scissors I use. But, I also noticed lots of other ways that left-handedness isn't accommodated. Doorknobs, water fountain buttons, hole-punched paper, even retractable desks on chairs once I got to high school were designed for right handed people! It's an illustration of the way a dominant way of thinking can overwhelm even our instinctive behaviors. I still write with my left hand, but I use all these tools made for right-handed people because to avoid using them, just because they weren't "made for me" would mean I didn't get to write at a desk or open doors, drink water or write on paper. This is similar to Rodriguez' point about the value and necessity of assimilation. If I insisted I would only use left-handed tools, I would probably be missing out on a public experience of "normalcy" or at least the equity of having access to everything that my right handed classmates get to use.

Education has a responsibility to accommodate as many private individualities as it can while still preparing students for the realities that await them after school. They should encourage kids to retain pride in their private individualities while giving them access to the public ones they'll need when they grow up.

Score explanation: This writer adequately identifies the theme in the quote from Richard Rodriguez, and recounts a relevant story from his or her own experience to respond to the prompt. The writer acknowledges that the cited experience is not exactly high stakes but still effectively connects it back to a parallel with the topic under discussion in Rodriguez' excerpt, namely the topic of bilingual education that allows for public and private identities to emerge.

Low-Scoring Response

What can one even do with a "private individuality"? To go to school one has to be public, to have a job one has to be public, to play a role in society, one has to be public. But why should that be different than a private identity? Why wouldn't you just occupy a role in a community that spoke the same original language as you? Birds of a feather can flock together and it doesn't have to be the end of the world.

When I was in elementary school, we had a choir concert where all the soloists were also in the choir, so for some songs we could come out to the front and sing into a microphone and for others we stood with the whole group. I was really nervous to leave the security of the whole choir to step out in front but it was important to me that I be able to stand out and be myself, to shine as a soloist. I wouldn't have wanted to be told I couldn't come out into a public identity because the chorus needed me or because it would affect my private identity. My private identity was waiting for me when I went home.

Score explanation: This writer struggled to accurately read and interpret the quote provided as part of the prompt. The writer misread the connotations of public and private, and brought in evidence that he or she wasn't able to explain for the reader in a meaningful way. The writing is controlled but not particularly clear.

SUMMING IT UP

- There are three types of free-response prompts:
  - **Synthesis:** You will read several sources of information on a topic and use at least three of them to support a thesis and argument.
  - **Analysis:** You will read a nonfiction piece of writing and analyze how the author develops an idea and purpose over the course of the given text.
  - **Argument:** You will create your own well-reasoned, evidence-based argument in response to a given prompt.
- You will have 2 hours and 15 minutes for the entire section—15 minutes to read all the passages, and 2 hours to write. Aim for an average of 40 minutes per essay.
- Close-read passages carefully; time spent reading the prompts, passages, and sources is not time wasted! You want to make sure you are responding to the question being asked, and that you fully understand the given documents and how the author has presented his or her ideas.
- Remember to make use of a variety of pre-writing tools and techniques: brainstorming, freewriting, and outlining. There is no "right" method—use the one that works best for you. Know your writing style before you go into the AP® Exam and use the tools that have brought you success so far in your academic writing.
- When working with practice prompts or even reading information from different sources in your everyday life, practice making synthesis moves, where you combine information from multiple sources and cite it appropriately.
- Study up on rhetorical techniques you'll need for the Analysis prompt. Some include allusion, imagery, irony, pacing, and colloquialism.
- Examine your personal experience, observations, and readings for the Argument prompt. The aim of the essay is to take a clear stance and back it up with solid examples. You want to prove your point—not just state it.
- Five varieties of argument that are useful to know: Fact, Definition, Value/Morality, Cause/Consequence, Policy/Proposal
- An argument must be debatable, and all evidence you provide must be related.
- Make time for revision, even if it's only five minutes. No one writes perfectly on the first try, so it's vital that you leave the time to check for spelling, grammar, and usage errors.

PART III
THREE PRACTICE TESTS

Practice Test 1

Chapter 4

ANSWER SHEET PRACTICE TEST 1

Section I: Multiple Choice

1. Ⓐ Ⓑ Ⓒ Ⓓ Ⓔ	15. Ⓐ Ⓑ Ⓒ Ⓓ Ⓔ	29. Ⓐ Ⓑ Ⓒ Ⓓ Ⓔ	43. Ⓐ Ⓑ Ⓒ Ⓓ Ⓔ
2. Ⓐ Ⓑ Ⓒ Ⓓ Ⓔ	16. Ⓐ Ⓑ Ⓒ Ⓓ Ⓔ	30. Ⓐ Ⓑ Ⓒ Ⓓ Ⓔ	44. Ⓐ Ⓑ Ⓒ Ⓓ Ⓔ
3. Ⓐ Ⓑ Ⓒ Ⓓ Ⓔ	17. Ⓐ Ⓑ Ⓒ Ⓓ Ⓔ	31. Ⓐ Ⓑ Ⓒ Ⓓ Ⓔ	45. Ⓐ Ⓑ Ⓒ Ⓓ Ⓔ
4. Ⓐ Ⓑ Ⓒ Ⓓ Ⓔ	18. Ⓐ Ⓑ Ⓒ Ⓓ Ⓔ	32. Ⓐ Ⓑ Ⓒ Ⓓ Ⓔ	46. Ⓐ Ⓑ Ⓒ Ⓓ Ⓔ
5. Ⓐ Ⓑ Ⓒ Ⓓ Ⓔ	19. Ⓐ Ⓑ Ⓒ Ⓓ Ⓔ	33. Ⓐ Ⓑ Ⓒ Ⓓ Ⓔ	47. Ⓐ Ⓑ Ⓒ Ⓓ Ⓔ
6. Ⓐ Ⓑ Ⓒ Ⓓ Ⓔ	20. Ⓐ Ⓑ Ⓒ Ⓓ Ⓔ	34. Ⓐ Ⓑ Ⓒ Ⓓ Ⓔ	48. Ⓐ Ⓑ Ⓒ Ⓓ Ⓔ
7. Ⓐ Ⓑ Ⓒ Ⓓ Ⓔ	21. Ⓐ Ⓑ Ⓒ Ⓓ Ⓔ	35. Ⓐ Ⓑ Ⓒ Ⓓ Ⓔ	49. Ⓐ Ⓑ Ⓒ Ⓓ Ⓔ
8. Ⓐ Ⓑ Ⓒ Ⓓ Ⓔ	22. Ⓐ Ⓑ Ⓒ Ⓓ Ⓔ	36. Ⓐ Ⓑ Ⓒ Ⓓ Ⓔ	50. Ⓐ Ⓑ Ⓒ Ⓓ Ⓔ
9. Ⓐ Ⓑ Ⓒ Ⓓ Ⓔ	23. Ⓐ Ⓑ Ⓒ Ⓓ Ⓔ	37. Ⓐ Ⓑ Ⓒ Ⓓ Ⓔ	51. Ⓐ Ⓑ Ⓒ Ⓓ Ⓔ
10. Ⓐ Ⓑ Ⓒ Ⓓ Ⓔ	24. Ⓐ Ⓑ Ⓒ Ⓓ Ⓔ	38. Ⓐ Ⓑ Ⓒ Ⓓ Ⓔ	52. Ⓐ Ⓑ Ⓒ Ⓓ Ⓔ
11. Ⓐ Ⓑ Ⓒ Ⓓ Ⓔ	25. Ⓐ Ⓑ Ⓒ Ⓓ Ⓔ	39. Ⓐ Ⓑ Ⓒ Ⓓ Ⓔ	53. Ⓐ Ⓑ Ⓒ Ⓓ Ⓔ
12. Ⓐ Ⓑ Ⓒ Ⓓ Ⓔ	26. Ⓐ Ⓑ Ⓒ Ⓓ Ⓔ	40. Ⓐ Ⓑ Ⓒ Ⓓ Ⓔ	54. Ⓐ Ⓑ Ⓒ Ⓓ Ⓔ
13. Ⓐ Ⓑ Ⓒ Ⓓ Ⓔ	27. Ⓐ Ⓑ Ⓒ Ⓓ Ⓔ	41. Ⓐ Ⓑ Ⓒ Ⓓ Ⓔ	55. Ⓐ Ⓑ Ⓒ Ⓓ Ⓔ
14. Ⓐ Ⓑ Ⓒ Ⓓ Ⓔ	28. Ⓐ Ⓑ Ⓒ Ⓓ Ⓔ	42. Ⓐ Ⓑ Ⓒ Ⓓ Ⓔ	

Section II: Free Response

Question 1

Question 2

Question 3

PRACTICE TEST 1

Section I: Multiple Choice

Time: 1 Hour • 55 Questions

Directions: This section consists of selections from prose passages and questions on their content, form, and style. After reading each passage, choose the best answer to each question and then fill in the corresponding circle on your answer sheet.

Questions 1-14. Read the following passage carefully before you decide on the answers to the questions.

This excerpt from the essay "A Plea for Captain John Brown," by Henry David Thoreau, was delivered to an audience in Concord, Massachusetts, on October 30, 1859, in defense of John Brown's raid on Harper's Ferry, which had taken place a few weeks earlier. John Brown, an abolitionist, along with 21 other men, captured and occupied the federal armory at Harper's Ferry, intending to arm slaves and foment a rebellion against the practice of slavery. Brown was charged with murder, treason, and inciting a slave insurrection. The short-lived rebellion is considered a major contributing event to the American Civil War, which began two years later.

Suppose that there is a society in this State that out of its own purse and magnanimity saves all the fugitive slaves that run to us, and protects our colored fellow-citizens, and leaves the other work to the government, so-called. Is not that government fast losing its occupation, and becoming contemptible to mankind? If private men are obliged to perform the offices of government, to protect the weak and dispense justice, then the government becomes only a hired man, or clerk, to perform menial or indifferent services. Of course, that is but the shadow of a government whose existence necessitates a Vigilant Committee. But such is the character of our Northern States generally; each has its Vigilant Committee. And, to a certain extent, these crazy governments recognize and accept this relation. They say, virtually, "We'll be glad to work for you on these terms, only don't make a noise about it." And thus the government, its salary being insured, withdraws into the back shop, taking the Constitution with it, and bestows most of its labor on repairing that. When I hear it at work sometimes, as I go by, it reminds me, at best, of those farmers who in winter contrive to turn a penny by following the coopering business. And what kind of spirit is their barrel made to hold? They speculate in stocks, and bore holes in mountains, but they are not competent to lay out even a decent highway. The only free road, the Underground Railroad, is owned and managed by the Vigilant Committee. They have tunnelled under the whole breadth of the land. Such a government is losing its power and respectability as surely as water runs out of a leaky vessel, and is held by one that can contain it.

I hear many condemn [John Brown and his] men because they were so few. When were the good and the brave ever in a majority? Would you have had him wait till that time came?—till you and I came over to him? The very fact that he had no rabble or troop of hirelings about him would alone distinguish him from ordinary heroes. His company was small indeed, because few could be found worthy to pass muster. Each one who there laid down his life for the poor and oppressed was a picked man, culled out of many thousands, if not millions; apparently a man of principle, of rare courage, and devoted humanity; ready to sacrifice his life at any moment for the benefit of his fellow-man. It may be doubted if there were as many more their equals in these respects in all the country—I speak of his followers only—for their leader, no doubt, scoured the land far and wide, seeking to swell his troop. These alone were ready to step between the oppressor and the oppressed. Surely they were the very best men you could select to be hung. That was the greatest compliment which this country could pay them. They were ripe for her gallows. She has tried a long time, she has hung a good many, but never found the right one before.

When I think of him, and his six sons, and his son-in-law, not to enumerate the others, enlisted for this fight, proceeding coolly, reverently, humanely to work, for months if not years, sleeping and waking upon it, summering and wintering the thought, without expecting any reward but a good conscience, while almost all America stood ranked on the other side—I say again that it affects me as a sublime spectacle. If he had any journal advocating 'his cause,' any organ, as the phrase is, monotonously and wearisomely playing the same old tune, and then passing round the hat, it would have been fatal to his efficiency. If he had acted in any way so as to be let alone by the government, he might have been suspected. It was the fact that the tyrant must give place to him, or he to the tyrant, that distinguished him from all the reformers of the day that I know.

It was his peculiar doctrine that a man has a perfect right to interfere by force with the slaveholder, in order to rescue the slave. I agree with him. They who are continually shocked by slavery have some right to be shocked by the violent death of the slaveholder, but no others. Such will be more shocked by his life than by his death. I shall not be forward to think him mistaken in his method who quickest succeeds to liberate the slave. I speak for the slave when I say that I prefer the philanthropy of Captain Brown to that philanthropy which neither shoots me nor liberates me. At any rate, I do not think it is quite sane for one to spend his whole life in talking or writing about this matter, unless he is continuously inspired, and I have not done so. A man may have other affairs to attend to. I do not wish to kill nor to be killed, but I can foresee circumstances in which both these things would be by me unavoidable. We preserve the so-called peace of our community by deeds of petty violence every day. Look at the policeman's billy and handcuffs! Look at the jail! Look at the gallows! Look at the chaplain of the regiment! We are hoping only to live safely on the outskirts of this provisional army. So we defend ourselves and our hen-roosts, and maintain slavery. I know that the mass of my countrymen think that the only righteous use that can be made of Sharp's rifles and revolvers is to fight duels with them, when we are insulted by other nations, or to hunt Indians, or shoot fugitive slaves with them, or the like. I think that for once the Sharp's rifles and the revolvers were employed in a righteous cause. The tools were in the hands of one who could use them.

The same indignation that is said to have cleared the temple once will clear it again. The question is not about the weapon, but the spirit in which you use it. No man has appeared in America, as yet, who loved his fellow-man so well, and treated him so tenderly. He lived for him. He took up his life and he laid it down for him. What sort of violence is that which is encouraged, not by soldiers, but by peaceable citizens, not so much by laymen as by ministers of the Gospel, not so much by the fighting sects as by the Quakers, and not so much by Quaker men as by Quaker women?

This event advertises me that there is such a fact as death,—the possibility of a man's dying. It seems as if no man had ever died in America before; for in order to die you must first have lived. I don't believe in the hearses, and palls, and funerals that they have had. There was no death in the case, because there had been no life; they merely rotted or sloughed off, pretty much as they had rotted or sloughed along. No temple's veil was rent, only a hole dug somewhere. Let the dead bury their dead. The best of them fairly ran down like a clock. Franklin,—Washington,—they were let off without dying; they were merely missing one day. I hear a good many pretend that they are going to die; or that they have died, for aught that I know. Nonsense! I'll defy them to do it. They haven't got life enough in them. They'll deliquesce like fungi, and keep a hundred eulogists mopping the spot where they left off. Only half a dozen or so have died since the world began. Do you think that you are going to die, sir? No! there's no hope of you. You haven't got your lesson yet. You've got to stay after school. We make a needless ado about capital punishment,—taking lives, when there is no life to take. Memento mori! We don't understand that sublime sentence which some worthy got sculptured on his gravestone once. We've interpreted it in a grovelling and snivelling sense; we've wholly forgotten how to die.

1. The main idea of this passage is best expressed as:
   - **A.** Citizens have a duty to protect their property and defend the Constitution.
   - **B.** Not every brave decision will also be a popular one.
   - **C.** The Vigilant Committee becomes necessary when government fails to act.
   - **D.** When the cause is righteous, the means are justified and even noble, even if it requires violence.
   - **E.** John Brown should be pardoned and regarded as a hero, because he knows what it means to truly live.

2. From the given lines (3–7) below, it is possible to infer which of the following conclusions?

   Is not that government fast losing its occupation, and becoming contemptible to mankind? If private men are obliged to perform the offices of government, to protect the weak and dispense justice, then the government becomes only a hired man, or clerk, to perform menial or indifferent services.

   - **A.** Thoreau thinks that the public should regard the government as their clerk, to assist them in their goals.
   - **B.** Thoreau accuses the government of neglecting its duties of providing security and ensuring fair treatment.
   - **C.** Thoreau is fearful of a harsh political response to his argument and wants to justify his argument.
   - **D.** Thoreau feels it is well past time for the government to take action and put an end to slavery.
   - **E.** Thoreau believes in a strong centralized government and is disappointed by the current administration.

3. In the first paragraph, Thoreau makes use of all the following devices EXCEPT:
   - **A.** Paradox
   - **B.** Simile
   - **C.** Comparison
   - **D.** Rhetorical questions
   - **E.** Figurative language

4. Thoreau most likely intends the following metaphor to suggest which of these answer choices?

   "When I hear it at work sometimes, as I go by, it reminds me, at best, of those farmers who in winter contrive to turn a penny by following the coopering business. And what kind of spirit is their barrel made to hold? They speculate in stocks, and bore holes in mountains, but they are not competent to lay out even a decent highway."

   - **A.** Governments aren't designed to be versatile, but should instead get very good at a specific array of tasks, the way responsible farmers are.
   - **B.** Farmers should focus on their main livelihood and not attempt other infrastructure improvements, instead leaving that to the government.
   - **C.** The government should focus on public works and not on agricultural concerns.
   - **D.** A farmer who picks up other trades in winter may lose sight of what he is supposed to do well; government is guilty of the same error.
   - **E.** The government, like an industrious farmer, is wisely finding work to do in its offseason but may find itself overextended.

5. The first paragraph of the passage undermines the public's faith in the efficiency and performance of government in order to
   A. call for the resignation of current political leaders.
   B. motivate his listeners to run for office.
   C. validate John Brown's decision to start an insurrection.
   D. promote Thoreau's candidacy for President.
   E. expose corruption in the nation's civil servants.

6. Throughout the passage, Thoreau builds his credibility in the eyes of his listeners by doing which of the following?
   A. Inviting others to join him at the conclusion of his speech
   B. Decrying Brown's methods, if not his motives
   C. Citing his personal experience as a life-long abolitionist
   D. Declaring himself morally superior
   E. Positioning himself alongside the listener

7. What narrative is Thoreau attempting to counter in his second paragraph?
   A. Brown's rebellion was just an ineffective bunch of stragglers.
   B. Brown's rebellion was ill-advised because it was so dangerous.
   C. Brown's rebellion was noble and necessary but his motives were misunderstood.
   D. Brown's rebellion needed to have been undertaken by fewer people in order to be meaningful.
   E. Brown's rebellion didn't deserve any attention because of its illegal nature.

8. The phrase "summering and wintering the thought" (lines 41–42) is an example of
   A. hyperbole.
   B. allusion.
   C. verbification.
   D. irony.
   E. narration.

9. The sentence "I shall not be forward to think him mistaken in his method who quickest succeeds to liberate the slave" (lines 55–56) most nearly means:
   A. Thoreau might disagree with Brown's methods but doesn't want to be the first to say so.
   B. Thoreau agrees that the ends justify the means and won't judge Brown's strategy.
   C. Thoreau thinks it's fair to acknowledge John Brown was overly hasty in his choice of tactics.
   D. Thoreau isn't ready to rush to judgment even though he thinks Brown was a hero.
   E. Thoreau wishes he had been able to advise Brown prior to the rebellion.

10. Which of the following phrases is an example of a juxtaposition?
   A. A man has a perfect right to interfere by force with the slaveholder, in order to rescue the slave.
   B. Any organ, as the phrase is, monotonously and wearisomely playing the same old tune.
   C. It was the fact that the tyrant must give place to him, or he to the tyrant.
   D. This event advertises me that there is such a fact as death.
   E. We preserve the so-called peace of our community by deeds of petty violence every day.

11. The word "deliquesce" (line 91) in context most nearly means to
    - **A.** solidify.
    - **B.** grow.
    - **C.** crumble.
    - **D.** dissolve.
    - **E.** decay.

12. Thoreau's redefinition of "live" and "die" in his final paragraph mostly appeals to
    - I. ethos
    - II. logos
    - III. pathos
    - **A.** I
    - **B.** II
    - **C.** III
    - **D.** I and III
    - **E.** I, II, and III

13. The tone of the passage can best be described as
    - **A.** outraged.
    - **B.** loquacious.
    - **C.** vengeful.
    - **D.** dispassionate.
    - **E.** vehement.

14. The sentences, "They who are continually shocked by slavery have some right to be shocked by the violent death of slaveholder, but no others. Such will be more shocked by his life than by his death" (lines 52–55) make use of which mode of rhetoric, primarily?
    - I. Ethos
    - II. Logos
    - III. Pathos
    - **A.** I
    - **B.** II
    - **C.** III
    - **D.** I and III
    - **E.** I, II, and III

Questions 15–27. Read the following passage carefully before you decide on the answers to the questions.

This excerpt is from "Louis Pasteur and His Work," by Patrick Geddes and J. Arthur Thomson. Louis Pasteur, a French biologist and chemist, lived from 1822–1895, and is known for his contributions to germ theory and clinical medicine.

Opposition was an ever-recurrent factor in Pasteur's life. He had to fight for his crystallographic[1] and chemical theories, and for his fermentation theory; he had to fight against the theory of spontaneous generation[2], and for his practice of inoculating as a preventive against splenic fever; he had to fight for each step. But no part of his work has met with so much opposition and adverse criticism as that concerning hydrophobia, though it is easy to exaggerate the importance of the discussion, in which Pasteur himself took little part. Feeling ran high in this country; hence, when it was announced that Pasteur—surely best qualified to speak—was to write the article Hydrophobia in "Chamber's Encyclopædia," a shower of letters inundated the office; hence the article in question includes an editorially demanded summary of the grounds of the opposition by one of ourselves, and to which therefore we may refer the reader.

While avoiding controversy and partisanship as far as may be, the question remains, What did Pasteur do in regard to hydrophobia? His claims are to have proved, first of all, that the disease was particularly associated with the nervous system. The virus is usually spread through the saliva, but it is not found in the blood or lymph, and it has its special seat in the nerves, brain, and spinal cord. Secondly, he showed that the virus might be attenuated in its virulence. The spinal cord of a rabbit which has died of rabies, is, when fresh, powerfully virulent, but when exposed for a couple of weeks to dry air at a constant temperature of 23°–24°C. it loses its virulence. Thirdly, he showed that inoculation with the attenuated virus rendered an animal immune from infection with rabies. To make the animal immune it has first to be inoculated with infected spinal cord fourteen days old, then with that of thirteen days, and so on till inoculation with almost freshly infected spinal cord is possible. In this way the animal becomes refractory to the infection, and if it be bitten it will not die. Fourthly, he showed that even if the organism had been bitten, it was still possible to save it, unless the wounds were near the head—that is, within close reach of the central nervous system. For in the case of a superficial wound, say on hand or leg, the virus takes some considerable time to spread, and during this period of spreading and incubation it is possible to forestall the virus by inoculation with that which has been attenuated. In this case there is obvious

1. Crystallography is the science dedicated to identifying the arrangement of atoms in the crystalline solids, for example the structure of snowflakes, diamonds, or table salt.

2. Before scientists like Pasteur confirmed that illness came from the spread of microscopic germs, many people believed that certain small organisms could simply arise from inanimate matter without being descended from similar organisms—this idea, originally proposed by scholars as far back as Aristotle, was intended to explain the origins of maggots in rotting meat or frogs by the side of a river, for example.

truth in the proverb, "He gives twice who gives quickly." And the outcome was, that while out of a hundred persons bitten, nineteen or twenty will in ordinary circumstances die, "the mortality among cases treated at the Pasteur Institute has fallen to less than 1–2 per cent." According to another set of statistics, a mortality of 40 per cent. has been reduced to 1.3 per cent.; and of 1673 patients treated by Pasteur's method only thirteen died.

As to the adverse criticism of Pasteur's inoculation against rabies, it consists, first and second, of the general argument of the anti-vaccinationists, and thirdly, of specific objections. To the two former the school of Pasteur, of course, replies that the value of human life answers the one, and the results of experience the other; but on these controversies we cannot enter here. The main specific objections we take to be three—that as the micro-organism of rabies has not really been seen, the theory and practice of Pasteur's anti-rabic method lack that stability which is desirable; that the statistics in favor of the Pasteur procedure have been insufficiently criticised; that there have been failures and casualties, sometimes of a tragic nature. In regard to this last point—that deaths have occurred as the result of the supposed cure, instead of from the original infection—we may note that the possibility of such casualties was admitted by the English Investigation Committee (1887), while, on the other hand, Dr. Armand Ruffer, who speaks with much authority, denies with all deliberateness that there is any known case in which death followed as the result of Pasteur's treatment.

Microscopic verification is, of course, most desirable, and statistics are proverbially difficult of criticism. But, on the whole, we think it likely that those who, like ourselves are not medical experts will incline to believe that Sir James Paget, Dr. Lauder Brunton, Professor George Fleming, Sir Joseph Lister, Dr. Richard Quain, Sir Henry Roscoe, and Professor Burdon Sanderson must have had grounds for saying, in the report which they presented to Parliament in 1887, "It may, hence, be deemed certain that M. Pasteur has discovered a method of protection from rabies comparable with that which vaccination affords against infection from small-pox."

So far a summary of Pasteur's personal life and scientific work, but is it not possible to make a more general and rational estimate of these? So much was his life centered in Paris that most people are probably accustomed to think of him as a townsman; but it is more biologically accurate to recognize him as a rustic, sprung from a strong, thrifty stock of mountain peasants. Nor can his rustic early environment of tanyard and farm, of village and country-side, be overlooked as a factor in developing that practical sense and economic insight which were so conspicuous in his life work. The tanner's son becomes the specialist in fermentation; the country boy is never throughout his life beyond hail of the poultry-yard and the farm-steading, the wine press and the silk nursery; brought up in the rural French atmosphere of careful thrift and minute economies, all centered not round the mechanism or exchange of town industries, but round the actual maintenance of human and organic life, he becomes a great life-saver in his generation.

In short, as we might almost diagrammatically sum it up, the shrewd, minutely careful, yet inquiring rustic, eager to understand and then to improve what he sees, passes in an ever-widening spiral from his rural centre upward, from tan-pit to vat and vintage, from manure-heaps, earthworms, and water-supply to the problems of civic sanitation. The rustic tragedies of the dead cow and the mad dog excite the explanation and suggest the prevention, of these disasters; from the poisoning of rats and mice he passes to suggestive experiments as to the rabbit-pest of Australia, and so in other cases from beast to man, from village to state. And on each radius on which he paused he left either a method or a clue, and set some other inquirer at work. On each radius of work he has left his disciples; for he founded not only an Institute, but a living school, or indeed whole schools of workers. We think of him, then, not only as thinking rustic, but as one of the greatest examples in science of the Rustic Thinker—a type of thinker too rare in our mechanical and urban generation, yet for whom the next generation waits.

As to his actual legacy to the world, let us sum it up briefly. There is the impulse which he gave, after the successful organization of his own Institute, to the establishment in other countries of similar laboratories of preventive medicine, and, one may also say, of experimental evolution. There is his educative work at Strasburg and Lille, at the Ecole Normale and the Sorbonne, and, above all, in the smaller yet world-wide circle of his immediate disciples. To general biology his chief contribution has been the demonstration of the part which bacteria play, not only in pathological and physiological processes, but in the wider drama of evolution. To the chemist he has given a new theory of fermentation; to the physician many a suggestive lesson in the etiology [inquiry into the causes] of diseases, and a series of bold experiments in preventive and curative inoculation, of which Roux's treatment of diphtheria and Professor Fraser's new remedy for snake-bite are examples at present before the public; to the surgeon a stable foundation, as Lister acknowledged, for antiseptic treatment; to the hygienist a multitude of practical suggestions concerning water-supply and drainage, disinfection and burial. On brewer, distiller, and wine-maker he has forced the microscope and its results; and he has shown both agriculturist and stock-breeder how some, at least, of their many more than ten plagues may be either averted or alleviated.

15. The main idea of the passage is best summarized by which of the following?
    - A. Louis Pasteur is an overrated scientist and people need to know the truth.
    - B. Pasteur's rabies work is more important than the rest of his discoveries.
    - C. Though he faced some controversies in his career, Pasteur helped establish modern medicine.
    - D. Without Pasteur, none of the ailments we consider "cured" would have been treated.
    - E. Louis Pasteur was a scientist from Paris who accomplished social mobility.

16. According to the passage, throughout his career Pasteur had to fight against all of the following EXCEPT:
    - A. People who doubted the results of his experiments
    - B. Outdated scientific concepts
    - C. People who objected to vaccinations
    - D. His own physical frailty
    - E. Particularly harmful and dangerous illnesses

17. The second paragraph relies on which of the following organizational strategies?
    - A. Order of importance
    - B. Sequence
    - C. Theme
    - D. Association
    - E. Reverse chronology

18. In context, "virulence" (line 18) most nearly means
    - A. requirements of treatment.
    - B. speed of transmission.
    - C. frequency of occurrence.
    - D. degree of symptoms experienced.
    - E. intensity of contagiousness.

19. The statistical results of Pasteur's experimentation are included in paragraph 2 in order to
    - A. demonstrate the effectiveness of his work.
    - B. bolster the reputation of the writers.
    - C. illustrate the wide application of his methods.
    - D. assuage the reader's concerns about catching rabies today.
    - E. demonstrate the risks inherent in the research.

20. What is the organizational function of paragraph 3?
    - A. To introduce specific examples of Pasteur's discoveries
    - B. To anticipate a counterargument from Pasteur's detractors
    - C. To transition in to the implications of Pasteur's work
    - D. To synthesize Pasteur's work with other scientific achievements
    - E. To persuade the reader of the superiority of Pasteur's findings

21. The authors of the passage respond to "the general argument of the anti-vaccinationists" (line 40) with what type of rhetoric in paragraph 3?

    I. Pathos

    II. Ethos

    III. Logos

    - A. I only
    - B. II only
    - C. III only
    - D. I and II
    - E. II and III

22. In the phrase "the rural French atmosphere of careful thrift and minute economies" (lines 74–75), the word "minute" most nearly means
   A. small in scale.
   B. minor in significance.
   C. fast-paced.
   D. short-term.
   E. silent.

23. Based on their interpretation of Pasteur's upbringing, what inference can you draw about the writers' attitude towards Pasteur's origins?
   A. They think his humble village was a major obstacle for him to overcome.
   B. From their perspective, Pasteur was a fish out of water in his village.
   C. Many of Pasteur's qualities as a scientist stem from the conditions in which he grew up.
   D. Nobody in his village was sufficiently grateful for all the progress Pasteur brought them.
   E. Pasteur was ill-prepared for the chaos and bustle of busy cities where he spent his career.

24. The following phrases: "as we might almost diagrammatically sum it up . . . passes in an ever-widening spiral from his rural centre upward . . . and on each radius on which he paused . . ." can best be described as
   A. allusion.
   B. extended metaphor.
   C. exposition.
   D. irony.
   E. parallelism.

25. Pasteur's legacy includes all of the following EXCEPT:
   A. An institute to continue the study of preventative medicine
   B. A cohort of scholars who continue pursuing his research
   C. A new understanding of prevention and treatment of common ailments
   D. A treatment for diphtheria, snake-venom, and polio
   E. Proof of the existence of bacteria

26. The primary mode of composition of the final paragraph is
   A. description.
   B. narration.
   C. summary.
   D. comparison and contrast.
   E. argument.

27. Based on the passage, Pasteur could be described as all of the following EXCEPT:
   A. Pugnacious
   B. Determined
   C. Economical
   D. Myopic
   E. Inquisitive

Questions 28-41. Read the following passage carefully before you decide on the answers to the questions.

Robert Louis Stevenson (1850–1895) was a Scottish writer, best known for Treasure Island *and* The Strange Case of Dr. Jekyll and Mr. Hyde. *This excerpt comes from a collection of essays he published on his life and the craft of writing.*

It was far indeed from being my first book, for I am not a novelist alone. But I am well aware that my paymaster, the Great Public, regards what else I have written with indifference, if not aversion; if it call upon me at all, it calls on me in the familiar and indelible character; and when I am asked to talk of my first book, no question in the world but what is meant is my first novel.

Sooner or later, somehow, anyhow, I was bound to write a novel. It seems vain to ask why. Men are born with various manias: from my earliest childhood, it was mine to make a plaything of imaginary series of events; and as soon as I was able to write, I became a good friend to the paper-makers. Reams upon reams must have gone to the making of 'Rathillet,' 'The Pentland Rising,' 'The King's Pardon' (otherwise 'Park Whitehead'), 'Edward Daven,' 'A Country Dance,' and 'A Vendetta in the West'; and it is consolatory to remember that these reams are now all ashes, and have been received again into the soil. I have named but a few of my ill-fated efforts, only such indeed as came to a fair bulk ere they were desisted from; and even so they cover a long vista of years. 'Rathillet' was attempted before fifteen, 'The Vendetta' at twenty-nine, and the succession of defeats lasted unbroken till I was thirty-one. By that time, I had written little books and little essays and short stories; and had got patted on the back and paid for them—though not enough to live upon. I had quite a reputation, I was the successful man; I passed my days in toil, the futility of which would sometimes make my cheek to burn—that I should spend a man's energy upon this business, and yet could not earn a livelihood: and still there shone ahead of me an unattained ideal: although I had attempted the thing with vigour not less than ten or twelve times, I had not yet written a novel. All—all my pretty ones—had gone for a little, and then stopped inexorably like a schoolboy's watch. I might be compared to a cricketer of many years' standing who should never have made a run. Anybody can write a short story—a bad one, I mean—who has industry and paper and time enough; but not every one may hope to write even a bad novel. It is the length that kills.

The accepted novelist may take his novel up and put it down, spend days upon it in vain, and write not any more than he makes haste to blot. Not so the beginner. Human nature has certain rights; instinct—the instinct of self-preservation—forbids that any man (cheered and supported by the consciousness of no previous victory) should endure the miseries of unsuccessful literary toil beyond a period to be measured in weeks. There must be something for hope to feed upon. The beginner must have a slant of wind, a lucky vein must be running, he must be in one of those hours when the words come and the phrases balance of themselves—even to begin. And having begun, what a dread looking forward is that until the book shall be accomplished! For so long a time, the slant is to continue unchanged, the vein to keep running, for so long a time you must keep at command the same quality of style: for so long a time your puppets are to be always vital, always consistent, always vigorous! I remember I used to look, in those days, upon every three-volume novel with a sort of veneration, as a feat—not possibly of literature—but at least of physical and moral endurance and the courage of Ajax.

...

My native air was more unkind than man's ingratitude, and I must consent to pass a good deal of my time between four walls in a house lugubriously known as the Late Miss McGregor's Cottage. And now admire the finger of predestination. There was a schoolboy in the Late Miss McGregor's Cottage, home from the holidays, and much in want of 'something craggy to break his mind upon.' He had no thought of literature; it was the art of Raphael that received his fleeting suffrages; and with the aid of pen and ink and a shilling box of water colours, he had soon turned one of the rooms into a picture gallery. My more immediate duty towards the gallery was to be showman; but I would sometimes unbend a little, join the artist (so to speak) at the easel, and pass the afternoon with him in a generous emulation, making coloured drawings. On one of these occasions, I made the map of an island; it was elaborately and (I thought) beautifully coloured; the shape of it took my fancy beyond expression; it contained harbours that pleased me like sonnets; and with the unconsciousness of the predestined, I ticketed my performance 'Treasure Island.' I am told there are people who do not care for maps, and find it hard to believe. The names, the shapes of the woodlands, the courses of the roads and rivers, the prehistoric footsteps of man still distinctly traceable up hill and down dale, the mills and the ruins, the ponds and the ferries, perhaps the Standing Stone or the Druidic Circle on the heath; here is an inexhaustible fund of interest for any man with eyes to see or twopence-worth of imagination to understand with! No child but must remember laying his head in the grass, staring into the infinitesimal forest and seeing it grow populous with fairy armies.

Somewhat in this way, as I paused upon my map of 'Treasure Island,' the future characters of the book began to appear there visibly among imaginary woods; and their brown faces and bright weapons peeped out upon me from unexpected quarters, as they passed to and fro, fighting and hunting treasure, on these few square inches of a flat projection. The next thing I knew I had some papers before me and was writing out a list of chapters. How often have I done so, and the thing gone no further! But there seemed elements of success about this enterprise. It was to be a story for boys; no need of psychology or fine writing; and I had a boy at hand to be a touchstone. Women were excluded. I was unable to handle a brig (which the Hispaniola should have been), but I thought I could make shift to sail her as a schooner without public shame. And then I had an idea for John Silver from which I promised myself funds of entertainment; to take an admired friend of mine (whom the reader very likely knows and admires as much as I do), to deprive him of all his finer qualities and higher graces of temperament, to leave him with nothing but his strength, his courage, his quickness, and his magnificent geniality, and to try to express these in terms of the culture of a raw tarpaulin. Such psychical surgery is, I think, a common way of 'making character'; perhaps it is, indeed, the only way. We can put in the quaint figure that spoke a hundred words with us yesterday by the wayside; but do we know him? Our friend, with his infinite variety and flexibility, we know—but can we put him in? Upon the first, we must engraft secondary and imaginary qualities, possibly all wrong; from the second, knife in hand, we must cut away and deduct the needless arborescence of his nature, but the trunk and the few branches that remain we may at least be fairly sure of.

28. Stevenson's use of "my paymaster, the Great Public" (line 2) is an example of

A. synecdoche.

B. allusion.

C. personification.

D. dramatic irony.

E. argument.

29. Based on the context, "indelible" (line 4) most nearly means

A. impossible to eat.

B. unaware.

C. not eligible.

D. related.

E. unforgettable.

30. What can be inferred from "I became a good friend to the paper-makers" (line 10)?

A. Long John Silver was inspired by a shop owner.

B. Stevenson liked to spend time in book stores.

C. As a writer, Stevenson purchased a lot of paper.

D. Stevenson traded tips on story-telling with other writers.

E. In addition to writing, Stevenson was interested in paper-making.

31. The sentence, "I had quite a reputation, I was the successful man; I passed my days in toil, the futility of which would sometimes make my cheek to burn—that I should spend a man's energy upon this business, and yet could not earn a livelihood" (lines 19–22) is an example of what kind of literary device?

A. Analogy

B. Anecdote

C. Antithesis

D. Irony

E. Paradox

32. Stevenson's use of em dashes ("Anybody can write a short story—a bad one, I mean—who has industry and paper and time enough") is intended to communicate

A. outrage.

B. disgust.

C. surprise.

D. clarification.

E. amusement.

33. The second paragraph makes use of all of the following EXCEPT:

A. Simile

B. Classification

C. Exemplification

D. Narrative

E. Comparison

34. Based on context, what is the nearest meaning for "lugubriously" (line 47)?

A. Excitedly

B. Devotedly

C. Sorrowfully

D. Animatedly

E. Vengefully

35. The meaning of the simile "harbours that pleased me like sonnets" (line 59) is most nearly that the

A. feeling of the author was similar to how he feels when he reads poetry.

B. imagery was visually rhythmic.

C. map seemed to have a rigid structure.

D. harbours had the same effect on the author as on a work of literature.

E. author always hoped to get back to writing poetry and the drawing helped him.

36. The main idea of the third paragraph is best expressed by which of the following?

A. A writer's practice begins when he or she is very young and has to continue through years of struggle.

B. The only writing worth having is spontaneously generated in the writer's brain.

C. Moments of inspiration are crucial for the initiate embarking on a literary career.

D. All great writing is drawn from dark and difficult emotional exploration.

E. To have any real success, a writer must have a mental repository of lived experience.

37. The chief effect of the classical allusions in Stevenson's essay ("the courage of Ajax," "more unkind than man's ingratitude," "all my pretty ones," "the art of Raphael") is to

A. suggest that Stevenson is a more serious writer than many of his contemporaries.

B. dismiss classic literature as less necessary than you might think.

C. hint that the reader needs to seek out more of the classics.

D. indicate Stevenson is more pretentious than he wants us to think.

E. elevate Stevenson's discussion beyond the "boys' fiction" genre in which he is often placed.

38. Stevenson's tone throughout the passage could be best described as

A. insouciant.

B. self-deprecating.

C. indignant.

D. deliberate.

E. thoughtful.

39. The primary mode of composition of the final paragraph is

A. argument.

B. process analysis.

C. definition.

D. description.

E. narration.

40. The sentence "Upon the first, we must engraft secondary and imaginary qualities, possibly all wrong; from the second, knife in hand, we must cut away and deduct the needless arborescence of his nature, but the trunk and the few branches that remain we may at least be fairly sure of" (lines 89–92) is an example of

A. parallelism.

B. irony.

C. simile.

D. anecdote.

E. personification.

41. The final paragraph makes use of all of the following EXCEPT:

A. Metaphor
B. Rhetorical questioning
C. Figurative language
D. Generalization
E. Solipsism

Questions 42–55. Read the following passage carefully before you decide on the answers to the questions.

George Eliot was the pen name of Mary Anne Evans (1819-1880), an English novelist, journalist and translator. She wrote seven novels, the best-known of which is Middlemarch. *This essay is in response to a work of design theory by Owen Jones,* The Grammar of Ornament.

IX. THE GRAMMAR OF ORNAMENT.

The inventor of movable types, says the venerable Teufelsdröckh[1], was disbanding hired armies, cashiering most kings and senates, and creating a whole new democratic world. Has any one yet said what great things are being done by the men who are trying to banish ugliness from our streets and our homes, and to make both the outside and inside of our dwellings worthy of a world where there are forests and flower-tressed meadows, and the plumage of birds; where the insects carry lessons of color on their wings, and even the surface of a stagnant pool will show us the wonders of iridescence and the most delicate forms of leafage? They, too, are modifying opinions, for they are modifying men's moods and habits, which are the mothers of opinions, having quite as much to do with their formation as the responsible father—Reason. Think of certain hideous manufacturing towns where the piety is chiefly a belief in copious perdition, and the pleasure is chiefly gin. The dingy surface of wall pierced by the ugliest windows, the staring shop-fronts, paper-hangings, carpets, brass and gilt mouldings, and advertising placards, have an effect akin to that of malaria; it is easy to understand that with such surroundings there is more belief in cruelty than in beneficence, and that the best earthly bliss attainable is the dulling of the external senses. For it is a fatal mistake to suppose that ugliness which is taken for beauty will answer all the purposes of beauty; the subtle relation between all kinds of truth and fitness in our life forbids that bad taste should ever be harmless to our moral sensibility or our intellectual discernment; and—more than that—as it is probable that fine

1. A reference to "Diogenes Teufelsdröckh," a fictional German philosopher from Thomas Carlyle's novel, *Sartorial Resartus* (or *The Tailor Re-Tailored*). In the novel, which is a satirical imitation of the work of other German philosophers like Goethe and Hegel, Teufelsdröckh is a professor of German idealism and "Things in General" and the writer of a book of philosophy called *Clothes, Their Origin and Influence*. The imaginary work-within-a-work says that meaning is derived from phenomena and changes over time as cultures remake themselves.

musical harmonies have a sanative influence over our bodily organization, it is also probable that just coloring and lovely combinations of lines may be necessary to the complete well-being of our systems apart from any conscious delight in them. A savage may indulge in discordant chuckles and shrieks and gutturals, and think that they please the gods, but it does not follow that his frame would not be favorably wrought upon by the vibrations of a grand church organ. One sees a person capable of choosing the worst style of wall-paper become suddenly afflicted by its ugliness under an attack of illness. And if an evil state of blood and lymph usually goes along with an evil state of mind, who shall say that the ugliness of our streets, the falsity of our ornamentation, the vulgarity of our upholstery, have not something to do with those bad tempers which breed false conclusions?

On several grounds it is possible to make a more speedy and extensive application of artistic reform to our interior decoration than to our external architecture. One of these grounds is that most of our ugly buildings must stand; we cannot afford to pull them down. But every year we are decorating interiors afresh, and people of modest means may benefit by the introduction of beautiful designs into stucco ornaments, paper-hangings, draperies, and carpets. Fine taste in the decoration of interiors is a benefit that spreads from the palace to the clerk's house with one parlor.

All honor, then, to the architect who has zealously vindicated the claim of internal ornamentation to be a part of the architect's function, and has labored to rescue that form of art which is most closely connected with the sanctities and pleasures of our hearths from the hands of uncultured tradesmen. All the nation ought at present to know that this effort is peculiarly associated with the name of Mr. Owen Jones[2]; and those who are most disposed to dispute with the architect about his coloring must at least recognize the high artistic principle which has directed his attention to colored ornamentation as a proper branch of architecture. One monument of his effort in this way is his "Grammar of Ornament," of which a new and cheaper edition has just been issued. The one point in which it differs from the original and more expensive edition, viz., the reduction in the size of the pages (the amount of matter and number of plates are unaltered), is really an advantage; it is now a very manageable folio, and when the reader is in a lounging mood may be held easily on the knees. It is a magnificent book; and those who know no more of it than the title should be told that they will find in it a pictorial history of ornamental design, from its rudimentary condition as seen in the productions of savage tribes, through all

2. Owen Jones (1809–1874) was a Welsh architect and design theorist, responsible for the popularization of design principles for interior decoration, patterning and ornamentation, as well as modern color theory. He was heavily involved in bringing the philosophy of Polychromy or "the practice of decoration in a variety of colors" to the United Kingdom after studying abroad. Historians often believed the Ancient Greeks and Romans had only sculpted in white, colorless marble, but have come to realize that they were proponents of polychrome work as well. He was also known for his role in organizing the Great Exhibition of 1851 and worked as a book designer and innovative binder. The scandal to which Eliot refers about "his coloring" referred to the palette Jones chose for the ironwork of the palace that housed the Exhibition—he used red, yellow and blue, which was shocking to the contemporary audience.

the other great types of art—the Egyptian, Assyrian, ancient Persian, Greek, Roman, Byzantine, Arabian, Moresque, Mohammedan-Persian, Indian, Celtic, Mediæval, Renaissance, Elizabethan, and Italian. The letter-press consists, first, of an introductory statement of fundamental principles of ornamentation—principles, says the author, which will be found to have been obeyed more or less instinctively by all nations in proportion as their art has been a genuine product of the national genius; and, secondly, of brief historical essays, some of them contributed by other eminent artists, presenting a commentary on each characteristic series of illustrations, with the useful appendage of bibliographical lists.

The title "Grammar of Ornament" is so far appropriate that it indicates what Mr. Owen Jones is most anxious to be understood concerning the object of his work, namely, that it is intended to illustrate historically the application of principles, and not to present a collection of models for mere copyists. The plates correspond to examples in syntax, not to be repeated parrot-like, but to be studied as embodiments of syntactical principles. There is a logic of form which cannot be departed from in ornamental design without a corresponding remoteness from perfection; unmeaning, irrelevant lines are as bad as irrelevant words or clauses, that tend no whither. And as a suggestion toward the origination of fresh ornamental design, the work concludes with some beautiful drawings of leaves and flowers from nature, that the student, tracing in them the simple laws of form which underlie an immense variety in beauty, may the better discern the method by which the same laws were applied in the finest decorative work of the past, and may have all the clearer prospect of the unexhausted possibilities of freshness which lie before him, if, refraining from mere imitation, he will seek only such likeness to existing forms of ornamental art as arises from following like principles of combination.

42. What do the opening sentences of the passage reveal about George Eliot's feelings about the value of architecture and design?

A. It is less significant than literary, political, and international revolution.

B. It is on par with major historical innovation and capable of major social change.

C. It is as inevitable as typography, commerce, and democracy.

D. It is even more important because it affects our daily lives.

E. It should be getting more attention from artists and literary thinkers.

43. This sentence, "They, too, are modifying opinions, for they are modifying men's moods and habits, which are the mothers of opinions, having quite as much to do with their formation as the responsible father—Reason" (lines 9–12) includes which of the following literary devices?

A. Irony

B. Synecdoche

C. Allusion

D. Simile

E. Metaphor

44. This sentence, "The dingy surface of wall pierced by the ugliest windows, the staring shop-fronts, paper-hangings, carpets, brass and gilt mouldings, and advertising placards, have an effect akin to that of malaria," (lines 13–16) uses which of the following rhetorical techniques?
   - **A.** Paradox
   - **B.** Narration
   - **C.** Hyperbole
   - **D.** Slanting
   - **E.** Colloquialism

45. In context, the word "sanative" (line 23) most nearly means
   - **A.** to make more intelligent.
   - **B.** to render more distinct.
   - **C.** to clean or improve.
   - **D.** to give a sensory experience.
   - **E.** to have a healing effect.

46. The main idea of the first paragraph can be summed up as:
   - **A.** There is synchronicity between our external and internal health, and what is harmful to our bodies is likely harmful to our spirits.
   - **B.** Poverty makes people less sensible of what is good and beautiful in the world around them.
   - **C.** There are objective standards of beauty and elegance that all good design should adhere to.
   - **D.** Some people are not capable of perceiving beauty but for most there is hope.
   - **E.** As long as the people concerned think something is beautiful, it doesn't matter what others think.

47. All of the following reasons are offered in support of Eliot's argument in the second paragraph EXCEPT:
   - **A.** Internal renovations can be done much more quickly than external ones.
   - **B.** It is more difficult to tear down and rebuild entire structures.
   - **C.** People redecorate their homes more frequently.
   - **D.** It is more affordable to implement design reform in simple features.
   - **E.** Interior decorating is more accessible across an entire society.

48. What is the relationship of the first two paragraphs to the second two paragraphs of the passage?
   - **A.** A broad overview of the topic pivoting to a vehement argument in favor of reform
   - **B.** An exploration of the history of interior design moving into a conversation with a prominent expert
   - **C.** A basic introduction to the concepts of internationally influenced design aesthetics that segues over to discussing recent developments in the field
   - **D.** A discussion of general philosophy transitions into a specific example of those principles being applied in the world of design
   - **E.** Eliot's explanation of recent trends in the design world opening outward into a larger examination of Owen's most significant work

49. What is the purpose of this passage?
   - **A.** To promote Owen Jones's design work to local businesses
   - **B.** An aesthetic treatise promoting polychromatic design
   - **C.** A set of principles by which young designers should abide
   - **D.** To review the latest edition of *The Grammar of Ornament*
   - **E.** A personal essay about Eliot's relationship to design

50. According to the passage, Owen Jones has documented artistic history from all of the following regions EXCEPT:

A. Africa

B. The Middle East

C. Western Europe

D. Asia

E. Pacific Islands

51. The purpose of *The Grammar of Ornament*, according to its author, is all of the following EXCEPT:

A. To help students learn through imitation

B. To demonstrate principles by way of specific examples

C. To identify global artistic themes

D. To provide further context for each instance of ornamental design

E. To aid students in inventing their own types of design and principles

52. In context, the word "appendage" (line 67) most nearly means

A. finger or digit.

B. additional material.

C. annotated index.

D. companion volume.

E. blank pages for the reader.

53. Through the use of the term "savage," the author can be understood to mean someone

A. with very poor manners.

B. from a culture outside of Western Europe.

C. whose traditions and practices are considered primitive.

D. who cannot read or write.

E. who was not raised in a social environment.

54. Which of the following is a reasonable inference from the passage?

A. Artists should be basing their work primarily on botanical influences.

B. Manufacturing will benefit from the influence of the natural world.

C. Cultures around the world have a similar relationship to nature as the United Kingdom does.

D. The beauty and diversity of nature is an ideal solution for human-made industrialized ugliness.

E. Owen Jones was a product of his time and his work soon became outdated.

55. Which of these choices best describes the different functions of the two footnotes?

A. One explains a particular reference, the other provides necessary background information.

B. One introduces a major character from literature, the other suggests further reading on the topics covered in the essay.

C. One provides context on the author of the essay, the other contextualizes the subject of it.

D. One speculates on the impact of the author's style, the other explains the origins of polychromy.

E. One engages with reader expectations, the other directs the reader how to interpret the essay itself.

STOP!
IF YOU FINISH BEFORE THE TIME IS UP, YOU MAY CHECK YOUR WORK IN THIS SECTION ONLY.

Section II: Free Response

Total Time: 2 hours, 15 minutes

Directions: The following prompt is based on the accompanying six sources. This question requires you to integrate a variety of sources into a coherent, well-written essay. When you synthesize sources, you refer to them to develop your position and cite them accurately. Your argument should be central; the sources should support the argument. Avoid merely summarizing sources. Remember to attribute both direct and indirect references.

Question 1
Suggested Time—40 Minutes

Schools have been debating the merits and disadvantages of requiring uniforms for decades; born out of a private school tradition that indicated status and scholarly seriousness, they have also been adopted by public schools to address a variety of problems. But are they successfully tackling these issues? Have uniforms done more harm than good in terms of student well-being, academic performance, or institutional values?

Carefully read the following six sources, including the introductory information for each source. Then synthesize and incorporate at least three of the sources into a coherent and well-written essay in which you develop a position that resists, advocates for, or promotes an alternative strategy for the practice of requiring school uniforms in public and private schools.

Your argument should be the main focus of the essay. Use the sources to inform and strengthen your argument. Avoid merely summarizing the sources. Indicate clearly which sources you are drawing from, whether through direct quotation, paraphrase or summary. You may cite the sources as Source A, Source B, etc. or by using the descriptions in parentheses.

Source A (Dept. of Education, Washington D.C.)

Source B (case studies)

Source C (Ruffner)

Source D (Student Editorial Board)

Source E (Wells)

Source F (survey)

Source A

Manual on School Uniforms, Department of Education, Washington D.C., 1996

Abstract:

In response to growing levels of violence in American schools, many communities are deciding to adopt school uniform policies as part of an overall program to improve school safety and discipline. This document provides the following guidelines for parents, teachers, and school leaders who may consider adopting a school-uniform policy: 1) Get parents involved from the beginning; 2) protect students' religious expression; 3) protect students' other rights of expression; 4) determine whether to implement a voluntary or mandatory policy; 5) consider whether to have an opt-out provision in the case of a mandatory policy; 6) do not require students to wear a message; 7) assist families that need financial help; and 8) treat school uniforms as part of an overall safety program. Proponents assert that school uniforms may decrease violence and theft among students over clothing; prevent the wearing of gang colors and insignia; instill student discipline; help students and parents resist peer pressure; help students focus on school work; and help school officials identify intruders.

Source B

Case Studies for Uniform Implementation

Kansas City, Missouri

Type: Mandatory uniform policy at George Washington Carver Elementary School

Opt-out: None. Carver is a magnet school to which parents and students apply knowing about the uniform policy.

Size of program: 320 elementary school students

Implementation date: 1990

Support for disadvantaged students: Students receive their uniforms at no cost to them. The state and school district pay for the uniforms primarily with magnet school funding.

Results: Philomina Harshaw, the principal for all six years that Carver has had uniforms, observed a new sense of calmness throughout the school after students began wearing uniforms. "The children feel good about themselves as school uniforms build a sense of pride." "It forces adults to know a child."

Memphis, Tennessee

Type: Voluntary uniform policy at Douglas Elementary School

Opt-out: Uniforms are voluntary

Size of program: 532 elementary school students

Implementation date: 1993

Support for disadvantaged students: Douglas has business partners in Memphis that have contributed financial support to purchase uniforms for needy families.

Results: According to Guidance Counselor Sharon Carter, "The tone of the school is different. There's not the competitiveness especially in grades 4, 5, and 6 about who's wearing what." Ninety percent of the students have elected to wear uniforms on school uniform days, Monday through Thursday. Fridays are "casual" days during which none of the students wear uniforms.

Seattle, Washington

Type: Mandatory uniform policy at South Shore Middle School

Opt-out: Yes, with parental consent

Size of program: 900 middle school students

Implementation date: 1995

Support for disadvantaged students: South Shore works with local businesses that contribute financial support to the uniform program. In addition, the administration at South Shore found that the average cost of clothing a child in a school with a prescribed wardrobe is less than in schools without such a program, sometimes 80 percent less. School officials believe that usability, reusability, and year-to-year consistency also increase the economy of the school's plan.

Results: The principal of South Shore, Dr. John German, reports that "this year the demeanor in the school has improved 98 percent, truancy and tardiness are down, and we have not had one reported incident of theft." Dr. German explains that he began the uniform program because his students were "draggin', saggin', and laggin'." "I needed to keep them on an academic focus. My kids were really into what others were wearing." Only five students have elected to attend another public school.

Source C

Letter to Parents from Louisa Ruffner, Principal at Luther Middle School

Luther Middle School is located in Baltimore, Maryland, and has been experiencing low graduation rates and increasing disciplinary issues stemming from the influence of local gang activity and community instability due to poverty. Many students hope to be the first generation in their families to go on to college.

Dear Parents, Guardians and Luther Community Members,

Next fall, Luther will be implementing a mandatory uniform policy at Luther Middle School. The PTA has had numerous conversations about the pros and cons of making this change and has ultimately decided the benefits more than outweigh the challenges that this transition may bring. Our sister school, Hendrickson High School, has seen an improvement in morale and student behavior since adopting a uniform policy five years ago. According to U.S. Department of Education software, Hendrickson High has seen a 47% drop in leaving class without permission, throwing objects has decreased by 68%, and fighting has diminished by 38%. Staff attribute these changes in large part to the adoption of a uniform code. Uniforms tend to create more of a sense of collective unity, minimize differences in taste and family income level, and encourage faculty to get to know students as a way to distinguish them as individuals through their behavior, not their clothes.

The Luther uniforms will consist of:

- Khaki slacks, dressy shorts, and skirts
- Hunter green polo shirts and blouses
- Charcoal grey hoodies, cardigans, tights, and knee-high socks

We know that not every family may find it easy to accommodate new clothing requirements, so we are also pleased to announce our partnership with LeHigh Schoolwear in downtown Baltimore, which will be providing every member of the class of 2004 with one complete uniform outfit (one bottom option, one top option, one layering option) free of charge. More options will be available for purchase, including long-sleeve tees, button downs and school gear with Luther name and logo), and we hope that graduating students will be willing to donate their uniforms to Luther upon graduation so we can also maintain a closet for future students in need.

Because each family will be provided with a set of clothing, and more options will be available at need-based discount or for retail purchase, we are making this policy mandatory. Students who come to school Monday through Thursday out of uniform will receive an in-school detention session with Mr. Lindsay that may also involve community service or school improvement projects.

We are excited to see the improvement in overall school climate and the greater focus on positive student behavior we expect as a result of this new policy. We will be having a two-part community meeting Thursday, March 12 at 2 pm and 7 pm to address any questions or concerns you or your student may have.

Source D

Statement from the Student Editorial Board, Alcott High School, Freedmont, Massachusetts

Philosopher Michel Foucault once said, "Schools serve the same social functions as prisons and mental institutions—to define, classify, control, and regulate people." Based on the administrative policies and personal values of faculty, staff, and administrators at Alcott High, we would assume this is not the underlying philosophy that our school operates on. And in general, we, the student editors of the Alcott High *Little Gazette* are fortunate to be able to disagree, both with the premise that schools *do* this, and with the implication that they *should* do this. But why then, given the administration's more student-focused attitude and intention to educate us as individuals with freedom of expression, are we locked into a mandatory uniform policy that in fact, defines, classifies, controls and regulates us?

While 92% of students have never received a disciplinary infraction for violating the uniform code, the 8% of students who have violated it received write-ups for all of the following: too-short sleeves, off-color skirts, too-short skirts, ripped slacks, the wrong color shoes, colorful undershirts, and oversized pants. We, the undersigned editors, do not wish to abolish the uniform codes. We understand there are benefits to unify and create a sense of community. But we object to the mandatory policy and the disciplinary responses as currently implemented according to the student manual, on the following grounds:

Sexism: The emphasis on covering up female students' bodies in the uniform code implies first, heteronormative attitudes about male students being "distracted" and female students being "responsible" for that distraction. If male students are misbehaving due to the proximity of female humans, why aren't they bearing the brunt of those consequences instead of female students whose learning is disrupted by being sent home or forced to wear a giant ugly sweater from the nurse's office?

Classism: What the administration doesn't seem to realize is that matching colors and requiring a certain kind of fit (no "oversized" clothing) or banning minor tears or rips is actually placing an undue burden on families of limited means, who are dependent on what they can find cheaply. This may mean a blue that is not quite navy, or a white that is actually "eggshell." This may mean buying a few sizes larger, or accepting hand me downs that don't exactly fit. If you're going to require specific types of clothes you have to be sensitive to the restrictions lower-income families are under. The "school-provided" options in the charity closet are always extremely worn, or in limited sizes themselves. The school may pride itself on taking care of needy families but if children of those families are punished for violating uniform code, the administration is making a hard situation worse.

Conformity: Students who are punished for wearing colorful undershirts or otherwise accessorizing their uniform are being given mixed messages about creativity and critical thinking. We are taught civil rights leaders who practiced nonviolent resistance and lobbied for changes to offensive policies are heroes, but then someone wearing a striped undershirt under their white polo is written up. Maybe we need to ban gang colors and maybe we need to agree on social norms and values we will all uphold, but are cool fashion choices really disturbing anyone's learning?

We hereby propose two changes to the uniform code. One, that undershirts and shoes be exempt from the requirements, and two, that the policy be amended to be voluntary, so that students do not face disciplinary action for violating it and instead are rewarded for positive actions like adhering to the code 4 weeks in a row, or finding code-approved ways to still express themselves while reflecting community values.

Source E

Student Essay: Pro Uniforms
Timothy Wells

Now that I'm in college, the impact of uniforms on my daily life is much less, but when I was in high school I was so glad when my school decided to implement uniforms after my freshman year. My high school, Bells Miller, is in a low-income area in a financially struggling city, and the influence of local gangs made walking to and from school like running through a war zone. Without a lot of productive after-school activities or jobs available for teens, the easiest way to stay safe and make money was to let one of the gangs take you in. Wearing blue or red told the other gang members to protect or harass you.

For a long time I refused to wear either. My dad has sickle cell anemia and I want to become a doctor and help develop treatments, so I didn't want to join either of the big gangs in my neighborhood. This led to me getting bullied a lot at school. It wasn't safe for me to go many places alone, but lots of people were scared to go with me, so I spent a lot of time by myself and trying to hide out. Once my school started requiring uniforms, it was harder to tell just from looking at people in school who belonged to which group, and it wasn't so obvious I was "neither," so my friends from middle school started to come back to hanging out with me again.

I know that my school's problems are bigger and more serious than just what kids wear to school, but I think fewer discipline problems at Bells Miller probably made it easier for cops to focus on dealing with the gang activities. It may also have reminded the gang members that we're just kids, and we need time to focus on school! I haven't felt scared or unsafe at school since the policy was officially adopted, so I think people who object to school uniforms should consider that issue along with everything else they think about when arguing against them.

Source F

A survey of students at 1,000 U.S. schools revealed the following:

- 86% say the uniform policy has made a significant, positive impact on peer pressure.
- 64% say the uniform policy has made a significant, positive impact on bullying.
- 85% say the uniform policy has made a significant, positive impact on classroom discipline.
- 83% say the uniform policy has made a significant, positive impact on image in the community.
- 79% say the uniform policy has made a significant, positive impact on student safety.
- 64% say the uniform policy has made a significant, positive impact on student achievement.
- 44% say the uniform policy has made a significant, positive impact on attendance.
- 86% of respondents say one of the main benefits is more cost-effective than regular apparel.
- 94% say it eliminates wardrobe battles with kids.
- 92% say it is easier to get kids ready in the morning.
- 90% say it is easier to shop for school clothes.

GO ON TO THE NEXT PAGE.

Question 2
Suggested Time—40 Minutes

In March of 1776, while John Adams was attending the Continental Congress, Abigail Adams, his wife, wrote him this letter.

Read the letter carefully. Then, in a well-developed essay, analyze the rhetorical strategies that Adams uses to convey her message. What does this letter tell us about the time in which it was written, about Abigail and John's relationship, and about Abigail herself?

Abigail Adams née Smith, was born in 1744 in Weymouth, Massachusetts. She was never sent to school, but was taught reading, writing and arithmetic at home. She married lawyer John Adams in 1764, they had five children, and he was later elected the second president of the United States in 1797.

Braintree, 31 March, 1776.

I wish you would ever write me a letter half as long as I write you, and tell me, if you may, where your fleet are gone; what sort of defense Virginia can make against our common enemy; whether it is so situated as to make an able defense. Are not the gentry lords, and the common people vassals? Are they not like the uncivilized vassals Britain represents us to be? I hope their riflemen, who have shown themselves very savage and even blood-thirsty, are not a specimen of the generality of the people. I am willing to allow the colony great merit for having produced a Washington; but they have been shamefully duped by a Dunmore.

I have sometimes been ready to think that the passion for liberty cannot be equally strong in the breasts of those who have been accustomed to deprive their fellow-creatures of theirs. Of this I am certain, that it is not founded upon that generous and Christian principle of doing to others as we would that others should do unto us.

Do not you want to see Boston? I am fearful of the small-pox, or I should have been in before this time. I got Mr. Crane to go to our house and see what state it was in. I find it has been occupied by one of the doctors of a regiment; very dirty, but no other damage has been done to it. The few things which were left in it are all gone. I look upon it as a new acquisition of property—a property which one month ago I did not value at a single shilling, and would with pleasure have seen it in flames.

The town in general is left in a better state than we expected; more owing to a precipitate flight than any regard to the inhabitants; though some individuals discovered a sense of honor and justice, and have left the rent of the houses in which they were, for the owners, and the furniture unhurt, or, if damaged, sufficient to make it good. Others have committed abominable ravages. The mansion-house of your President is safe, and the furniture unhurt; while the house and furniture of the Solicitor General have fallen a prey to their own merciless party. Surely the very fiends feel a reverential awe for virtue and patriotism, whilst they detest the parricide and traitor.

I feel very differently at the approach of spring from what I did a month ago. We knew not then whether we could plant or sow with safety, whether where we had tilled we could reap the fruits of our own industry, whether we could rest in our own cottages or whether we should be driven from the seacoast to seek shelter in the wilderness; but now we feel a temporary peace, and the poor fugitives are returning to their deserted habitations.

Though we felicitate ourselves, we sympathize with those who are trembling lest the lot of Boston should be theirs. But they cannot be in similar circumstances unless pusillanimity and cowardice should take possession of them. They have time and warning given them to see the evil and shun it.

I long to hear that you have declared an independency. And, by the way, in the new code of laws which I suppose it will be necessary for you to make, I desire you would remember the ladies and be more generous and favorable to them than your ancestors. Do not put such unlimited power into the hands of the husbands. Remember, all men would be tyrants if they could. If particular care and attention is not paid to the ladies, we are determined to foment a rebellion, and will not hold ourselves bound by any laws in which we have no voice or representation.

That your sex are naturally tyrannical is a truth so thoroughly established as to admit of no dispute; but such of you as wish to be happy willingly give up the harsh title of master for the more tender and endearing one of friend. Why, then, not put it out of the power of the vicious and the lawless to use us with cruelty and indignity with impunity? Men of sense in all ages abhor those customs which treat us only as the vassals of your sex; regard us then as beings placed by Providence under your protection, and in imitation of the Supreme Being make use of that power only for our happiness.

April 5.

I want to hear much oftener from you than I do. March 8th was the last date of any that I have yet had. You inquire of me whether I am making saltpeter. I have not yet attempted it, but after soap-making believe I shall make the experiment. I find as much as I can do to manufacture clothing for my family, which would else be naked. I know of but one person in this part of the town who has made any. That is Mr. Tertius Bass, as he is called, who has got very near a hundred-weight which has been found to be very good. I have heard of some others in the other parishes. Mr. Reed, of Weymouth, has been applied to, to go to Andover to the mills which are now at work, and he has gone.

I have lately seen a small manuscript describing the proportions of the various sorts of powder fit for cannon, small-arms, and pistols. If it would be of any service your way I will get it transcribed and send it to you. Every one of your friends sends regards, and all the little ones. Adieu.

GO ON TO THE NEXT PAGE.

Question 3
Suggested Time—40 Minutes

In 1859, John Stuart Mill (1806-1873) wrote *On Liberty*, in which he said,

> "If it were only that people have diversities of taste, that is reason enough for not attempting to shape them all after one model. But different persons also require different conditions for their spiritual development; and can no more exist healthily in the same moral, than all the variety of plants can exist in the same physical, atmosphere and climate. The same things which are helps to one person towards the cultivation of his higher nature, are hindrances to another. . . . Unless there is a corresponding diversity in their modes of life, they neither obtain their fair share of happiness, nor grow up to the mental, moral, and aesthetic stature of which their nature is capable."

Philosophy professor Kwame Anthony Appiah uses this quote as evidence of the longevity of the idea that diversity is essential to the success of not only individuals, but of communities that cultural preservationists (people seeking to keep a culture from being "contaminated") hope to protect from outside influences like globalization (the arrival of goods, services, or values from the larger world).

Write an essay that argues your position on the importance of either preserving or diversifying a community or culture through the process of globalization. Use relevant examples from your experience, observations, or readings to support your argument appropriately.

STOP!
IF YOU FINISH BEFORE THE TIME IS UP,
YOU MAY CHECK YOUR WORK IN THIS SECTION ONLY.

ANSWER KEY AND EXPLANATIONS

Section I: Multiple Choice

1. D	12. D	23. C	34. C	45. E
2. B	13. E	24. B	35. A	46. A
3. A	14. B	25. D	36. C	47. A
4. D	15. C	26. C	37. E	48. D
5. C	16. D	27. D	38. B	49. D
6. E	17. B	28. A	39. E	50. E
7. A	18. E	29. E	40. A	51. A
8. C	19. A	30. C	41. E	52. B
9. B	20. B	31. D	42. B	53. C
10. E	21. E	32. D	43. E	54. D
11. E	22. A	33. B	44. C	55. A

1. **The correct answer is D.** It best captures the main overall message of the passage, even though it does not specifically refer to John Brown. Choice A is incorrect because it is the opposite of what Thoreau is arguing—he thinks the government focuses on defending the Constitution to the exclusion of engaging with its values. Choice B is incorrect because it is an oversimplification of one of Thoreau's ideas, not his main idea. Choice C is incorrect because it is the main idea of Thoreau's first paragraph, not the text as a whole. Choice E is incorrect because it overstates Thoreau's position—he is not calling for Brown's pardon.

2. **The correct answer is B.** From these extracted lines, it is clear Thoreau is suggesting that government is "becoming contemptible" when private citizens have to uphold the laws in order to ensure justice. Choice A is incorrect because Thoreau does not think it's a good thing that the public is coming to regard government as contemptible. Choice C is incorrect because it is not supported by the text—Thoreau does not seem fearful, nor is he justifying himself. Choice D is incorrect because, while Thoreau might believe this as demonstrated by his argument elsewhere in the passage, these particular lines do not support this inference. Choice E is incorrect because Thoreau is not making a broader statement about the role of government or particular leaders, but referring to a specific set of circumstances.

3. **The correct answer is A.** Paradox, or a statement that appears to be contradictory but later turns out to contain some degree of truth, is the device Thoreau is *not* using in this passage. Choice B is incorrect because Thoreau does use a simile, a comparison using "like" or "as," when he says, "as surely as water runs out of a leaky vessel." Choice C is incorrect because Thoreau does use comparison, when he says the government reminds him of a farmer in winter. Choice D is incorrect because Thoreau opens the

passage with rhetorical questions, which the reader doesn't need to answer since he will address them himself. Choice E is incorrect because both the simile and comparison in this case are examples of figurative language.

4. **The correct answer is D.** Thoreau's metaphor is pointing out that farmers who make barrels may do so without knowing what the barrel is meant to hold, i.e., what it's for. And government, in parallel, knows how to deal with money and making tunnels, but is failing to provide what people actually need. Choice A is incorrect because it misreads the comparison, which is not suggesting government be good at fewer things. Choice B is incorrect because the target of the metaphor is not the farmer. Choice C is incorrect because it is an overly literal reading of the excerpt. Choice E is incorrect because Thoreau is not complimenting either the farmer or the government.

5. **The correct answer is C.** It correctly identifies the rhetorical link between Thoreau's decision to start with critique to make the case for why John Brown's rebellion was necessary. Choice A is incorrect because Thoreau isn't discussing specific leadership but an overall pattern in government in this paragraph. Choice B is incorrect because it is not supported by the passage—this is not the kind of action Thoreau is hoping to inspire. Choice D is incorrect because there is no evidence Thoreau hopes to run for office. Choice E is incorrect because Thoreau is not exposing corruption as much as cowardice in American leadership—and in any case, his purpose for the passage as a whole is larger.

6. **The correct answer is E.** Thoreau aligns himself with his listeners several times, by saying "until you or I came over to him" and using "we" repeatedly. Choice A is incorrect because it is not supported by the passage, which actually ends with Thoreau starting to confront his audience. Choice B is incorrect because Thoreau overtly defends Brown's methods, due to the urgency of the issues at stake. Choice C is incorrect because Thoreau acknowledges he has not always been writing and speaking out about slavery, thus excusing his listener from having done so. Choice D is incorrect because Thoreau carefully avoids taking a moral high ground at any point.

7. **The correct answer is A.** It correctly paraphrases Thoreau's topic sentence in that paragraph, which suggests that he was hearing many people dismiss the rebellion for having small numbers, and reflects the argument Thoreau was building that only the best and bravest were chosen for the mission. Choice B is incorrect because Thoreau is not arguing the rebellion was not dangerous. Choice C is incorrect because this is not the idea Thoreau is trying to reject or respond to. Choice D is incorrect because it is not supported by the passage—neither Thoreau nor Brown's detractors thought the rebellion should have had fewer people. Choice E is incorrect because the nature of the rebellion is not under discussion in this paragraph.

8. **The correct answer is C.** In that phrase, "summer" and "winter" are changed from nouns to verbs via verbification. Choice A is incorrect because it is not an exaggeration for effect. Choice B is incorrect because this is not an allusion to an outside concept or piece of writing. Choice D is incorrect because it is not supported by the context of the passage. Choice E is incorrect because this phrase in and of itself is not narrating a sequence of events.

9. **The correct answer is B.** "Forward" in this sentence means "inappropriate" or "in a hurry to . . . ," so Thoreau is saying he will not rush to tell a man he's wrong if that man is making the most progress toward liberation. Choices A and D are incorrect

because each misinterprets "forward" based on context. Choice C is incorrect because it is not supported by the passage. Choice E is incorrect because it is not an accurate reading of the sentence.

10. **The correct answer is E.** The juxtaposition occurs from the close proximity of "so-called peace" and "deeds of petty violence." Choice A is incorrect, though it is an example of parallelism. Choice B is incorrect; it is an example of metaphor. Choice C is incorrect, though it does feature an inversion. Choice D is incorrect because it is not bringing two contrasting ideas together for added meaning.

11. **The correct answer is E.** You may have interpreted "deliquesce" via its root, *liqui–* to accurately select this answer; context clues included the comparison to fungi and the earlier discussion of rotting or sloughing off. Choices A, C, and D are incorrect—the mention of "eulogists mopping" serves to eliminate each one. Choice B is incorrect; though the inference is reasonable based on the fungi reference, it is not ultimately supported by the broader context of the paragraph, which is about dying, not living or prospering.

12. **The correct answer is D.** By questioning the very meaning of living and dying, Thoreau seeks to elicit an emotional response from the listeners (pathos) as well as their understanding of what it means to do the right thing (ethos) by making the best use of one's life. Choice A is incorrect because ethos is not the only answer. Choice B is incorrect because these definitions do not appeal to the listener's sense of logic. Choice C is incorrect because pathos is not the only answer. Choice E is incorrect because it includes logos.

13. **The correct answer is E.** It most accurately sums up the tone of the passage overall. Choice A is incorrect because it doesn't reflect the entire passage—*some* paragraphs are outraged, but that is not the only register in which Thoreau works. Choice B is incorrect because Thoreau is not merely talkative. Choice C is incorrect because Thoreau is not seeking revenge upon those who will condemn Brown. Choice D is incorrect because dispassionate means to lack passion, to be detached.

14. **The correct answer is B.** Thoreau is using a logical construction to persuade his readers—if they are upset about the very concept of slavery, then they can be shocked by an attack on a slaveowner. But if they are not outraged about the daily violence and death that slavery entails, they can't logically be outraged by the death of a slaveowner. This logic is intended to confront listeners with the double standard at work (where the life of the white slave owner is worth more to them than the enslaved people John Brown was attempting to free). Choices A, C, D, and E are incorrect because they don't identify the logos present in the extract.

15. **The correct answer is C.** It correctly sums up the larger overarching idea the passage is seeking to convey. Choice A is incorrect because it is not supported by the passage. Choice B is incorrect because while there is a paragraph about Pasteur's rabies research, it is not presented as most important, nor is that the main idea of the entire passage. Choice D is incorrect because the passage does not go so far as to say that nobody else could have done the work Pasteur did. Choice E is incorrect because while it mentions specific facts, it is not the most accurate or the most reflective of the ideas in the passage.

16. **The correct answer is D.** It correctly identifies the one option not discussed in the passage—there is no mention of Pasteur's physical health. Choices A and B are incorrect because both options are mentioned in the

first paragraph. Choices C and E are incorrect and are covered later in the passage when the writers describe specific objections to Pasteur's work and the difficulty of the work he undertook.

17. **The correct answer is B.** The paragraph uses transitions like "first of all," "Secondly," "Thirdly," Fourthly," etc. Choice A is incorrect because the paragraph is not organized using order of importance, even if it were possible to determine which step in an experiment or proof was most significant. Choice C is incorrect because while some of the passage is organized by type of research, this paragraph is not. Choice D is incorrect because the links between sentences are not based on a writer's understanding but on the order in which they happened. Choice E is incorrect because the order of events is chronological, not backward.

18. **The correct answer is E.** In context, the passage is discussing the way the rabies virus was most intense on the first day it was exposed to the air but less intense, and therefore less prone to being spread, after that. Choice A is incorrect because in context, this use of virulence has nothing to do with treatment. Choice B is incorrect because contagion is about more than just speed; it also relates to the capacity for infection. Choice C is incorrect because the rabies virus does not occur more often when it is virulent, but it spreads more quickly and with a greater degree of potency. Choice D is incorrect because the passage is not examining the experience of symptoms as described by a patient.

19. **The correct answer is A.** The presence of actual data serves to document the results of Pasteur's experiments. Choice B is incorrect—since it's not suggested that either of the writers was involved with Pasteur's work, directly referring to data doesn't enhance their credibility as scientists. Choice C is incorrect because these results are specific; they are not presented as a transition to how the methodology could be further applied. Choice D is incorrect because the statistics only offer reassurance about a cure, they don't speak to a lowered risk of contracting the illness. Choice E is incorrect because there is no discussion of the risk to the scientist himself.

20. **The correct answer is B.** The purpose of paragraph 3, as indicated by the topic sentence, is to address the arguments of opponents to Pasteur's rabies vaccine. Choice A is incorrect because the passage has already been discussing specific examples, and this paragraph is moving more deeply into the conversation, not introducing new examples. Choice C is incorrect because the paragraph is not serving to apply Pasteur's discovery to other contexts. Choice D is incorrect because the paragraph does not mention other discoveries or attempt to examine them together. Choice E is incorrect because the paragraph is summarizing views of people who disagree with Pasteur.

21. **The correct answer is E.** By responding with "To the two former the school of Pasteur, of course, replies that the value of human life answers the one, and the results of experience the other," the authors invoke Pasteur on the grounds of ethos, placing value on human life rather than the lives of individual humans, and logos, the scientific evidence. Choice A is incorrect because the authors are not using an emotional appeal. Choices B and C are incorrect because they omit one of the correct options. Choice D is incorrect because it is the wrong combination of options.

22. **The correct answer is A.** *Minute* here means "small, or on a micro scale." Choice B is incorrect because no diminutive implications

are being made about the importance of the economies in the village. Choices C and D are incorrect because *minute*, as in a unit of time, is not the correct definition in context. Choice E is incorrect because it is not a definition supported by the passage.

23. **The correct answer is C.** It accurately reflects the connotations of "Rustic Thinker," as the writers dub Pasteur—every aspect of his childhood and youth informed his priorities and mindset as a scientist and researcher. Choice A is incorrect; the writers are more generous with his village. Choice B is incorrect because there's no evidence they thought Pasteur was unusual in his hometown. Choice D is incorrect because it is not supported by the passage. Choice E is incorrect because the writers clearly think Pasteur was well-prepared by his upbringing.

24. **The correct answer is B.** As the writers signal with "diagrammatically," they are offering a visualization of Pasteur's progress throughout his career as a spiral with multiple arms. Choice A is incorrect because the image is not a reference to another work or concept. Choice C is incorrect because the writers are using a metaphorical shorthand rather than explaining what actually took place in a coherent narrative. Choice D is incorrect because it is not ironic that there should be a visualization of Pasteur's career, given the scientific nature of his work. Choice E is incorrect because the tense of each section is actually inconsistent and not precisely in parallel.

25. **The correct answer is D.** Of the accomplishments listed, Choice D is the only one attributable to a different scientist, and *not* mentioned in the passage. Choices A, B, C, and E are all mentioned in the final paragraphs.

26. **The correct answer is C.** The writers signal very clearly that their purpose for the paragraph is "to sum up." Choice A is incorrect because the passage is condensed and list-based, not overly descriptive. Choice B is incorrect because the writers are not presenting this series of events as though it is unfolding over a set amount of time or gradually; they are looking back and accounting for it all at once. Choice D is incorrect because neither Pasteur nor his work is being compared with anyone else. Choice E is incorrect because the facts are more or less objectively stated; the writers are not overtly advancing a specific argument.

27. **The correct answer is D.** No mention is made of Pasteur's literal eyesight, nor a figurative lack of perception. Choice A is incorrect because the opening paragraph describes him as fighting all kinds of barriers to the acceptance of his work. Choice B is incorrect because the scientific process he undertook clearly suggests he was resilient. Choice C is incorrect because the passage repeatedly mentions his thrifty qualities. Choice E is incorrect because the passage describes him as "eager to understand."

28. **The correct answer is A.** In representing all of his public as one paymaster, Stevenson is representing many with just one part. Choice B is incorrect because the author is not using allusion for emphasis in this instance. Choice C is incorrect because the author is not giving human qualities to something inanimate. Choice D is incorrect because the author is not revealing information to the audience unbeknownst to a character. Choice E is incorrect because the author is not making an argument with this phrase.

29. **The correct answer is E.** *Indelible*, in context, means "impossible to remove." Choice A is incorrect—you might have chosen it if you mistook *indelible* for *inedible*. Choice B is incorrect because it is not supported by the passage. Choice C is

incorrect and is trying to trip you up based on visual similarity. Choice D is incorrect because *familiar* would make it redundant in context.

30. **The correct answer is C.** In addition to befriending the sellers (literally or figuratively), Stevenson also mentions that he purchased "reams and reams" of paper from them. Choice A is incorrect because Stevenson has not yet introduced his most famous character. Choice B is incorrect because it is not supported by the passage. Choice D is incorrect because there is no evidence the paper-sellers were also writers. Choice E is incorrect because it reads the phrase too literally.

31. **The correct answer is D.** Although Stevenson was developing a reputation as a writer, he was not actually successful enough to make all the hard work add up to supporting himself; this is ironic. Choice A is incorrect because he is not comparing the experience to anything else. Choice B is incorrect—if he had recounted a story in which someone described him as a writer while he confessed to having made no money from it, that would be an anecdote about the same experience. Choice C is incorrect because he is not presenting the antithesis to an argument in progress. Choice E is incorrect because this is not a question without an obvious—or with a seemingly contradictory—answer.

32. **The correct answer is D.** Em dashes function the same way commas or parentheses do, to frame an aside that interrupts an ongoing narrative. Here, Stevenson is clarifying what he means by a short story. Choices A, B, and C are incorrect because he does not appear to be making an observation with any feeling behind it. Choice E is incorrect because while he might be intending to amuse the reader, there is little indication Stevenson himself found humor in it.

33. **The correct answer is B.** In this paragraph, Stevenson does *not* make an effort to group his stories or material thematically or make categorical statements. He does use simile ("like a schoolboy's watch"), examples (naming the titles and genres of his works), a narrative (anchoring these examples in a chronological structure), and comparative moves ("I might be compared to a cricketer . . ."), so choices A, C, D, and E are incorrect.

34. **The correct answer is C.** The context clue to help you identify lugubrious with sadness or sorrow is that it refers to the way the cottage was referred to as "The Late Miss McGregor's." Choices A, B, D, and E are all unsupported by the passage.

35. **The correct answer is A.** It accurately reads the simile as comparing the author's feelings about the harbor drawing to his feelings about sonnets. Choices B and C are incorrect because they literally attribute the qualities of a sonnet to the harbor drawing. Choice D is incorrect because it misattributes the implications of the simile. Choice E is incorrect because it is not supported by the passage.

36. **The correct answer is C.** The author describes the process of the established writer's hard work in contrast to the burst of luck and struggle for endurance that brand new writers experience. Choice A is incorrect—it seems to refer to the previous paragraph. Choice B is incorrect because it overstates Stevenson's claim. Choices D and E are incorrect because they are not supported by the passage.

37. **The correct answer is E.** While Stevenson is mostly discussing adventure novels and acknowledging his lack of success, the references that indicate he was well read and well educated add a layer of seriousness to

his discussion. Choice A is incorrect because there is no implied or explicit comparison with other writers. Choice B is incorrect because classic literature is hardly less necessary if you still need to be well-read enough to catch the allusions. Choice C is incorrect because it is overstating the effect of the allusions. Choice D is incorrect because there is no indication that Stevenson is pretentious.

38. **The correct answer is B.** Despite appearing somewhat pompous, Stevenson also goes to great lengths to downplay the time and energy he put in to writing and developing his craft. He makes jokes at his own expense despite his later success as a commercial novelist. Choice A is incorrect because Stevenson's tone is neither uniformly light and breezy nor always casual, and he's surely not indifferent—he has moments of seriousness, and if he were indifferent, he wouldn't be writing the piece in the first place. Choice C is incorrect because Stevenson is not reacting to anything that might render him indignant. Choice D is incorrect because Stevenson's tone is too casual to be described as deliberate. Choice E is incorrect because Stevenson is maintaining a joking tone—he is not being entirely profound or deeply considered.

39. **The correct answer is E.** In this paragraph, Stevenson is describing his process of creation by arranging details according to a chronological structure. Choice A is incorrect because Stevenson is not attempting to make any argument via his recounting. Choice B is incorrect because he is not analyzing the steps of composing. Choice C is incorrect because Stevenson is not defining what composition looks like. Choice D is incorrect because there is not a significant amount of description in this paragraph, particularly compared with others in the passage.

40. **The correct answer is A.** The author has constructed a parallel set of metaphorical instructions for modeling a character on an acquaintance and a good friend, respectively, by describing how to modify their characteristics by adding or removing detail. Choice B is incorrect because the process does not seem to contradict what has come before. Choice C is incorrect because it's not a comparison using like or as, but a conceit in which the author imagines the characters as trees. Choice D is incorrect because there is insufficient detail to consider this an anecdote. Choice E is incorrect because Stevenson is not giving the trees human characteristics, but imagining humans in a state of "arborescence."

41. **The correct answer is E.** The author does not ruminate on the value or meaning of the self as a construct, though he uses metaphor (see the previous tree metaphor), asks rhetorical questions, uses other forms of figurative language, and generalizes about what boys like in adventure stories, so choices A, B, C, and D are incorrect.

42. **The correct answer is B.** By comparing the two innovations, Eliot is not seeking to rank them, but to validate the study and importance of design and architecture alongside other major social evolutions. Choice A is incorrect because she is not suggesting it is less important, as indicated by the level of detail. Choice C is incorrect because Eliot is crediting the people behind these developments and not citing them as inevitable. Choice D is incorrect because Eliot is not saying one is more significant than the other. Choice E is incorrect because Eliot doesn't initiate an argument about who should be giving architecture more attention at this point in her essay.

43. **The correct answer is E.** Eliot is equating "moods and habits" with mothers and "Reason" with fathers in terms of their relationship to opinions. Choice A is incorrect

because she is not playing the personifications off one another in unexpected ways. Choice B is incorrect because she is not using a part to stand in for a whole. Choice C is incorrect because she is not referring to another literary work. Choice D is incorrect because she is not using *like* or *as* to achieve the comparison.

44. **The correct answer is C.** Saying the effect of poor internal decoration is "akin to that of malaria" is an overstatement for effect, not a valid observation. Choice A is incorrect because it is not a contradiction, but a hyper-extended comparison. Choice B is incorrect because the writer is not describing a linear series of events. Choice D is incorrect because the writer is not setting up a reversal of meaning. Choice E is incorrect because the language is somewhat formal, not casual or regionally inflected.

45. **The correct answer is E.** "Sanative" comes from the same root as "sanitize" but here is not so much about physical cleanliness as physical or emotional health. Choice A is incorrect; good design does not make you smarter. Choice B is incorrect; it is not supported by context. Choice C is incorrect because it's not referring to external improvements. Choice D is incorrect because it is not supported by the passage.

46. **The correct answer is A.** The driving idea of this paragraph is to establish the relationship between internal health, external health, and one's environment. Choice B is incorrect because Eliot is making the opposite point, that even people without access to beauty can appreciate it. Choice C is incorrect because this is not the argument Eliot is developing. Choice D is incorrect because this is not the topic Eliot is pursuing in this paragraph. Choice E is incorrect because it is directly contradicted by Eliot in this paragraph.

47. **The correct answer is A.** It is the only reason that is not supported in the passage—Eliot is saying that artistic reform philosophy can be applied more quickly to interior decor than to external architecture, not that the actual renovation will be speedier. Choices B, C, D, and E are incorrect, since they are part of the evidence provided by Eliot in support of her analysis.

48. **The correct answer is D.** It most accurately captures the nature of the first two paragraphs and how they are crafted to give rise to the latter two, by moving from a general philosophy into a specific exhibit to consider. Choice A is incorrect because it misstates the function of the later paragraphs. Choice B is incorrect because it misstates both the intent of the first half and the format of the second half—it is not a conversation. Choice C is incorrect because the first half provides no specific discussion of aesthetics and the second half doesn't get into specific techniques or trends. Choice E is incorrect because it fails to identify either the content or the form of each half.

49. **The correct answer is D.** Though not explicitly labeled as such, and featuring a significant digression from the author, this is a book review, as indicated by the specific discussion of the physical properties of the book, as well as its contents. Choice A is incorrect because it underevaluates the purpose of the passage. Choice B is incorrect because there are no specific aesthetic descriptions of polychromatic design. Choice C is incorrect because there are no principles explicitly articulated. Choice E is incorrect because George Eliot is not truly present as a viewer or personal voice in the essay.

50. **The correct answer is E.** Jones has studied work from each of the following regions or cultures: the Egyptian, Assyrian, ancient Persian, Greek, Roman, Byzantine, Arabian, Moresque, Mohammedan-Persian, Indian, Celtic, Medieval, Renaissance, Elizabethan,

and Italian. The only area missing is the Pacific Islands, which would not have been as readily accessible to a British designer in the 19th century. Choices A, B, C, and D are accounted for.

51. **The correct answer is A.** Jones explicitly does *not* want students to learn only through imitation of existing artistic works, but to acquire the principles and an understanding of global artistic practices so they can originate their own designs in the future, as described in choices B, C, D, and E.

52. **The correct answer is B.** In tis context, an appendage refers to an "appendix," or additional material commonly found in the backmatter of a printed volume. Choice A is incorrect based on the context of the passage. Choice C is incorrect based on the information that it's a bibliographic appendix, not an index. Choice D is incorrect because there is no support for the idea that there's a second volume to accompany the main book. Choice E is incorrect because it is not supported by the passage.

53. **The correct answer is C.** Based on the context clues throughout the passage, "savage" is not just intended to refer to groups in specific geographical areas, but anyone who has not been part of "civilization" as George Eliot would have experienced it. We would of course not use this terminology today—more correct vocabulary, depending on the specific tribal group under discussion, could include indigenous, native, or even simply "early civilization," if referring to a group in the past. Choices A, B, D, and E *might* all have been considered primitive or "savage," in Eliot's time, but choice C is the only one would cover *all* of that.

54. **The correct answer is D.** It is the most accurate summation of one of the main ideas in Eliot's work, without overstating the significance or being too specific in its conclusion. Choice A is incorrect because it too broadly applies one of the key concepts from later in the passage. Choice B is incorrect because it over evaluates Eliot's discussion of industrial spaces. Choice C is incorrect because it is an assumption not entirely supported by the passage. Choice E is incorrect because the rest of Jones' career is not discussed in the passage.

55. **The correct answer is A.** The first footnote explains Eliot's reference to a fictional work within a work, and the second introduces the reader to Owen Jones and his historical context. Choice B is incorrect because the second footnote is not suggesting further reading, and the first choice option overstates the significance of Eliot's allusion. Choice C is incorrect because neither footnote provides more information about George Eliot. Choice D is incorrect because the purpose of the second footnote is broader than just introducing polychromy. Choice E is incorrect because there is no discernable difference in relationship to the reader between the two footnotes.

Section II: Free Response

Question 1

High-Scoring Sample Essay

While originally school uniforms were only for religious or expensive private schools, in the past few decades many types of schools and communities in the United States have considered adopting standardized outfits for their students. The U.S. Department of Education encourages communities considering the practice to be sure to consider parental involvement, protection of religious freedoms and self-expression, whether policies should be voluntary or mandatory, and how to make sure families in need of financial help are not disadvantaged as a result (Source A). These are all good considerations, and there are others, but they omit some important perspectives in the process. Clearly schools are struggling due to a variety of internal and external factors, and I don't doubt they all think they're doing providing the very best for their students—but is that what's happening?

First let's look at some of the reasons schools typically decide to adopt uniforms. According to the Department of Education's case studies, reasons include morale, school unity, and a sense that students are being invested in by their community (Source B). One school implementing a new policy even hoped it would "encourage factually to get to know students . . . as individuals through their behavior, not their clothes" (Source C). These are some optimistic reasons to consider standardizing student wardrobe, but as a group of protesting students writing an op ed for their school paper wrote, "Why then, given the administration's more student-focused attitude and intention to educate us as individuals with freedom of expression, are we locked into a mandatory uniform policy that in fact, defines, classifies, controls, and regulates us?" Even when administrators have the best of intentions, students may perceive these types of policies as oppressive, and even offensive, for reason we'll get to in a minute.

To be frank, the next category of reasons in the uniform discussion are probably more compelling to parents and teachers than to students—both groups of adults say that part of the appeal of uniforms is the convenience and improved experience of getting kids ready for school in the morning (Source F). But doesn't that sound like a parenting problem, not to have a good routine in progress by the time your kid is ready for middle school or high school? What's so wrong with just having them pick out their clothes the night before, or giving the kids the freedom to deal with consequences if being picky about clothes makes them late?

Speaking of consequences, the most major reason schools consider uniforms is their perceived positive impact on discipline. And indeed, accounts like this one from former public school student Timothy Wells (Source E) suggest that the implementation of uniforms seriously cut down on gang visibility and related bullying. Faculty members can cite statistics, and principals can say that before uniforms, students were "draggin', saggin', and laggin'," (Source B) but students are also quick to respond that many of the criterion for uniforms have sexist and even racist implications for the student body. Only girls have their sleeves and skirt-length scrutinized, and it seems problematic that a teacher or principal would mention saggy pants. Has any research really proven that uniforms prevent these "distractions" from happening anyway? What about the negative messages that the students at Alcott High noticed—a detention is way more distracting than a tank top, if you ask me.

It seems obvious from the variety of parent, administration, law-maker and student perspectives available that often, uniforms have a positive effect on morale and a cohesive community feel in schools. But what each of these fails to do is examine the problems that uniforms cannot, and should not, solve. Gang activity is a community security issue and should be dealt with by law enforcement. Low-income families need social services that are taxpayer funded and don't draw attention to the kids growing up in these families. Administrators need to examine the conscious and unconscious bias that may exist in their policy language when it targets specific groups for infractions without stopping to think what message that sends. The conversation around school uniforms needs to move away from mandatory vs voluntary and closer to, what other contributing factors are affecting the educational experience of our students. It isn't fair to put the burden of addressing all those issues on the bodies of middle and high school students, and then give them detention if it doesn't work.

Reader Response for the High-Scoring Sample Essay

This essay effectively synthesizes multiple sources in order to take a stance—not for or against uniforms, but for a revamped process of deciding whether to even consider them. The evidence and explanations are appropriate, relevant, and convincing. The student uses transitions appropriately, along with the five-paragraph structure. She successfully represents multiple sides of the discussion. Her prose is well organized thematically, and while not flawless, demonstrates the writer's ability to use a range of effective writing techniques.

Middle-Scoring Sample Essay

Many different teachers think that uniforms are great (Source B) but lots of students think they are a bad idea (Source D). On the plus side, they help with discipline and let everyone look the same, but on the downside they can be expensive, and even if the school provides clothes, some people will still have more and everybody will know. Still I found the personal essay in Source E very persuasive—nobody's right to wear a hoodie with words on it is more important than kids like Timothy feeling safe. I also liked how he didn't try to change people's minds but asked them to just think about his point of view. The grown-ups in Source B were encouraging too—they seemed to really think that uniforms made a big difference at their school.

I don't think there should be one rule for everybody, but I think uniforms could be good at my school. I wouldn't mind having fewer options because I could still change when I got home or wear different stuff on the weekends. A lot of people do care about designers at my school, and I think kids who don't have as much money feel bad. We don't have to much discipline issues but sometimes when people get on campus and nobody knows who they are it can be a little weird. One of the administrators in Source B said he liked being able to identify intruders which I think makes sense and would be a good reason. All in all, I won't ask my school for uniforms but if they decided to do them, I would support it.

Reader Response for the Middle-Scoring Sample Essay

This writer adequately identifies the main issue and introduces a few sources to explain it, but stops short of actually synthesizing the content or responding to it in a more significant way. The argument is generally clear and there are some lapses in diction and syntax, but generally the writer is able to convey his ideas appropriately. The essay's structure indicates an understanding of what functions various paragraphs can serve, but perhaps exhibits symptoms of a time crunch, as it is not very developed.

Low-Scoring Sample Essay

School should not have uniforms because it gets in the way of students who need to be creative, like when students talk about how it makes their morning easier they forget that sometimes art needs to be challenging, like at my school it is the hardest class but being able to express myself is too important. Schools need to listen to their students because nobody can afford uniforms and it's not cheaper for everyone. What if I need to be able to wear a shirt of any color? With words on it? How can I come to school in the same clothes as everyone else when I'm not just like anyone else? Uniforms may be good for parents but they are bad for students.

Reader Response for the Low-Scoring Sample Essay

This writer took a strong stance against uniforms but missed many of the components of the prompt—the writer neglected to include references to sources and didn't cover multiple facets of the issue or develop ideas in a logical, well-organized way. The essay lacks structure and also exhibits syntax and style issues inappropriate for this context.

Question 2

High-Scoring Sample Essay

In this letter, which Abigail Adams wrote to her husband John while he was contributing to the Continental Congress prior to the declaration of American independence, her writing style reflects the capacity women have always had to be informed and resilient as they advocate for themselves and others. She uses rhetoric of persuasion, description, and an appeal to ethos and pathos to make her point in hopes of winning John over to her cause.

Adams shows that she is informed when she asks specific questions about geography, defense, ad political leadership. She builds her authority not only by her knowledge of current events but also with her exceptional vocabulary using words like felicitate and pusillanimity. She uses active, not passive, rhetoric to push Adams to declare independence and offers to pass on information that could be helpful to revolutionary leaders in charge of munitions, which shows pragmatism and a lack of fear.

We also see how she was required to be resilient as Adams manages in the same letter to balance concerns of state with concerns of home, reporting on the condition of the family house that has been left to the occupying force. She was prepared to move on and consider the house lost but now is prepared to restore it—she shows an understanding of narrative techniques and how to prioritize in order of importance (the president's house comes before the solicitor general). She also remembers to provide a homey update for her husband to let him know how her domestic concerns are going too, about saltpeter and making clothes for the family. It is hard to imagine how the revolution could have functioned if the wives of men who history finds so memorable weren't at home sewing clothes and keeping track of family property.

Abigail Adams was also a feminist advocate. Using both philosophical rhetoric and figurative language, Abigail declares men to be a tyrannical sex and insists that John should do better, or women are determined not to be restrained by laws that don't represent them. She draws a parallel between the British, who are less passionate about freedom because they have always had it, and the men in charge of the Constitution, who may make the same mistake about women's rights. A very famous phrase from this letter is "remember the ladies," which is an appeal to both pathos, because it refers to her, but also ethos, because equality is something all men believe in. She even sneaks in an appeal to logos, by trying to suggest men can reinterpret their "protector status" and use their power for good, rather than just trying to get them to give up power.

The fact that women like Abigail exist should had made every man involved in creating the Constitution ashamed to exclude them. For modern women, the fact that we are not fighting a new fight but continuing a very, very old one can either inspire hope or despair. I choose to be hopeful, because people like Abigail, who continue learning and demanding a voice their whole lives, were able to overcome much tougher obstacles than mine.

Reader Response for the High-Scoring Sample Essay

This writer has effectively identified multiple rhetorical strategies at work in Abigail Adams' letter to her husband, John, and used them to create an interpretive argument about the significance of Adams and her rhetoric. The writer has developed the analysis with appropriate examples, referred to the source text explicitly, and successfully structured the essay with cohesive chronological and thematic organization. The prose is consistently well articulated, even if not perfect.

Middle-Scoring Sample Essay

One interesting thing that Abigail Adams does is start her letter about one thing, and then finish it, and then add another note. This tells me that she was very busy, because she had to record the important stuff and then the little stuff later, or put it all down at once and not worry about being organized. It also tells us that women weren't actually fighting the war, but the stuff she knew about the politics and the army says women weren't safe. It's clear that Abigail had a lot of education because how else would she know how to write like this? They also lived on a farm, or would if they got their house back.

Abigail writing to John shows some neediness in the way she says she wants to hear from him more. He's very busy and it's like using bad rhetoric to just try to make him feel bad and want to come home. I would say she has a lot of ideas but if she really wanted to use them she should just go to Boston or wherever and try to get stuff done herself. Writing letters is not as useful even if you do now good words and have ideas. Her style is personably but sometimes insistent, and she really wants Adams to "remember the ladies" and not do what every other government does.

Reader Response for the Middle-Scoring Sample Essay

This writer does identify some rhetorical strategies, and evaluates the impact of those strategies on the effectiveness of the letter. The writing contains lapses in diction and syntax but is generally clear. The writer implicitly refers to the passage but doesn't do more than the minimum to engage with it, and falls short of advancing an argument of his or her own to interpret the passage.

Low-Scoring Sample Essay

This letter from Abigail Adams to her husband the president shows that women are not involved in politics and are more focused on stuff at home like their families and their houses. They have to sit at home and wait for news and don't stay very informed because they have more important things to do and are removed from the war. Abigail is living in her big house and looking forward to gardening and farming while John is doing important things in the Navy. She uses personal stories and narrative information and metaphor.

Reader Response for the Low-Scoring Sample Essay

This writer struggles to accurately close-read the passage, and provides only cursory attempts at identifying rhetorical techniques. The writer generalizes about Abigail Adams' concerns as relates to the plight of other women during wartime, and incorrectly attempts to summarize the letter's content. The diction is too informal, and the essay itself is too brief.

Question 3

High-Scoring Sample Essay

Scholars like John Stuart Mill have been trying to decided what to do about human liberty for centuries. For actual hundreds of years they have been debating what's ok and what's wrong for a visiting culture to do with an established culture, and recently professor Kwame Anthony Appiah has joined the debate. Mill decided that different people have diverse needs and for any civilization to reach its full potential, it has to be receptive to different ways of doing things. Appiah's point is similar, but he's more worried about resisting "cultural preservationists" who want to actually prevent new information and technologies from reaching cultures they've decided should stay pure. This idea of purity is dangerous. It facilitates cultures drawing firm lines between "themselves" and "the other" which is so often dangerous. But let's be clear, there are different kinds of contamination too.

Let's first look at colonialism, one of the original forms of cultural contamination. It gave the "colonized" culture no chance to look over their weapons or art or food or traditions and say "We'll take the farming implements but not the diseases please!" It's true that some members of the colonized culture probably found things they liked either during initial trades or after the takeover, but this is the kind of contamination that makes preservationists angry, because it involves steamrolling over one kind of culture with another. And that we should all be able to agree is wrong.

But later, different groups settled in proximity to one another, and the kind of contamination was more symbiotic. Think of neighboring towns with factories that meet needs the other one has, or a village with great textiles getting friendly with a village that has good dyeing abilities. This is what both Mill and Appiah would think of as useful and important. It's more like cross-pollinating than being contaminated, because what's coming in to either culture isn't bad, and it's wanted. I have to come down on the side of this collaborative mode, because it also allows for the spread of technology, which nobody should "own", copyrights and patents aside. America doesn't have an exclusive right to use the technology we use or the medicine we have, and it's not wrong to take that to a place that doesn't have it and share it.

Finally this brings us to cultural appropriation. As we learned to live in proximity without combining cultures, and as people figured out the difference between being inclusive and being overrun, we started to see problems like appropriation, where instead of one group replacing another group's culture with their own, they would just harvest the parts they like, like with Katy Perry or the Kardashians, or Gwen Stefani. On the one hand, cross-pollination might have led each of them to aspects of another culture that they like, but you have to think about the benefit to the other culture. It should be mutual, and if it's not, then the "visitor" shouldn't get to profit from whatever they take. It's sort of a forcible contamination that makes it hard for the appropriated culture to hold on to the traditions they decided not to modernize or lose track of.

In conclusion, Mill is right that people have different needs, and Appiah is right to be protective of people's ability to learn and grow. But the people with *more* knowledge have a strong obligation to be generous, and not greedy. They should give as much as they take, as long as it's wanted, and be thoughtful about how their addition might impact the community they're going into. They should also make a mutual effort to exchange ideas, if not assimilate, because you never know what's going to spark someone's imagination or lead to an important innovation. Contamination is inevitable, but collaboration is even better.

Reader Response for the High-Scoring Sample Essay

This writer more than effectively met the criteria for this prompt—he engaged with the provided source excerpts, provided his own observations and experience, and organized his essay thoughtfully and competently. The writer took a stance and developed his position by considering multiple perspectives. Though the tone of the essay was a little informal, the writer demonstrated an appropriate ability to manage effective writing strategies, especially in the limited time allotted.

Middle-Scoring Sample Essay

I definitely think we need to keep older cultures alive—Mills and Appiah are right that different groups need different things but I think they forgot how sad people are when we lose a language or a craft. My people used o do really great bead work but gradually we forgot how, and even though I know how to do things my people didn't used to know, like use technology and travel on airplanes, I would really like to still know how to do bead work. But just protecting us from TV and iPhones wouldn't have kept us doing beadwork for ever, you know? So I have to say also that cultures have to be free to expand.

According to Mills, people won't even be happy if they don't "cultivate of his higher nature," and "obtain their fair share." So I think it's right that some people should keep practicing the traditional arts and everybody else should be free to try new things. You can't stop progress or city hall, and sometimes it's better to let it in ad see what people decide to keep. Globalization is hard for traditional people but being bored and not having any skills is hard for young people, who need to grow up to the status of which they are capable, says Mills. Given all that I have to say that cultures are responsible for maintaining what's important to them, and so am I.

Reader Response for the Middle-Scoring Sample Essay

This writer adequately responds to the prompt by identifying relevant personal experience and connecting it to the main ideas provided by Appiah and Mill. The connection may be strained and more implicit than explicit, but it is present. The language contains lapses in clarity and organization but is generally competent. The writer did successfully take a position, acknowledge multiple sides, and ultimately come to a decision about his or her own argument.

Low-Scoring Sample Essay

According to John Stuart Mill people are like plants and need different things to survive, which I have seen in my life because I like different things from other people around me. But I also only need the basics, like food and shelter and water and clothing. Most people need those. We just like the other stuff like entertainment and culture. I would have to say that Mills is wrong because Appiah is wrong too, and sometimes things have to stay the same or else they get lost and what if they are important? Then it's not good for people who would have been better off with just survival type stuff.

Reader Response for the Low-Scoring Sample Essay

This writer does refer to the writers from the prompt and starts to make a connection to his or her own experience, but does not actually introduce or support an argument in this brief essay. The essay's syntax is clumsy and unpolished, and the writer needed to engage more thoughtfully with the prompt text.

Chapter 5

Practice Test 2

ANSWER SHEET PRACTICE TEST 2

Section I: Multiple Choice

1. Ⓐ Ⓑ Ⓒ Ⓓ Ⓔ	15. Ⓐ Ⓑ Ⓒ Ⓓ Ⓔ	29. Ⓐ Ⓑ Ⓒ Ⓓ Ⓔ	43. Ⓐ Ⓑ Ⓒ Ⓓ Ⓔ
2. Ⓐ Ⓑ Ⓒ Ⓓ Ⓔ	16. Ⓐ Ⓑ Ⓒ Ⓓ Ⓔ	30. Ⓐ Ⓑ Ⓒ Ⓓ Ⓔ	44. Ⓐ Ⓑ Ⓒ Ⓓ Ⓔ
3. Ⓐ Ⓑ Ⓒ Ⓓ Ⓔ	17. Ⓐ Ⓑ Ⓒ Ⓓ Ⓔ	31. Ⓐ Ⓑ Ⓒ Ⓓ Ⓔ	45. Ⓐ Ⓑ Ⓒ Ⓓ Ⓔ
4. Ⓐ Ⓑ Ⓒ Ⓓ Ⓔ	18. Ⓐ Ⓑ Ⓒ Ⓓ Ⓔ	32. Ⓐ Ⓑ Ⓒ Ⓓ Ⓔ	46. Ⓐ Ⓑ Ⓒ Ⓓ Ⓔ
5. Ⓐ Ⓑ Ⓒ Ⓓ Ⓔ	19. Ⓐ Ⓑ Ⓒ Ⓓ Ⓔ	33. Ⓐ Ⓑ Ⓒ Ⓓ Ⓔ	47. Ⓐ Ⓑ Ⓒ Ⓓ Ⓔ
6. Ⓐ Ⓑ Ⓒ Ⓓ Ⓔ	20. Ⓐ Ⓑ Ⓒ Ⓓ Ⓔ	34. Ⓐ Ⓑ Ⓒ Ⓓ Ⓔ	48. Ⓐ Ⓑ Ⓒ Ⓓ Ⓔ
7. Ⓐ Ⓑ Ⓒ Ⓓ Ⓔ	21. Ⓐ Ⓑ Ⓒ Ⓓ Ⓔ	35. Ⓐ Ⓑ Ⓒ Ⓓ Ⓔ	49. Ⓐ Ⓑ Ⓒ Ⓓ Ⓔ
8. Ⓐ Ⓑ Ⓒ Ⓓ Ⓔ	22. Ⓐ Ⓑ Ⓒ Ⓓ Ⓔ	36. Ⓐ Ⓑ Ⓒ Ⓓ Ⓔ	50. Ⓐ Ⓑ Ⓒ Ⓓ Ⓔ
9. Ⓐ Ⓑ Ⓒ Ⓓ Ⓔ	23. Ⓐ Ⓑ Ⓒ Ⓓ Ⓔ	37. Ⓐ Ⓑ Ⓒ Ⓓ Ⓔ	51. Ⓐ Ⓑ Ⓒ Ⓓ Ⓔ
10. Ⓐ Ⓑ Ⓒ Ⓓ Ⓔ	24. Ⓐ Ⓑ Ⓒ Ⓓ Ⓔ	38. Ⓐ Ⓑ Ⓒ Ⓓ Ⓔ	52. Ⓐ Ⓑ Ⓒ Ⓓ Ⓔ
11. Ⓐ Ⓑ Ⓒ Ⓓ Ⓔ	25. Ⓐ Ⓑ Ⓒ Ⓓ Ⓔ	39. Ⓐ Ⓑ Ⓒ Ⓓ Ⓔ	53. Ⓐ Ⓑ Ⓒ Ⓓ Ⓔ
12. Ⓐ Ⓑ Ⓒ Ⓓ Ⓔ	26. Ⓐ Ⓑ Ⓒ Ⓓ Ⓔ	40. Ⓐ Ⓑ Ⓒ Ⓓ Ⓔ	54. Ⓐ Ⓑ Ⓒ Ⓓ Ⓔ
13. Ⓐ Ⓑ Ⓒ Ⓓ Ⓔ	27. Ⓐ Ⓑ Ⓒ Ⓓ Ⓔ	41. Ⓐ Ⓑ Ⓒ Ⓓ Ⓔ	55. Ⓐ Ⓑ Ⓒ Ⓓ Ⓔ
14. Ⓐ Ⓑ Ⓒ Ⓓ Ⓔ	28. Ⓐ Ⓑ Ⓒ Ⓓ Ⓔ	42. Ⓐ Ⓑ Ⓒ Ⓓ Ⓔ	

Section II: Free Response

Question 1

Question 2

Question 3

PRACTICE TEST 2

Section I: Multiple Choice

Time: 1 Hour • 55 Questions

Directions: This section consists of selections from prose passages and questions on their content, form, and style. After reading each passage, choose the best answer to each question and then fill in the corresponding circle on your answer sheet.

Questions 1-13. Read the following passage carefully before you decide on the answers to the questions.

This excerpt is from an essay by Edgar Allan Poe called "Instinct vs. Reason—A Black Cat," *which was first published in an issue of* Alexander's Weekly Messenger *on January 29, 1840. The essay is an investigation into the differences between human logic and animal instinct: a common theme for the author. While Poe has written on the subject in a variety of essays, such as "Eureka" and even in fiction, in his short story "The Black Cat," this essay never attained the same level of popularity as did most of his works.*

The line which demarcates the instinct of the brute creation from the boasted reason of man, is, beyond doubt, of the most shadowy and unsatisfactory character—a boundary line far more difficult to settle than even the North-Eastern or the Oregon. The question whether the lower animals do or do not reason, will possibly never be decided—certainly never in our present condition of knowledge. While the self-love and arrogance of man will persist in denying the reflective power to beasts, because the granting it seems to derogate from his own vaunted supremacy, he yet perpetually finds himself involved in the paradox of decrying instinct as an inferior faculty, while he is forced to admit its infinite superiority, in a thousand cases, over the very reason which he claims exclusively as his own. Instinct, so far from being an inferior reason, is perhaps the most exacted intellect of all. It will appear to the true philosopher as the divine mind itself acting *immediately* upon its creatures.

The habits of the lion-ant, of many kinds of spiders, and of the beaver, have in them a wonderful analogy, or rather similarity, to the usual operations of the reason of man—but the instinct of some other creatures has no such analogy—and is referable only to the spirit of the Deity itself, acting *directly*, and through no corporal organ, upon the volition of the animal. Of this lofty species of instinct the coral-worm affords a remarkable instance. This little creature, the architect of continents, is not only capable of building ramparts against the sea, with a precision of purpose, and scientific adaptation and arrangement, from which the most skillful engineer might imbibe his best knowledge—but is gifted of prophecy. It will foresee, for months in advance, the pure accidents which are to happen to its dwelling, and aided by myriads of its brethren, all acting as if with one mind (and *indeed* acting with only one—with the mind of the Creator) will work diligently to counteract influences which exist alone in the future. There is also an immensely wonderful consideration connected with the cell of the bee. Let a mathematician be required to solve the problem of the shape best calculated in such a cell as the bee wants, for the two requisites of strength and space—and he will find himself involved in the very highest and most abstruse questions of analytical research. Let him be required to tell the number of sides which will give to the cell the greatest space, with the greatest solidity, and to define the exact angle at which, with the same object in view, the roof must incline—and to answer the query, he must be a Newton or a Laplace. Yet since bees were, they have been continually solving the problem. The leading distinction between instinct and reason seems to be, that, while the one is infinitely the more exact, the more certain, and the more far-seeing in its sphere of action—the sphere of action in the other is of the far wider extent. But we are preaching a homily, when we merely intended to tell a short story about a cat.

1. Which of the following is the closest definition of the word "reason" (line 2) as it is used in the passage?

A. Justification

B. Ability to comprehend one's existence

C. Ability to empathize with others

D. Sanity

E. Spatial awareness

2. Which of the following best expresses the main idea of the passage?

A. Humans, being rational beings, are superior to animals.

B. Animals, equipped with sharper teeth and claws, are superior to humans.

C. Science still has a long way to go in the study of human and animal development.

D. Reason is more exact than instinct, but instinct can understand things that science cannot.

E. Bees actually have a highly sophisticated understanding of mathematics, as evidenced by their hives.

3. In line 20, the author uses the phrase "architect of continents" to refer to the

A. coral-worm, because of its ability to fortify its home against the sea and predict future environmental dangers.

B. coral-worm, because of its ability to calculate the strongest shape in which to build the cells of its protective structure.

C. Deity, for imbuing creatures with remarkable instinct.

D. Deity, for predicting future environmental dangers that threaten species.

E. bee, which is able to conduct analytical research.

4. Based on this passage, the author would be most likely to agree with which of the following statements?
   - A. People should put more effort toward using animals for labor, as they are naturally much stronger than humans.
   - B. People should abandon the study of science and mathematics in favor of developing instincts in the style of animal instinct.
   - C. Instinct is a valuable tool, but future events can only be predicted by science.
   - D. Animals lose their powers of instinct when they become domesticated by people.
   - E. Because of their need to feel like the superior species, people often do not give enough to credit the importance of animal instinct.

5. To what does the author of this passage attribute animal instinct?
   - A. Science and reason
   - B. Evolution
   - C. A divine plan
   - D. The volition of the animal
   - E. Language

6. The phrase "of the most shadowy and unsatisfactory character" (lines 2–3) refers to which of the following?
   - A. The self-centered and boastful nature of man
   - B. The distinction between instinct and reason
   - C. The distinction between natural instinct and divine intervention
   - D. The natural mysteries that science has yet to explain
   - E. The question of how much animals really know

7. The author's view of animals could be described as all of the following EXCEPT:
   - A. Willing to entertain the possibility that animal instinct may be more powerful than human reason
   - B. Filled with wonder at the power of animal instinct
   - C. Resentful that animals have a closer relationship with the Creator than humans do
   - D. Characterized by the belief that in some respects, animals are wiser than humans
   - E. Characterized by the belief that human reason excels in its exactitude

8. What is the relationship between the first and second paragraphs of this passage?
   - A. The first paragraph establishes a claim and the second paragraph provides examples to support it.
   - B. The first paragraph establishes one viewpoint on an issue and the second paragraph provides a counter-viewpoint.
   - C. The first paragraph establishes a claim and the second paragraph goes back through history to explain why this claim came to be the case.
   - D. The first paragraph is emotional and the second paragraph is more conciliatory.
   - E. The first paragraph asks a question that the second paragraph seeks to answer.

9. In line 31, the word "abstruse" most closely means

A. laudable.

B. obscure.

C. grandiose.

D. unnecessary.

E. preposterous.

10. From the passage, we can infer all of the following EXCEPT:

A. Instinct helps bees build hives in much the same way that mathematics helps humans build homes.

B. Humans' belief in their own superiority as a species may prevent them from learning all that animals have to teach them.

C. Black cats are instinctively capable of predicting weather patterns that science cannot; therefore it is advised to keep one as a pet.

D. Despite the fact that they lack reason, God has a close relationship with animals.

E. The true philosopher values animal instinct more than the common man does.

11. How is the passage organized?

A. Chronologically

B. Thematically

C. Disjointedly

D. By free association

E. In list form

12. The tone of the passage can best be described as

A. autobiographical.

B. philosophical.

C. journalistic.

D. historical.

E. scientific.

13. This passage makes use of all of the following EXCEPT:

A. Citing examples

B. Metaphor

C. Simile

D. Abstract generalization

E. Irony

Questions 14–25. Read the following passage carefully before you decide on the answers to the questions.

Emily Post was an American author who famously wrote her book about proper etiquette in 1922. She lived from 1872–1960. This is an excerpt from her "Etiquette in Society, in Business, in Politics and at Home."

New York, more than any city in the world, unless it be Paris, loves to be amused, thrilled and surprised all at the same time; and will accept with outstretched hand any one who can perform this astounding feat. Do not underestimate the ability that can achieve it: a scintillating wit, an arresting originality, a talent for entertaining that amounts to genius, and gold poured literally like rain, are the least requirements.

Puritan America on the other hand demanding, as a ticket of admission to her Best Society, the qualifications of birth, manners and cultivation, clasps her hands tight across her slim trim waist and announces severely that New York's "Best" is, in her opinion, very "bad" indeed. But this is because Puritan America, as well as the general public, mistakes the jester for the queen.

As a matter of fact, Best Society is not at all like a court with an especial queen or king, nor is it confined to any one place or group, but might better be described as an unlimited brotherhood which spreads over the entire surface of the globe, the members of which are invariably people of cultivation and worldly knowledge, who have not only perfect manners but a perfect manner. Manners are made up of trivialities of deportment which can be easily learned if one does not happen to know them; manner is personality—the outward manifestation of one's innate character and attitude toward life. A gentleman, for instance, will never be ostentatious or overbearing any more than he will ever be servile, because these attributes never animate the impulses of a well-bred person. A man whose manners suggest the grotesque is invariably a person of imitation rather than of real position.

Etiquette must, if it is to be of more than trifling use, include ethics as well as manners. Certainly what one is, is of far greater importance than what one appears to be. A knowledge of etiquette is of course essential to one's decent behavior, just as clothing is essential to one's decent appearance; and precisely as one wears the latter without being self-conscious of having on shoes and perhaps gloves, one who has good manners is equally unself-conscious in the observance of etiquette, the precepts of which must be so thoroughly absorbed as to make their observance a matter of instinct rather than of conscious obedience.

Thus Best Society is not a fellowship of the wealthy, nor does it seek to exclude those who are not of exalted birth; but it *is* an association of gentle-folk, of which good form in speech, charm of manner, knowledge of the social amenities, and instinctive consideration for the feelings of others, are the credentials by which society the world over recognizes its chosen members.

14. In line 8, "Best Society" most closely means

A. a collection of people who embody Puritan values.

B. those born into elevated wealth and status.

C. those with the most interesting stories of adventures and travel.

D. those who embody good manners, etiquette, and consideration for others.

E. those who have worked hard to achieve celebrity status.

15. Who is most likely the intended audience for this passage?

A. Future historians who wish to learn more about Best Society in New York

B. New Yorkers contemporary to the author who wish to improve their manners and etiquette

C. Europeans wishing to learn more about the United States

D. Women seeking tips on how to be fashionably dressed

E. Poor people who want to give the appearance of being wealthy

16. In lines 5–6, the phrase "gold poured literally like rain" can be described as which of the following?

A. Hyperbole

B. Sarcasm

C. Irony

D. Juxtaposition

E. Abstract generalization

17. The author views Best Society as all of the following EXCEPT:

A. An association of gentle-folk

B. A brotherhood of cultivation and knowledge

C. A group of people born with impeccable manners

D. A collection of men and women who value etiquette

E. People who strive to embody, as opposed to imitate, the ideals of good etiquette

18. In lines 18–19, "the outward manifestation of one's innate character" refers to which quality?

A. Manner

B. Puritan values

C. Originality

D. Knowledge of foreign cultures

E. Ethics

19. Which of the following best describes the author's tone in this passage?

A. Hysterical

B. Exploratory

C. Measured

D. Technical

E. Adulatory

20. Which of the following most closely describes the relationship between the second and third paragraphs?
    A. The second paragraph explains the Puritan viewpoint on Best Society, and the third paragraph provides examples to support that viewpoint.
    B. The second paragraph describes Puritan life in America, and the third paragraph condemns the Puritan lifestyle.
    C. The second paragraph caricatures Puritans as overly prim, and the third paragraph likens the members of Best Society to court jesters.
    D. The second paragraph asserts that Puritans value good breeding and propriety, and the third paragraph counters that New York's Best Society values manners, culture, and knowledge above status and wealth.
    E. The second paragraph establishes the Puritan viewpoint on Best Society, and the third paragraph describes the history of Best Society within the Puritan community.

21. Which of the following statements is best supported by this passage?
    A. New York's Best Society values people who have good manners, charming demeanors, and interesting anecdotes to tell.
    B. New York's Best Society is open to those of all social classes, but is not open to women.
    C. Members of New York's Best Society should take a special interest in supporting the arts.
    D. Puritans disapprove of New York's Best Society largely because of their differences in religious belief.
    E. Good etiquette refers chiefly to manners, not ethics.

22. In line 22, the word "grotesque" most likely refers to all of the following EXCEPT:
    A. Loud, obnoxious behavior
    B. Braggadocio
    C. An overly servile attitude
    D. Interest in the history of war
    E. Chewing with one's mouth open

23. In lines 10–11, what does the author most likely mean when she asserts that "… Puritan America, as well as the general public, mistakes the jester for the queen"?
    A. Best Society is often misunderstood by those who value a cheap imitation of good manners over the real thing.
    B. Puritans, as well as many other Americans, will never amount to Best Society because they overlook the importance of providing entertainment as well as having good manners.
    C. Puritans, as well as many other Americans, will never amount to Best Society until they embrace democratic ideals and stop romanticizing a monarchical government.
    D. Puritans, as well as many other Americans, misunderstand Best Society because they believe that manners can be taught, when in fact true manners are something certain people innately possess.
    E. Best Society is largely viewed by the general public as a joke because it lacks a spokesman or manifesto.

24. Which of the following does the author NOT employ in this passage?
    A. Hyperbole
    B. Simile
    C. Personification
    D. Rhetorical questions
    E. Compound sentences

25. From this passage, which of the following can be inferred about the author?
    A. She is a Puritan, and wishes to speak out against the vulgarities of society in New York.
    B. She is of modest birth but attained Best Society status anyway, and now wishes to teach others how to do the same.
    C. She is an expert on etiquette, and is writing the text as a way to teach others proper etiquette.
    D. She is an expert on etiquette, and is protesting the exclusion of women from the brotherhood of Best Society.
    E. She is of modest birth, and wishes to speak out against the classism of Best Society.

Questions 26–34. Read the following passage carefully before you decide on the answers to the questions.

This passage is an excerpt from the introduction to Frederick Douglass' autobiographical narrative of his childhood as a slave and his journey to freedom. This passage describes the town of Douglass' birth. My Bondage and My Freedom *was published in 1855.*

In Talbot county, Eastern Shore, Maryland, near Easton, the county town of that county, there is a small district of country, thinly populated, and remarkable for nothing that I know of more than for the worn-out, sandy, desert-like appearance of its soil, the general dilapidation of its farms and fences, the indigent and spiritless character of its inhabitants, and the prevalence of ague and fever.

The name of this singularly unpromising and truly famine stricken district is Tuckahoe, a name well known to all Marylanders, black and white. It was given to this section of country probably, at the first, merely in derision; or it may possibly have been applied to it, as I have heard, because some one of its earlier inhabitants had been guilty of the petty meanness of stealing a hoe—or taking a hoe that did not belong to him. Eastern Shore men usually pronounce the word *took*, as *tuck; Took-a-hoe*, therefore, is, in Maryland parlance, *Tuckahoe.* But, whatever may have been its origin—and about this I will not be positive—that name has stuck to the district in question; and it is seldom mentioned but with contempt and derision, on account of the barrenness of its soil, and the ignorance, indolence, and poverty of its people. Decay and ruin are everywhere visible, and the thin population of the place would have quitted it long ago, but for the Choptank river, which runs through it, from which they take abundance of shad and herring, and plenty of ague and fever.

It was in this dull, flat, and unthrifty district, or neighborhood, surrounded by a white population of the lowest order, indolent and drunken to a proverb, and among slaves, who seemed to ask, *"Oh! what's the use?"* every time they lifted a hoe, that I—without any fault of mine was born, and spent the first years of my childhood.

The reader will pardon so much about the place of my birth, on the score that it is always a fact of some importance to know where a man is born, if, indeed, it be important to know anything about him. In regard to the *time* of my birth, I cannot be as definite as I have been respecting the *place*. Nor, indeed, can I impart much knowledge concerning my parents. Genealogical trees do not flourish among slaves. A person of some consequence here in the north, sometimes designated *father*, is literally abolished in slave law and slave practice. It is only once in a while that an exception is found to this statement. I never met with a slave who could tell me how old he was. Few slave-mothers know anything of the months of the year, nor of the days of the month. They keep no family records, with marriages, births, and deaths. They measure the ages of their children by spring time, winter time, harvest time, planting time, and the like; but these soon become undistinguishable and forgotten. Like other slaves, I cannot tell how old I am. This destitution was among my earliest troubles. I learned when I grew up, that my master—and this is the case with masters generally—allowed no questions to be put to him, by which a slave might learn his age. Such questions deemed evidence of impatience, and even of impudent curiosity. From certain events, however, the dates of which I have since learned, I suppose myself to have been born about the year 1817.

26. Which of the following most accurately describes the relationship between tone and subject in this passage?

A. The tone is bored, to characterize the monotonous Maryland landscape.

B. The tone builds excitement, to characterize an impending important moment in the author's life.

C. The tone is disillusioned, to reflect the hopelessness of growing up in an impoverished slave community.

D. The tone is nostalgic, to symbolize fond memories of the author's childhood and family.

E. The tone is angry, to indicate the resentment the author still feels for his parents.

27. What is the general tone of the passage?

A. Scientific

B. Autobiographical

C. Journalistic

D. Philosophical

E. Analytical

28. Which of the following is used most extensively in the passage?
   A. Animal imagery
   B. Religious language
   C. Environmental imagery
   D. Rhetorical questions
   E. Hyperbole

29. In lines 31–32, the author uses the phrase "A person of some consequence here in the north, sometimes designated *father*" for what purpose?
   A. To describe a father-like figure peculiar to the north to readers outside the north who have no knowledge of such a figure
   B. To impress the importance of religious education as well as familial education
   C. To use irony to convey how rare it is for slaves to grow up knowing their fathers
   D. To speak about a friend the author has in the North so important to him that he is practically family
   E. To speculate as to where his father, from whom he was separated as a young slave, might be today

30. In line 24, the phrase "without any fault of mine" refers to
   A. being born into slavery.
   B. the naming of the town "Tuckahoe" after the practice of stealing hoes, as the author was not yet born and could not be at fault.
   C. the lack of information regarding the author's family tree.
   D. the author's childhood, during which he did nothing wrong and was undeserving of the harsh conditions under which he lived.
   E. the fact that the slave community was surrounded by an impoverished white population.

31. Which of the following rhetorical devices does NOT appear in the passage?
   A. Symbolism
   B. Personification
   C. Colloquialism
   D. Mixed metaphors
   E. Compound sentences

32. From the context of the passage, we can infer that the author
   A. returned to Maryland as an adult to help impoverished black communities fight famine.
   B. suffered from ague and fever as a child.
   C. was profoundly affected by growing up in Tuckahoe despite his poor quality of life.
   D. learned his exact age and birthday only years after moving to the north.
   E. harbored great resentment toward his master because he did not permit the author to ask questions.

33. What is the primary purpose of this passage?

A. To educate those who do not know about the horrors of slavery

B. To provide background for readers of the author's biography on the details of his early life

C. To chastise the citizens of Tuckahoe for not leaving despite the prevalence of disease

D. To begin a historical narrative of Maryland's impoverished small towns

E. To educate the reader on the relationships between slaves and impoverished white communities

34. In line 23, what is the purpose of the phrase "Oh, what's the use?"

A. To present the exhaustion of slaves as a symbol for the decrepitude of the town

B. To showcase the author's ambivalence about the plight of the town

C. To imply that nihilism is the only reasonable viewpoint for those who grow up in poverty

D. To personify the soil, which has been worked too hard

E. To illustrate the lethargy that waterborne illnesses cause

Questions 35–43. Read the following passage carefully before you decide on the answers to the questions.

This is an excerpt from An Inquiry Into the Nature and Causes of the Wealth of Nations, *by Adam Smith. Smith was a Scottish philosopher and economist who lived from 1723–1790. His book, commonly referred to as* The Wealth of Nations, *was published in 1776 and deals with the philosophical aspect of the economy.*

The real price of every thing, what every thing really costs to the man who wants to acquire it, is the toil and trouble of acquiring it. What every thing is really worth to the man who has acquired it and who wants to dispose of it, or exchange it for something else, is the toil and trouble which it can save to himself, and which it can impose upon other people. What is bought with money, or with goods, is purchased by labour, as much as what we acquire by the toil of our own body. That money, or those goods, indeed, save us this toil. They contain the value of a certain quantity of labour, which we exchange for what is supposed at the time to contain the value of an equal quantity. Labour was the first price, the original purchase money that was paid for all things. It was not by gold or by silver, but by labour, that all the wealth of the world was originally purchased; and its value, to those who possess it, and who want to exchange it for some new productions, is precisely equal to the quantity of labour which it can enable them to purchase or command.

Wealth, as Mr Hobbes says, is power. But the person who either acquires, or succeeds to a great fortune, does not necessarily acquire or succeed to any political power, either civil or military. His fortune may, perhaps, afford him the means of acquiring both; but the mere possession of that fortune does not necessarily convey to him either. The power which that possession immediately and directly conveys to him, is the power of purchasing a certain command over all the labour, or over all the produce of labour which is then in the market. His fortune is greater or less, precisely in proportion to the extent of this power, or to the quantity either of other men's labour, or, what is the same thing, of the produce of other men's labour, which it enables him to purchase or command. The exchangeable value of every thing must always be precisely equal to the extent of this power which it conveys to its owner.

35. In the context of this passage, what is the function of labor?

A. The amount of labor a person exerts is equal to the amount of power they wield.

B. Labor is the most basic currency used to accumulate wealth.

C. The system of currency was invented for people who did not want to perform labor.

D. Labor is related to the personal pursuit of self-betterment and has no correlation to wealth or power.

E. The more labor a person does and the less wealth they own, the higher their status is in society.

36. What is the tone of the passage?

A. Technical

B. Hysterical

C. Matter of fact

D. Autobiographical

E. Scientific

37. This passage is best described as a(n)

A. how-to guide on transforming labor into wealth.

B. warning against employing others to do labor that you can do yourself.

C. philosophical reasoning on the relationship between labor and wealth.

D. negative judgment about the correlation between wealth and labor in society.

E. illustration of the development of labor over the course of human history.

38. In line 2, "toil and trouble" most closely means

A. an allusion to a Shakespeare play, implying a relationship between wealth and the arts.

B. the amount of labor that can be saved by expending a given amount of wealth.

C. the problems that result from gaining additional wealth.

D. the physical unhealthiness that results from laboring too much when one could have expended wealth instead.

E. the problems that result from the transition of labor as official currency to wealth as official currency.

39. According to Hobbes, which of the following is NOT true of power?

A. Accumulation of wealth leads to an increase in power in politics and the military.

B. Accumulation of wealth leads to control over labor in the market.

C. The amount of power a person holds is directly proportional to his wealth.

D. A person can exchange an amount of wealth for an equal amount of power.

E. A amount of power a person holds is equal to the amount of labor he can pay others to do for him.

40. The author develops the passage by moving from

A. specific evidence to broad generalization.

B. illustration of the correlation between labor and wealth to illustration of the correlation between wealth and power.

C. definition of the meaning of labor to definition of the meaning of power.

D. personal experience with wealth to a broad perspective on wealth.

E. pastoral imagery to concrete facts.

41. Which of the following statements is the author of this passage most likely to agree with?

A. When considering hiring employees, one should carefully consider the worth of labor versus the worth of the wealth one would have to spend.

B. One should always expend wealth in order to gain power.

C. Economic success is not as important as holding sway within local government.

D. Wealth is only an indicator of power when it is being gained or expended.

E. Those employed by the government have the greatest amount of wealth.

42. Who is most likely the intended audience for this passage?

A. Experienced economists seeking philosophical input to get a fresh perspective

B. Experienced philosophers seeking economic input to get a fresh perspective

C. Politicians who wish to learn more about the role of wealth in positions of political power

D. The general public interested in the relationship between labor and wealth, with no philosophical or economic training

E. Future historians who wish to learn about the function of labor during the author's time

43. The relationship of the first paragraph to the second paragraph is most closely defined as follows:

A. The first paragraph develops an argument; the second paragraph supports that argument with statistics.

B. The first paragraph establishes a philosophical viewpoint; the second paragraph establishes an unrelated viewpoint.

C. The first paragraph develops a theory; the second paragraph contradicts that theory.

D. The first paragraph establishes a theory; the second paragraph develops a related theory created by another philosopher.

E. The first paragraph develops a theory; the second paragraph blames that theory on Hobbes' argument.

Questions 44–55. Read the following passage carefully before you decide on the answers to the questions.

Mary Kingsley was an explorer and scientific writer who traveled and wrote about West Africa extensively during the late 19th century. This excerpt, from Travels in West Africa (Congo Français, Corisco, and Cameroons), *published in 1896, details her first voyage.*

It was the beginning of August '93 when I first left England for "the Coast." Preparations of quinine with postage partially paid arrived up to the last moment, and a friend hastily sent two newspaper clippings, one entitled "A Week in a Palm-oil Tub," which was supposed to describe the sort of accommodation, companions, and fauna likely to be met with on a steamer going to West Africa, and on which I was to spend seven to *The Graphic* contributor's one; the other from *The Daily Telegraph*, reviewing a French book of "Phrases in common use" in Dahomey. The opening sentence in the latter was, "Help, I am drowning." Then came the inquiry, "If a man is not a thief?" and then another cry, "The boat is upset." "Get up, you lazy scamps," is the next exclamation, followed almost immediately by the question, "Why has not this man been buried?" "It is fetish that has killed him, and he must lie here exposed with nothing on him until only the bones remain," is the cheerful answer. This sounded discouraging to a person whose occupation would necessitate going about considerably in boats, and whose fixed desire was to study fetish. So with a feeling of foreboding gloom I left London for Liverpool—none the more cheerful for the matter-of-fact manner in which the steamboat agents had informed me that they did not issue return tickets by the West African lines of steamers. I will not go into the details of that voyage here, much as I am given to discursiveness. They are more amusing than instructive, for on my first voyage out I did not know the Coast, and the Coast did not know me and we mutually terrified each other.

I fully expected to get killed by the local nobility and gentry; they thought I was connected with the World's Women's Temperance Association, and collecting shocking details for subsequent magic-lantern lectures on the liquor traffic; so fearful misunderstandings arose, but we gradually educated each other, and I had the best of the affair; for all I had got to teach them was that I was only a beetle and fetish hunter, and so forth, while they had to teach me a new world, and a very fascinating course of study I found it. And whatever the Coast may have to say against me—for my continual desire for hair-pins, and other pins, my intolerable habit of getting into water, the abominations full of ants, that I brought into their houses, or things emitting at unexpectedly short notice vivid and awful stenches—they cannot but say that I was a diligent pupil, who honestly tried to learn the lessons they taught me so kindly, though some of those lessons were hard to a person who had never previously been even in a tame bit of tropics, and whose life for many years had been an entirely domestic one in a University town.

One by one I took my old ideas derived from books and thoughts based on imperfect knowledge and weighed them against the real life around me, and found them either worthless or wanting. The greatest recantation I had to make I made humbly before I had been three months on the Coast in 1893. It was of my idea of the traders. What I had expected to find them was a very different thing to what I did find them; and of their kindness to me I can never sufficiently speak, for on that voyage I was utterly out of touch with the governmental circles, and utterly dependent on the traders, and the most useful lesson of all the lessons I learnt on the West Coast in 1893 was that I could trust them. Had I not learnt this very thoroughly I could never have gone out again and carried out the voyage I give you a sketch of in this book.

44. Which of the following best describes the tone of the passage?

A. Comedic

B. Diaristic

C. Scientific

D. Measured

E. Fearful

45. In line 13, the use of the word "cheerful" is an example of

A. irony.

B. syllogism.

C. metaphor.

D. alliteration.

E. allusion.

46. In line 20, the word "discursiveness" in context most closely means

A. hysteria.

B. exaggeration.

C. digression.

D. complaint.

E. confusion.

47. In line 26, the phrase "fearful misunderstandings arose" refers to which of the following?

A. The author telling the residents of the Coast that she collects beetles, and their misunderstanding that she collects poisonous snakes

B. The author believing she has learned to say, "Is this fresh water?" in the native language of the Coast, when in fact she has learned to say, "Help, I'm drowning"

C. The lessons the natives of the Coast unsuccessfully attempted to teach the author

D. The author's belief that the natives of the Coast were untrustworthy

E. The author's belief that the natives of the Coast might kill her, and their belief that she might be a Prohibition activist, i.e., a temperance lecturer collecting information to use in an anti-liquor campaign

48. At the beginning of the passage, the author's attitude toward her voyage can best be described as
  A. horror and dread.
  B. trepidation.
  C. extreme excitement.
  D. apathy.
  E. irritation at the logistical difficulties of the journey.

49. Which of the following is NOT a major point of this passage?
  A. Even in the tame parts of the Coast, there are many new customs to learn for a Western woman.
  B. The author found the natives of the Coast to be ultimately trustworthy.
  C. The author found that all the preconceived ideas she'd had from books before embarking upon her trip to the Coast were either incorrect or incomplete.
  D. The author found that other writers' experiences, despite the fact that they had spent less time at sea than she planned to, helped prepare her for her journey.
  E. The author had preconceived ideas about the natives of the Coast, and they had preconceived ideas about her, too.

50. What is the primary purpose of the anecdote described in lines 10–12 of the passage, "'Get up, you lazy scamps' … 'Why has not this man been buried?'"
  A. Establishing humor and voice
  B. Warning others not to venture to the Coast
  C. Providing anecdotes to support the author's claim that the extant literature did not fully prepare her for her trip
  D. Depicting a common scene the author encountered on the Coast
  E. Giving an example of the local dialect of the coast

51. The passage can be best described as a(n)
  A. letter to a friend from the Coast.
  B. introduction to a longer work about the Coast and the people who live there.
  C. speech given to encourage more young people to travel.
  D. section from the author's memoir, which focuses on the author's life as a whole, and not merely her voyage to the Coast.
  E. historical narrative about the Westerners who went to the Coast before the author did.

52. This passage uses all the following stylistic features EXCEPT:
  A. Parenthetical asides
  B. Humor
  C. Repetition for emphasis
  D. Compound sentences
  E. Personal voice

53. In line 28, what does the word "fetish" mean in context?
   A. Interest in beetle collection
   B. Religious factors
   C. Documentation of terrain unfamiliar to the locals
   D. Obsession with the natives of the Coast
   E. Intolerable Western habits

54. Which of the following most closely describes the shift in the author's perspective over the course of her journey?
   A. She began her journey afraid of the Coast, but ended it with a commitment to return.
   B. She began her journey as an advocate for the temperance movement, but ended it with a newfound respect for personal liberty.
   C. She began her journey as a tourist, and returned to become a professional writer.
   D. She began her journey with excitement, but ended with disdain for the natives of the Coast.
   E. She began her journey thinking the Coast would be comparatively tame, and was shocked and horrified by the customs she encountered.

55. In lines 29–30, the phrase "whatever the Coast may have to say against me" employs which of the following rhetorical devices?
   A. Metaphor
   B. Personification
   C. Irony
   D. Simile
   E. Sarcasm

STOP!
IF YOU FINISH BEFORE THE TIME IS UP,
YOU MAY CHECK YOUR WORK IN THIS SECTION ONLY.

Section II: Free Response

Total Time: 2 Hours, 15 minutes

Directions: The following prompt is based on the accompanying six sources. This question requires you to synthesize a variety of sources into a coherent, well-written essay. When you synthesize sources, you refer to them to develop your position and cite them accurately. Your argument should be central; the sources should support the argument. Avoid merely summarizing sources. Remember to attribute both direct and indirect references.

Question 1
Suggested Time—40 Minutes

Around the world, different countries have adopted various approaches to structured school calendars. Some still adhere to the semester method, with a long summer holiday, while others have arranged their terms to involve more short-term breaks and extended class sessions. Education experts still debate the effectiveness of each option. Now's your chance to weigh in.

Carefully read the following six sources, including the introductory information for each source. Then synthesize and incorporate at least three of the sources into a coherent and well-written essay in which you develop a position on the structure of school calendars. Your argument should be the focus of the essay.

Use the sources to inform and strengthen your argument. Avoid merely summarizing the sources. Indicate clearly which sources you are drawing from, whether through direct quotation, paraphrase, or summary. You may cite the sources as Source A, Source B, etc., or by using the descriptions in parentheses.

Source A (California Department of Education)

Source B (Lenilworth)

Source C (Montessori)

Source D (Thomas)

Source E (National Center for Education Statistics)

Source A

California Department of Education: Year-Round Education Guide

Introduction

Year-round education (YRE) is not a typical alternative way to deliver the curriculum. It is, however, an alternative way to construct the school calendar. It may have positive effects on student achievement, especially for disadvantaged students.

Both traditional and some year-round school calendars can have 180 days of instruction. The traditional calendar, of course, is divided into nine months of instruction and three months of vacation during the summer. Year-round calendars break these long instructional/vacation blocks into shorter units. The most typical instructional/vacation year-round pattern is called the 60/20 calendar (60 days of instruction followed by 20 days of vacation and the second most popular is the 45/15). There are numerous other possible patterns, but they are not common.

Year-round education is also known by the number of "tracks" it uses. A school using a "single track" year-round calendar is simply changing the instructional/vacation sequence of the school year; all the students and staff are in school or vacation at the same time. But a school using a "multitrack" year-round calendar does something quite different; it divides the entire student body and staff into different tracks (from four to five). If, for example, a school is using a four-track system, then at any one time three of the four tracks are attending school while the fourth is on vacation. The rotation sequence depends on the year-round calendar being used. In the 60/20 calendar, one track returns from vacation and one track leaves every 20 days.

The advantage of a multitrack system is that it expands the seating capacity of a school facility. For example, if a school with a seating capacity of 1,000 uses a four-track system, it could potentially enroll 1,333 students, increasing its capacity by 33 percent. In practice, four-track plans typically expand the seating capacity by about 25 percent.

For many, however, the advantages of multitrack year-round education are compromised by the disadvantages. For instance, lengthening the school year beyond 180 days by using on-site classrooms is thwarted by the available-day limitations of each multitrack year-round education track. And offering mandatory remediation sessions, when all classrooms are used all year, is likewise a challenge. A district considering the implementation of multitrack year-round education must consider both its facility needs and its instructional objectives and then choose a course that provides each of its students with the maximum opportunity to learn.

The ability of year-round education to relieve overcrowding has overshadowed its effectiveness as an educational strategy. Yet there are, in fact, compelling reasons year-round education should be considered in its single-track form simply for its educational benefits, especially for at-risk students.

Source B

The Case Against Year Round Schooling
Principal Mac Lenilworth

While the California Department of Education seems to think the administrative hassles of multi-track "Year Round Education" are worth it, I want to make sure parents and students of Curie High School, where I'm the principal, know that we are committed to a traditional schedule for the foreseeable future. And I wanted to make sure they know why.

Year-round schooling places undue burdens on kids and parents—different kids in the same family may wind up on different tracks, which makes scheduling vacations or even doctor's visits more difficult. After-school activities may face lags in attendance and participation, and certain programs may be totally inaccessible if a student is in the wrong rotation to be involved. If half the track team is going to still come to practice when they're off for a three week spring break rotation, that's not much of a break for them either!

Further, the workload for teaching and administrative staff is too likely to become overwhelming. Rather than keeping all four sections of 10th grade English in sync, for example, a teacher might be in Quarter 1 with one group, Quarter 2 with another, and her 3rd group might be out for three weeks in a row! Teachers may need to give up their offices, which is detrimental to their planning and respite opportunities. Many of our teachers also depend on a summer schedule for professional development, or just to spend time with their own families!

The challenges of maintaining a facility that's well-run and in excellent condition are made much more difficult by year round programs. We use the summer for vital maintenance and repair initiatives that may be too dangerous to implement while students are present.

This is not the right program for Curie High, and I hope the community will come out and support adherence to a traditional schedule at the next PTA and School Board double session.

Source C

Dr. Maria Montessori, *Dr. Montessori's Own Handbook*

FREEDOM

It is necessary for the teacher to guide the child without letting him feel her presence too much, so that she may be always ready to supply the desired help, but may never be the obstacle between the child and his experience. A lesson in the ordinary use of the word cools the child's enthusiasm for the knowledge of things, just as it would cool the enthusiasm of adults. To keep alive that enthusiasm is the secret of real guidance, and it will not prove a difficult task, provided that the attitude towards the child's acts be that of respect, calm and waiting, and provided that he be left free in his movements and in his experiences.

Then we shall notice that the child has a personality which he is seeking to expand; he has initiative, he chooses his own work, persists in it, changes it according to his inner needs; he does not shirk effort, he rather goes in search of it, and with great joy overcomes obstacles within his capacity. He is sociable to the extent of wanting to share with every one his successes, his discoveries, and his little triumphs. There is therefore no need of intervention. "Wait while observing." That is the motto for the educator.

Let us wait, and be always ready to share in both the joys and the difficulties which the child experiences. He himself invites our sympathy, and we should respond fully and gladly. Let us have endless patience with his slow progress, and show enthusiasm and gladness at his successes. If we could say: "We are respectful and courteous in our dealings with children, we treat them as we should like to be treated ourselves," we should certainly have mastered a great educational principle and undoubtedly be setting an example of good education.

What we all desire for ourselves, namely, not to be disturbed in our work, not to find hindrances to our efforts, to have good friends ready to help us in times of need, to see them rejoice with us, to be on terms of equality with them, to be able to confide and trust in them—this is what we need for happy companionship. In the same way children are human beings to whom respect is due, superior to us by reason of their "innocence" and of the greater possibilities of their future. What we desire they desire also.

As a rule, however, we do not respect our children. We try to force them to follow us without regard to their special needs. We are overbearing with them, and above all, rude; and then we expect them to be submissive and well-behaved, knowing all the time how strong is their instinct of imitation and how touching their faith in and admiration of us. They will imitate us in any case. Let us treat them, therefore, with all the kindness which we would wish to help to develop in them. And by kindness is not meant caresses. Should we not call anyone who embraced us at the first time of meeting rude, vulgar and ill-bred? Kindness consists in interpreting the wishes of others, in conforming one's self to them, and sacrificing, if need be, one's own desire. This is the kindness which we must show towards children.

Source D

"A Teacher's Perspective"

Lorena Thomas

Have you ever tried to pick up where you left off with a group of ten year olds, three months after the fact? It is a very particular exercise in frustration that I'm all too familiar with. My school district has recently been considering the adoption of a year-round program, single track, which would give us 60 days "on" and 20 days "off", cutting the typically 10 week summer break down to just 4 weeks in the process. Notice there are still 4 unstructured weeks there! I say that to forestall the inevitable parental complaint of "what about our vacation?" I get it—you want you and your kids in a minivan on the road, pursuing family quality time with the zeal of the Scooby gang in the Mystery Machine. You can still do that! Surely after a month you'll be ready to come home and shower without kids bouncing on hotel room beds while you rinse!

Shorter breaks mean kids remember more. Period. It also gives us more time to find out what students are missing and get them caught up—if you're only doing diagnostics at the beginning of the semester, you might miss a student falling behind, but if you're checking in every time they come back from a few weeks away, you're able to implement catch-up lessons on the fly, which is more effective for student retention as well.

It's also a great use of school space; rather than leaving school buildings empty all summer, we keep them in more constant use. This also has benefits for low-income families who can't afford to keep their kids in summer camps and sometimes rely on lunchtime meal assistance. Working parents don't have to use up their own limited vacation and leave time all at once; they can choose when to coordinate with their kids' schedules.

And this may be a selfish reason, but financially year-round schooling is easier on teachers as well. We don't have to fill up long summer periods without a paycheck by taking on work that may hasten our rates of burnout, we can enjoy shorter time away and come back refreshed and ready to be our best selves with your kids!

Source E

Data Extract: Instructional Days and Hours, Y-RE Policy by State

State	Year-Round Schooling?	Instructional Days in Calendar	Instructional Hours, Grades 9–12
Alabama	No	180	720
Alaska	No	180	720
Arkansas	Yes	178	1080
California	Yes	180	1056
Colorado	No	160	900
Connecticut	No	180	1032
Florida	Yes	180	1032
Georgia	No	180	900
Hawaii	No	180	990
Illinois	Yes	180	990
Iowa	Yes	180	990
Kentucky	No	170	1062
Louisiana	No	177	1062

GO ON TO THE NEXT PAGE.

Question 2
Suggested Time—40 Minutes

In the passage below from a 1905 letter to the Reverend Joseph J. Twichell, American author Mark Twain develops an argument that, since pessimism is appropriate for anyone over the age of 48, the addressee is naive for believing that American citizens are generally honest.

Read the passage carefully. Then, develop an essay in which you analyze the author's position and describe his relationship to the recipient of the letter.

DEAR JOE,—I have a Puddn'head maxim:

"When a man is a pessimist before 48 he knows too much; if he is an optimist after it, he knows too little."

It is with contentment, therefore, that I reflect that I am better and wiser than you. Joe, you seem to be dealing in "bulks," now; the "bulk" of the farmers and U. S. Senators are "honest." As regards purchase and sale with money? Who doubts it? Is that the only measure of honesty? Aren't there a dozen kinds of honesty which can't be measured by the money-standard? Treason is treason—and there's more than one form of it; the money-form is but one of them. When a person is disloyal to any confessed duty, he is plainly and simply dishonest, and knows it; knows it, and is privately troubled about it and not proud of himself. Judged by this standard—and who will challenge the validity of it?—there isn't an honest man in Connecticut, nor in the Senate, nor anywhere else. I do not even except myself, this time.

Am I finding fault with you and the rest of the populace? No—I assure you I am not. For I know the human race's limitations, and this makes it my duty—my pleasant duty—to be fair to it. Each person in it is honest in one or several ways, but no member of it is honest in all the ways required by—by what? By his own standard. Outside of that, as I look at it, there is no obligation upon him.

Am I honest? I give you my word of honor (private) I am not. For seven years I have suppressed a book which my conscience tells me I ought to publish. I hold it a duty to publish it. There are other difficult duties which I am equal to, but I am not equal to that one. Yes, even I am dishonest. Not in many ways, but in some. Forty-one, I think it is. We are certainly all honest in one or several ways—every man in the world—though I have reason to think I am the only one whose black-list runs so light. Sometimes I feel lonely enough in this lofty solitude.

Yes, oh, yes, I am not overlooking the "steady progress from age to age of the coming of the kingdom of God and righteousness." "From age to age"—yes, it describes that giddy gait. I (and the rocks) will not live to see it arrive, but that is all right—it will arrive, it surely will. But you ought not to be always ironically apologizing for the Deity. If that thing is going to arrive, it is inferable that He wants it to arrive; and so it is not quite kind of you, and it hurts me, to see you flinging sarcasms at the gait of it. And yet it would not be fair in me not to admit that the sarcasms are deserved. When the Deity wants a thing, and after working at it for "ages and ages" can't show even a shade of progress toward its accomplishment, we—well, we don't laugh, but it is only because we dasn't. The source of "righteousness"—is in the heart? Yes. And engineered and directed by the brain? Yes. Well, history and tradition testify that the heart is just about what it was in the beginning; it has undergone no shade of change. Its good and evil impulses and their consequences are the same today that they were in Old Bible times, in Egyptian times, in Greek times, in Middle Age times, in Twentieth Century times. There has been no change.

Meantime, the brain has undergone no change. It is what it always was. There are a few good brains and a multitude of poor ones. It was so in Old Bible times and in all other times—Greek, Roman, Middle Ages and Twentieth Century. Among the savages—all the savages—the average brain is as competent as the average brain here or elsewhere. I will prove it to you, some time, if you like. And there are great brains among them, too. I will prove that also, if you like.

Well, the 19th century made progress—the first progress after "ages and ages"—colossal progress. In what? Materialities. Prodigious acquisitions were made in things which add to the comfort of many and make life harder for as many more. But the addition to righteousness? Is that discoverable? I think not. The materialities were not invented in the interest of righteousness; that there is more righteousness in the world because of them than there, was before, is hardly demonstrable, I think. In Europe and America, there is a vast change (due to them) in ideals—do you admire it? All Europe and all America, are feverishly scrambling for money. Money is the supreme ideal—all others take tenth place with the great bulk of the nations named. Money-lust has always existed, but not in the history of the world was it ever a craze, a madness, until your time and mine. This lust has rotted these nations; it has made them hard, sordid, ungentle, dishonest, oppressive.

Did England rise against the infamy of the Boer war? No—rose in favor of it. Did America rise against the infamy of the Phillipine war? No—rose in favor of it. Did Russia rise against the infamy of the present war? No—sat still and said nothing. Has the Kingdom of God advanced in Russia since the beginning of time?

Or in Europe and America, considering the vast backward step of the money-lust? Or anywhere else? If there has been any progress toward righteousness since the early days of Creation—which, in my ineradicable honesty, I am obliged to doubt—I think we must confine it to ten per cent of the populations of Christendom, (but leaving, Russia, Spain and South America entirely out.) This gives us 320,000,000 to draw the ten per cent from. That is to say, 32,000,000 have advanced toward righteousness and the Kingdom of God since the "ages and ages" have been flying along, the Deity sitting up there admiring. Well, you see it leaves 1,200,000,000 out of the race. They stand just where they have always stood; there has been no change.

N. B. No charge for these informations. Do come down soon, Joe.

GO ON TO THE NEXT PAGE.

Question 3
Suggested Time—40 Minutes

The passage below is an excerpt from the 1932 essay "In Praise of Idleness," by Bertrand Russell. Read the passage carefully. Then write an essay in which you develop a position on Russell's argument that "there is far too much work done in the world, immense harm is caused by the belief that work is virtuous …" Drawing from your own reading, experience, and observations, develop a clear argument defending, debating, or qualifying Russell's opinion. Use appropriate, specific evidence to illustrate and develop your position.

> "Like most of my generation, I was brought up on the saying "Satan finds some mischief still for idle hands to do." Being a highly virtuous child, I believed all that I was told and acquired a conscience which has kept me working hard down to the present moment. But although my conscience has controlled my *actions,* my *opinions* have undergone a revolution. I think that there is far too much work done in the world, that immense harm is caused by the belief that work is virtuous…" Bertrand Russell, "In Praise of Idleness"

In his 1932 essay "In Praise of Idleness," Bertrand Russell questions the idea that work and productivity are inherently virtuous, and argues that society's goal should be to allow its citizens the maximum amount of liberty to pursue the things that bring them happiness. Drawing from your own reading, experience, and observations, develop a clear argument defending, debating, or qualifying Russell's position.

STOP!
IF YOU FINISH BEFORE THE TIME IS UP,
YOU MAY CHECK YOUR WORK IN THIS SECTION ONLY.

ANSWER KEY AND EXPLANATIONS

Section I: Multiple Choice

1. B	12. B	23. A	34. A	45. A
2. D	13. E	24. D	35. B	46. C
3. A	14. D	25. C	36. C	47. E
4. E	15. B	26. C	37. C	48. B
5. C	16. A	27. B	38. B	49. D
6. B	17. C	28. C	39. A	50. A
7. C	18. A	29. C	40. B	51. B
8. A	19. C	30. A	41. A	52. C
9. B	20. D	31. D	42. D	53. B
10. C	21. A	32. C	43. D	54. A
11. B	22. D	33. B	44. B	55. B

1. **The correct answer is B.** It best captures the meaning of "reason" as defined by the passage. Choice A is incorrect because it refers to another definition of "reason" not mentioned in the passage. Choice C is incorrect because, in this passage, the author is focusing on humans' relationship with the world, not with one another. Choice D is incorrect because, while sanity may be commonly used as a synonym for "reason," the author does not state so explicitly anywhere in the passage. Instead, reason is compared to instinct. Choice D is incorrect because spatial awareness refers to one's ability to be aware of objects or beings surrounding one in space. This is a different kind of awareness than the logic, or ability to make decisions, the author describes in the passage.

2. **The correct answer is D.** It best captures the overall point of the passage instead of referring to only portions of the author's argument. Choice A is incorrect because it is the opposite of what the author is arguing: the author states that while animals may appear inferior to humans because they lack reason, instinct can be just as powerful a survival tool. Choice B is incorrect because it refers to the physical strength of animals, which the author does not address. Choice C is incorrect because, while it may be inferred from context, it is not the primary point. Choice E is incorrect because it is an example supporting the overall point—but not the overall point itself.

3. **The correct answer is A.** A close reading of lines 19–23 of the second paragraph will make it clear that the author states this directly. Choice B is incorrect because the author attributes mathematical inclinations in constructing hives to bees, not coral-worms. Choice C is incorrect because, although the author does state that the Deity imbues animals with instinct, at no point does he refer to the Deity as the "architect of continents." Similarly, Choice E is also incorrect for that reason. Additionally, it

is the coral-worm (not the Deity) that the author states has the ability to predict future dangers.

4. **The correct answer is E.** Since the author states that humans assume animals are inferior and feel that reason is superior to instinct, we can infer that he would also believe that humans overlook the importance of animal instinct. Choice A is incorrect because the author does not address physical strength. Choice B is incorrect because the author argues that reason is important as well as instinct. Choice C is incorrect because it contradicts the author's point that certain animals can, through instinct, predict future events. Choice D is incorrect because the author does not address the subject of domestication in this passage.

5. **The correct answer is C.** The author argues that, as animals do not possess human reason, their instinctual logic is divinely given. Choice A is incorrect because the author argues that animals have no concept of science or reason. Choice B is incorrect because the author does not address evolution. Similarly, Choice D is incorrect because the author does not give an opinion about whether animals have free will. Choice E is incorrect because the author does not address the issue of animals' language.

6. **The correct answer is B.** In (lines 2–3), containing the phrase "of the most shadowy and unsatisfactory character," the subject of the sentence is the line that separates instinct and reason. Choice A is incorrect because, while the author does address human arrogance later in the passage, it does not appear in this sentence. Choice C is incorrect because the author argues that divine intervention causes animal instinct, not that animal instinct and divine intervention are easily confused with each other. Choice D is incorrect because the author does not argue that science will someday teach us the difference between reason and instinct. Choice E is incorrect because, while the author does claim that animals may know more than we think they do, he does not ascribe this specific phrase to that phenomenon.

7. **The correct answer is C.** It is the only of the four choices that the author does not directly or indirectly state in the passage. Choice A is incorrect because it is the author's main thesis statement in the passage. Choice B is incorrect because the writer's tone implies that he finds animal instinct interesting. Choice D is incorrect because his argument that animal instinct may in some respects be superior to human reason implies a belief that animals may be in some ways wiser than humans. Choice E is incorrect because, citing the examples of the coral-worm and the bee, the author illustrates examples of animals using instinct the way humans use reason.

8. **The correct answer is A.** The first paragraph makes the argument that, while humans believe themselves superior to animals, animal instinct is often as wise as human reason. Then, the second paragraph gives the examples of the bee and the coral-worm to illustrate this. Choice B is incorrect because the second paragraph supports, and does not dispute, the first paragraph. Choice C is incorrect because the second paragraph has a philosophical tone, and does not address history. Choice D is incorrect because both paragraphs employ a measured tone. Choice E is incorrect because the two paragraphs provide an argument and then support it with facts, but the first paragraph does not pose a question.

9. **The correct answer is B.** *Abstruse* is a synonym for "obscure," or "difficult to understand." Choice A is incorrect because *laudable* means "deserving of praise." Choice

C is incorrect because *grandiose* means "magnificent to an excessive or pretentious degree." Choice D is incorrect because *unnecessary* means "not needed." Choice E is incorrect because *preposterous* means "completely ridiculous."

10. **The correct answer is C.** The question asks which of the statements CANNOT be assumed after reading the passage, and while the author does ascribe the ability to predict weather patterns to coral-worms, he says nothing about black cats except for a brief mention at the end of the passage. Choices A, B, D and E can all be concluded from the information given in the passage.

11. **The correct answer is B.** The author expresses a thesis, and then talks about various points of that thesis. Choice A is incorrect because the passage does not proceed chronologically, or over a period of time. Choice C is incorrect because the author's thoughts are related to each other. Choice D is incorrect because the author structures his sentences to appeal to a broad audience, instead of structuring them based on his personal abstract mental connections. Choice E is incorrect because the passage is structured in paragraphs, not lists.

12. **The correct answer is B.** The author is addressing a subject related to the fundamentals of reality and human knowledge. Choice A is incorrect because the author is not talking about himself or telling a personal story. Choice C is incorrect because, while there are scientific observations here, the passage is primarily dedicated to a better understanding of how we think about the world as opposed to the concrete, reportable facts. Choice D is incorrect because the author is discussing a timeless phenomenon, not one that happened at an earlier point in history, and the goal of the passage is to talk about how humans perceive the world, not educate readers on something that happened in history. Choice E is incorrect because, similarly to choice C, there are elements of scientific reasoning within the passage, but the overall tone can best be described as philosophical.

13. **The correct answer is E.** Irony, or an author's choice to use words to signify meaning that is usually the opposite of what those words convey, is not present in this passage. Choice B is incorrect because metaphor is a rhetorical device in which an author gives something a description that does not literally fit it as a form of symbolism. Describing the coral-worm as the "architect of continents" is a metaphor because coral-worms are not literally architects. Choice C is incorrect, since a simile is a rhetorical device comparing one thing to another unrelated thing, using words such as *as* or *like* ("crazy like a fox," for example.) The comparison of the boundary line between instinct and reason in (lines 1–2) to the boundary line between the North-Eastern and the Oregon is a simile because the geographical line and the philosophical line are not literally related, but both have hazy boundaries.

14. **The correct answer is D.** It best sums up the overall point of the passage. Good manners, proper etiquette and consideration for others are all important aspects of what characterizes "Best Society" in the author's view. Choice A is incorrect because the author states that Puritans disapprove of Best Society, so it is unlikely that Best Society adheres to their values. Choice B is incorrect because the author argues that one does not need to be born into wealth or status in order to become a member of Best Society. Choice C may be a tempting answer, because the author believes that members of Best Society will be able to entertain and interest others;

but she later goes on to say that this must be in balance with being interested in and considerate for others, so being able to tell interesting stories is a comparatively small part of being a member of Best Society. Choice E is incorrect because achieving or aspiring to celebrity status is not necessary to qualify as Best Society.

15. **The correct answer is B.** The author presents this passage as a way for the general public to understand what goes into becoming part of Best Society, and therefore it is most likely intended for a contemporary audience seeking to understand Best Society or improve their etiquette. Choice A is incorrect because, while future historians may be interested in learning about the culture of the author's time, there is nothing in her tone to suggest that they are the primary intended audience. Choice C is incorrect because, aside from the brief comparison of New York to Paris, there is nothing in the passage that mentions Europe or any ways in which New York is culturally unique. Choice D is incorrect because the passage deals primarily with proper behavior, not fashionable dress. Choice E is incorrect because, while people who want to give the appearance of having refined manners might certainly be interested in reading the passage, the author argues that wealth and status have little to do with achieving Best Society.

16. **The correct answer is A.** Despite the use of *literally*, the author does not mean that people should actually pour gold over their guests, but rather purposely exaggerates the degree to which hosts should go out of their way to amuse and delight their guests. This is hyperbole, or an intentional embellishment or exaggeration. Choice B is incorrect because the author does not use this phrase in order to mock or ridicule anything. Choice C is incorrect because, though the author does use words that she does not literally mean, the definition of irony is the use of language that typically means the opposite of what the speaker uses it to mean, and "gold poured literally like rain" does not convey the opposite of "abundant entertainment." Choice D is incorrect because *juxtaposition* means the contrasting of two different things. While there is a comparison between *gold* and *rain* here, their relationship is closer to that of a simile; the author does not seek to show how different gold is from rain. Choice E is incorrect because the author is speaking about the particulars of successfully entertaining guests, as opposed to the general idea.

17. **The correct answer is C.** The author distinguishes between *manner* and *manners*: manner is an innate part of one's character, but manners can easily be learned, so it is not necessary to be born with them. Choice A is incorrect because in (line 34) the author describes Best Society as "an association of gentle-folk." Choice B is incorrect because in the third paragraph, the author describes an interest in the pursuit of knowledge as something common to all members of Best Society. Choice D is incorrect because the importance of etiquette in Best Society is a major point of the passage. Choice E is incorrect because the author states in (lines 25–26), "Certainly what one is, is of far greater importance than what one appears to be," implying that part of belonging to Best Society is truly believing in, and not just mimicking, its ideals.

18. **The correct answer is A.** In (lines 17–19), the subject of the sentence is *manner*. Choice B is incorrect because the author establishes in the first paragraph that Puritan values are very different from those of Best Society. Choices C, D, and E are all incorrect because, while they are important aspects

of Best Society, they are not what is being discussed in the context of the sentence.

19. **The correct answer is C.** The author presents her viewpoint as fact, not colored by her own personal opinion or experiences. Choice A is incorrect because *hysterical* means "characterized by extreme emotion," and though the author feels strongly about her argument, her prose is fairly unemotional. Choice B is incorrect because *exploratory* suggests that the author is working her way toward a new idea through writing, but this passage is more *explanatory*—the author firmly believes in what she is arguing and has written the passage in order to explain Best Society to others. Choice D is incorrect because the author is speaking to a general audience. Choice E is incorrect because *adulatory* means "full of praise," and while we can infer that the author admires Best Society, most of the passage seeks to define, not excessively praise, it.

20. **The correct answer is D.** The second and third paragraphs can best be described as a juxtaposition of what Puritans and many Americans may think of when they think of Best Society, and what Best Society *actually* means. Choice A is incorrect because, while the second paragraph does indeed address the Puritans' idea of Best Society, the third paragraph disputes, instead of supporting, this idea. Choice B is incorrect because, while it describes a juxtaposition similar to the one in the passage, the author does not at any point condemn the Puritan lifestyle in general. She merely argues that their idea of Best Society is wrong. Choice C is incorrect because, while we could infer from the second paragraph that the author may think Puritans are overly prim and strict, the third paragraph argues that Best Society members are the opposite of—not similar to—court jesters. Choice E is incorrect because the third paragraph does not address the history of Best Society at all, and the second paragraph makes the point that the Puritan community frowns on Best Society, so it does not make sense that it would have a major history within that community.

21. **The correct answer is A.** Since the author stresses the importance of a member of Best Society being charming, considerate, and well-mannered, we can infer that its members value those qualities among each other. Choice B is incorrect because there is no evidence in this passage to support the claim that Best Society is not open to women. Choice C is incorrect because there is little mention of the arts in this passage, and while we may assume that an appreciation of the arts is part of being well-mannered, there is nothing in the passage that explicitly connects Best Society with the arts. Choice D is incorrect because, while Puritans disapprove of Best Society from a social standpoint, the author does not explicitly address a difference in religion. Choice E is incorrect because the author states directly that good ethics are an extension of good manners.

22. **The correct answer is D.** In this context, *grotesque* has a meaning slightly different from its typical use: here it means a demeanor that *intends* to be Best Society but is a hideous, comically distorted version of it. An interest in war history can be expressed in a grotesque fashion, but it could also be expressed in the form of interesting anecdotes, which would be an important part of any member of Best Society's demeanor. Choices A, B, C, and E are all examples of grotesque misinterpretation of etiquette or manners.

23. **The correct answer is A.** The phrase "mistakes the jester for the queen" is a metaphor meaning that many people mistake imitators of Best Society for those with truly refined etiquette. Choice B is incorrect because the

author does not directly make the argument that Puritans can never be members of Best Society, nor does she state that any Puritans want to be a part of Best Society. Choice C is incorrect because the phrase "mistakes the jester for the queen" is a metaphor, not a literal comment on forms of government. Choice D is incorrect because the passage argues that manners *can* in fact be taught. Choice E is incorrect because at no point does the author address the general public's opinion on the validity of Best Society, and in fact we can infer that Best Society is not literally a formal club that needs a manifesto or spokesperson, but rather a loose association of those who value the same kinds of etiquette and ethics.

24. **The correct answer is D.** A rhetorical question is a question posed for dramatic effect, and this passage does not include any sentences ending with a question mark, rhetorical or otherwise. Choice A and B are incorrect because the phrase "gold poured literally like rain" in the first paragraph is an example of both hyperbole and simile. Choice C is incorrect because "personification" means attributing human characteristics to non-human beings or things, or using a human as a symbol for a larger entity. In the first paragraph, the phrase "New York . . . loves to be amused, thrilled, and surprised all at the same time" uses New York to symbolize the typical New Yorker. Choice E is also incorrect. A compound sentence is a sentence consisting of two or more independent clauses—normally joined by a coordinating conjunction: *and*, *or*, *nor*, *for*, *but*, or *yet*. There are several such sentences in the passage.

25. **The correct answer is C.** Since she is writing this passage to educate the reader on what proper etiquette and Best Society are, we can assume she is an expert. Choice A is incorrect because there is no evidence to suggest the author is a Puritan, and in fact because she is presumably a member of Best Society, which is looked down on by those who hold Puritanical values, she is very likely not a Puritan. Choice B is incorrect because the author mentions nothing about her own status or that of her family. Choice D is incorrect because, from the passage, we cannot infer that women are excluded from Best Society, and the author at no point makes a case for their inclusion. Similarly to Choice B, Choice E is incorrect because we have no data about the author's own familial status, and because she is not making a case against Best Society, but rather for it.

26. **The correct answer is C.** The author speaks with disillusionment, or a sense of having become jaded, in order to reflect his distaste for the impoverished community in which he grew up. Choice A is incorrect because, although the Maryland landscape could possibly be described as monotonous from the author's description, the point of the passage is not how boring it is but rather the injustice of growing up in a slave community. Choice B is incorrect because the author's tone is not excited, nor is there any indication of an important event in the passage. Choice D is incorrect because, as he did not enjoy growing up in Tuckahoe, the author is clearly not nostalgic (wistful, remembering fondly) about his childhood. Choice E is incorrect because, although the author may certainly be angry, that anger is directed toward poverty and slavery, not towards his parents.

27. **The correct answer is B.** The tone is autobiographical because the author is recollecting scenes from his own life. Choice A is incorrect because the author does not address a scientific problem or use technical language. Choice C may be a tempting choice since the author does describe a cultural problem, but since he draws nearly entirely from his own life

to depict it, "journalistic" is not an apt word to describe the passage. Similarly, Choice D is incorrect: while the passage takes on some elements of a philosophical problem, the direct and personal tone keeps this from being a mainly philosophical passage. Choice E is incorrect because, while the author expresses his opinion, he primarily simply presents his experience from his own life and allows the reader to draw her own conclusion.

28. **The correct answer is C.** Environmental imagery, or descriptions of the author's surroundings, are heavily present in the passage. Choice A is incorrect because there are only one or two passing mentions of animals, and unlike the environment, they are not symbolic of the meaning of the passage. Choice B is incorrect because the passage does not adopt a religious tone, nor does it employ religious symbolism. Choice D is incorrect because, although there are one or two rhetorical questions in the passage, they are not a predominant part of the passage from start to finish. Choice E is incorrect, because while the passage makes occasional use of metaphor, the passage is heavily grounded in reality, and hyperbole is a rhetorical tool that uses purposeful exaggeration to make a point.

29. **The correct answer is C.** This is an ironic statement suggesting that "father" is a foreign concept, when in fact the author understands that most people are born with or have knowledge of their fathers. He employs irony to make the point that slaves almost never knew their fathers. Choice A is incorrect because the author is not creating a juxtaposition (or contrast) between people who grow up in the North versus people who grow up in the South; he is comparing people who grow up as slaves to people who do not. Choice B is incorrect because the author is referring to "father" as it is used in the familial sense, not in the religious sense. Choice D is incorrect because it suggests that the author is using hyperbole to convey a friendship so close that it was like family, when in fact he is speaking about his literal father. Choice E is incorrect because there is no evidence in the passage that the author wonders where his father is—he merely addresses the fact that he has no knowledge of his father.

30. **The correct answer is A.** In the sentence that contains the phrase "without any fault of mine," the subject is his birth into slavery. Choices B, C, D, and E all occur in other sentences, which have different subjects.

31. **The correct answer is D.** Mixed metaphors, or the combination of two different metaphors that, together, make no sense, do not appear in this passage. Choice A is incorrect because the passage uses the bleakness of the environment to symbolize the bleakness of life in Tuckahoe. Choice B is incorrect because, in the third paragraph, the author uses personification in the image of the farmer lifting the hoe, which represents the desperation of all the people in the town. Choice C is incorrect because in the third paragraph, the author uses the phrase "drunken to a proverb," which is an example of colloquialism, or familiar speech. Choice D is incorrect because there are several compound sentences in this passage.

32. **The correct answer is C.** We can infer that the author sees his childhood in Tuckahoe as an important, if unhappy, time in his life because he states that "it is always a fact of some importance to know where a man is born," and because he chooses to begin his biography with a depiction of that town. Choice A is incorrect because there is no evidence in the passage to support the claim that the author eventually returned to Tuckahoe later in life. Choice B is incorrect because, although he asserts that ague and

fever plagued the town in general, the author gives no indication that he himself suffered from these ailments. Choice D is incorrect because the author states that to this day he does not know the date and year of his birth. Choice E is incorrect because, although it is reasonable to imagine that a slave would resent his master for not permitting him to ask questions, there is no indication of resentment over this particular point in the passage.

33. **The correct answer is B.** The author establishes the town of Tuckahoe as a setting to give context to his own life. Choices A and D are incorrect because they both infer that the author is mostly focused on the town or on slavery in general, when the passage primarily focuses on the author's own experience with both. Choice C is incorrect, because the author states why the citizens of Tuckahoe stay there despite the ague and fever they get from the river: the river also gives them a source of food.

34. **The correct answer is A.** The phrase "Oh, what's the use?" might as well be a motto for the town, as is indicated by the desert-like conditions and impoverished slaves the author describes elsewhere in the passage. Choice B is incorrect because ambivalence, or the state of having conflicting or mixed feelings about something, does not accurately depict how the author feels about the town. Choice C is incorrect because the author does not address nihilism in the text or suggest that it is the only reasonable viewpoint for those who live in Tuckahoe. Choice D is incorrect because the passage is about Tuckahoe and the people who live there, and does not address the history or scientific makeup of the soil. Choice E is incorrect because the sentence in which this phrase occurs is talking about the soil, not the river-borne illness.

35. **The correct answer is B.** The author says that the true cost of anything is the amount of labor a person is willing to spend on it. Therefore, labor is the most basic level of currency. Choice A is incorrect because the author establishes a connection between labor and wealth, and cites Hobbes as saying that wealth is equal to power, but does not assert that labor is *equal* to power. Choice C is incorrect because, while the author may certainly believe that the currency system was instituted as a stand-in for labor, this does not address the function of labor itself. Choice D and Choice E are both incorrect because they are the opposite of points argued in the passage.

36. **The correct answer is C.** The passage is straightforward and direct. Choices A and E are both incorrect because the passage does not use terms or previously established theories that only a specialist would understand. Choice B is incorrect because the passage does not convey strong emotion; it is too measured to be called hysterical. Choice D is incorrect because the author is speaking about a general premise, not himself or his particular experiences and recollections. Choice E is incorrect because there isn't a significant amount of technical language or jargon.

37. **The correct answer is C.** The tone is philosophical and the goal is to come to an understanding about the relationship between wealth, labor, and power. Choice A is incorrect because the passage does not provide tips or directions on how to turn labor into wealth; it merely explores the concepts from a philosophical standpoint. Choices B and D are incorrect because the passage does not express any personal opinions the author may hold. Choice E is incorrect because the passage does not talk about the history of wealth or labor

in human society, and deals primarily with their contemporary definitions.

38. **The correct answer is B.** In the sentence in question, toil and trouble refers to the labor one could spare oneself by paying someone else to do a given job. Choice A is incorrect because, although the phrase "toil and trouble" does appear in the Shakespeare play *Macbeth*, there is no indication that this is anything more than coincidence. Choices C and D are both incorrect because they refer to problems not addressed at all in this passage: the complications that come with excess wealth and the risk of physical injury that comes with labor. Choice E is incorrect because, while the passage establishes labor as the most basic form of currency, it does not describe the creation of a money system or the problems that may have come with it.

39. **The correct answer is A.** The author cites Hobbes as stating that, while wealth does provide power in the labor industry, this power doesn't necessarily carry over into the military or government. Choices B, C, D, and E are all parts of Hobbes's theory, clearly stated in the second paragraph of the passage, and therefore they are incorrect.

40. **The correct answer is B.** The author talks about the relationship between labor and wealth, and then cites Hobbes to talk about the relationship between wealth and power. Choice A is incorrect because the author speaks in abstract generalities for nearly all of the passage, and has very few specific examples. Choice C is incorrect because, while the author does discuss labor in the first paragraph and power in the second, he does not *define* the terms but rather *juxtaposes*, or contrasts, them to a related concept. Choice D is incorrect because the author does not draw on personal experience at any point in the passage. Choice E is incorrect because pastoral imagery, or the depiction of rural, farm-like landscapes, often used as a symbol for innocence, is not present anywhere in the passage.

41. **The correct answer is A.** It depicts a real-world situation that most closely embodies the author's belief that there is a trade-off between expending labor and expending wealth. Choice B is incorrect because, according to the passage, there is a direct relationship between labor and wealth but not a direct relationship between wealth and power; therefore, a person cannot expend labor to get power in the same way that a person can expend labor to get wealth. Choice C is incorrect because the passage does not express an opinion on whether wealth or power is better or more important. Choice D is incorrect because it argues that wealth only equates to power when a person is in the process of getting or losing it, but we know from Hobbes that wealth is not necessarily an indication of all types of power. Choice E is incorrect, similarly, because Hobbes argues that greater amounts of wealth do not lead to greater amounts of political power, so we can't infer that everyone in a political position has a lot of wealth.

42. **The correct answer is D.** The passage uses general language and presents the relationship between wealth, power, and labor as philosophical points of interest. Choices A, B, and C are all incorrect because there is no indication in the language that the passage is particularly geared toward economists, financial planners, or advanced philosophers—although it might be of interest to all three. Similarly, choice E is incorrect because the passage does not approach the relationships between labor, power, and wealth from an anthropological standpoint: the author doesn't talk specifically about his culture and how his contemporaries think about these concepts, but instead talks about

them in more universal terms. However, future historians might find the passage interesting anyway.

43. **The correct answer is D.** In the first paragraph, the author develops a theory about the relationship between labor and wealth, and in the second paragraph he cites a theory developed by Hobbes about the relationship between wealth and power. Choice A is incorrect because the second paragraph deals with a separate theory, and doesn't provide statistics to support the theory established in the first paragraph. Choice B is incorrect, because while the theories in the two paragraphs are distinct, they are related to each other. Choice C is incorrect because Hobbes's theory doesn't disagree with the author's theory—it simply addresses a different angle of the problem. Choice E is incorrect because the author does not criticize Hobbes's theory of wealth and power.

44. **The correct answer is B.** The tone is diaristic because the passage is a daily record of the author's experiences as she travels to the Coast. Choice A may be tempting, because there are interjections of humor in the passage, but it does not characterize the overall tone, nor is making the reader laugh at the point of the passage. Choice C is incorrect because the passage depends most heavily on the author's descriptions and experiences, not on scientific data. Choice D is incorrect, because the tone is heavily influenced by the writer's personal impressions and not meant to be entirely objective. Choice E is incorrect because although the author does state at certain points that she is nervous before embarking upon her trip, fear does not characterize the tone of the passage as a whole.

45. **The correct answer is A.** The author uses the word *cheerful* to describe something which is the opposite of cheerful, and the definition of irony in this context is the use of a word or phrase to describe its opposite for rhetorical effect. Choice B is incorrect because a syllogism involves reaching a conclusion based on two facts both assumed to be true, and this sentence does not have this structure. Choice C is incorrect because a metaphor involves comparing one thing to another, and there is no comparison in this sentence. Choice D is incorrect because alliteration occurs when multiple words in the same sentence or phrase begin with the same sound (such as "curious crocodiles"). Choice E is incorrect because an allusion would involve the author using a word or phrase to implicitly call something else to the reader's mind, and there is no evidence of that in this sentence.

46. **The correct answer is C.** In this context, *discursiveness* means "rambling from one subject to another" or "digression." *Hysteria* (choice A) means "extreme emotion." *Exaggeration* (choice B) means "representing something as more extreme than it really is." *Complaint* (choice D) means "a statement of dissatisfaction" or "an ailment." *Confusion* (choice E) means "disorientation" or "doubt." Therefore, *digression* (choice C) is the best answer.

47. **The correct answer is E.** The phrase "so fearful misunderstandings arose" refers to the first two sections of this compound sentence: the fact that the author was worried that the natives might kill her, and the fact that they worried she would attempt to prevent them from consuming alcohol. Choice A is incorrect because, while the author does state that she collects beetles while on the Coast, there is no mention of the natives believing that she collects poisonous snakes in this passage. Choices B and D are both incorrect because, while they are mentioned in other sentences in the passage, they do not

occur in this particular sentence and "fearful misunderstandings" that arose do not apply to them. Choice C is incorrect because the author states the opposite: in fact, the natives successfully taught her many lessons.

48. **The correct answer is B.** At the beginning of the passage, the author describes her nervousness about the Coast: therefore, the best description of her feelings is "trepidation," or "apprehension." Choice A is incorrect because at no point in the passage does the author voice horror. Choice C is incorrect because, while she may indeed be excited about the trip, that excitement is initially overshadowed by her nervousness. Choice D is incorrect because "apathy," or "lack of interest," is the opposite of the enthusiasm that characterizes the author's tone throughout the passage. Choice E is incorrect because, while the beginning of the passage does address the logistical difficulties of the journey, the author does not express impatience about that aspect of the trip.

49. **The correct answer is D.** A primary point of the passage is that the author held many misconceptions about what the Coast would be like until she spent time there, despite the fact that she had read many books on the subject, and Choice D states the opposite. choice A is incorrect because lines 24-27 list the ways in which, even in this more Westernized part of the Coast, the author's habits differed from the natives' habits. Choice B is incorrect because the fact that the author found the natives to be trustworthy is the major conclusion of the passage. Choice C is incorrect because it states the opposite of Choice D—the fact that the author found all the research she'd done before her journey to be either unhelpful or incomplete. Choice E is incorrect because (line 26), in which the author and the natives simultaneously misunderstand things about each other, shows that both she and the natives had preconceived ideas about what the other would be like.

50. **The correct answer is A.** The author begins with this anecdote in order to establish a light, playful tone and include humorous color in the passage. Choice B is incorrect because the playful tone and use of irony indicates that the author is including this quote about a dead man who hasn't been buried as a humorous aside about the strange subjects her native language phrasebook uses, not as a serious description to ward off potential visitors. Choice C is incorrect because the phrase refers to a language book, not to research materials about the Coast. Choice D is incorrect because the author tells this anecdote before she has left for the Coast, so it is not a description of something she is actually seeing. Choice E is incorrect because, while this may be a direct quote from the author's phrasebook, it is an English translation and does not use any dialect unfamiliar to an English-speaking reader.

51. **The correct answer is B.** This passage is most likely the beginning to a longer work about the Coast and what the author finds there. Choices A and C are both possibilities, as the author adopts a conversational tone as if the passage were meant to be read aloud or intended for a friend. However, the author's goal is to give potential travelers to the Coast the valuable and complete information she did not have before setting out, so the passage is not intended to be read privately by just one person. Also, nowhere in the passage does she explicitly encourage young people to travel. Choice D is incorrect because, while the author does include personal anecdotes, the main subject is the place that she describes in this passage. Choice E is incorrect because the author is speaking primarily to contemporaries, and talking about contemporary perceptions as opposed to historical facts.

52. **The correct answer is C.** The author does not repeat words or phrases in order to emphasize them at any point in this passage. All the other rhetorical devices listed appear in this passage.

53. **The correct answer is B.** During the period in which the author wrote this piece, the term "fetish" was used to describe religious practices. Despite the fact that the author does not mention religion in connection with fetish at any point in the piece, we can still figure this out from context. Choice A, beetle collection, must be incorrect because the author states that she is interested in collecting beetles AND fetish. There would be no need for her to state twice that she wanted to collect beetles. Choice C, documentation of unfamiliar terrain, does not make sense given the fact that she wants to study the fetishes of the locals. If they are locals, the terrain in which she studies them would not be unfamiliar to them. Similarly, choice D is out of the running: there is no reason why the natives would be obsessed with learning about themselves and their own customs. Choice E is also not possible, because the natives—not being Western—could not possibly have intolerable Western habits. Therefore, choice B is the only logical option.

54. **The correct answer is A.** The author begins her journey nervous and unsure of what will happen, but ends her journey excited to return. Choice B is incorrect because the author states in the passage that the natives mistakenly believed she was a member of the Temperance movement—however, they soon learned that she was not. Choice C is incorrect because the author indicates at the beginning of the passage that she was a writer prior to undertaking this trip. Choice D is incorrect because she states that at the end of the trip she had learned that the natives were trustworthy, therefore it is not very likely that she felt disdainful towards them. Choice E is incorrect because, although the author does say at the beginning of the passage that the area where she will be traveling is comparatively tame, she does not return to this claim after describing her travels there, nor does she express horror at what she finds during her journey.

55. **The correct answer is B.** In this instance she is attributing human desires and thoughts to a non-human entity, which is an example of personification. Metaphor (the comparison of one thing to another), irony (the use of a word or phrase to describe something to which the opposite meaning could be more logically applied), simile (the comparison of one thing to another using connecting phrases such as "like" or "as if to"), and sarcasm (the use of ironic language to convey a mocking tone), are all absent from this sentence.

Section II: Free Response

Question 1

High-Scoring Sample Essay

No single educational policy is ever going to work for all schools in a given district, let alone all the schools in the country! Even so, some schools have been considering adopting a different school calendar than the American norm (which involves school from Labor Day to Memorial Day, with a winter break in December and January. There are reasons to approve and dismiss this plan, which we should tackle categorically.

First there's the argument put forth by schools—that year-round schooling provides greater continuity of learning, prevents burnout for both students and staff, and makes most efficient use of school facilities, and even has some additional benefits for at-risk families (Sources A and D). You could also argue that it upholds Montessori values of more effectively letting children find real world inspiration to keep them learning, by letting them have experiential learning more frequently (Source C). These are some compelling arguments, especially for a school board to consider, but they fail to take into account how students react to the idea of going to school all year.

For their part, students probably initially react to this idea with dread—as do some principals, who suggest it makes after school or extra-curriculars harder to maintain and cause difficulties for multi-child families. We can't help it—once you're used to the idea of being free from June to August, it's hard to understand any other way. Even if, as students must realize, they are actually getting the same amount of school days (180 days, in most states, according to Source E), but distributed with more frequent 3 week breaks. Imagine a 3 week break every 3 months! You could still travel, and go to camp, and sleep late, and overdose on cartoons, but in smaller installments, more often!

Parents are the final group to convince, and for them many concerns are logistical. Maybe the pros include access to less exhausted teachers, but the cons include the difficulty of schedule time off for the whole family. If parents are low income, they may have a harder time lining up intermittent childcare if they can't send their kids to the kinds of programs that are available only in long blocks of summer. But parents should also be sympathetic to what teacher Lorena Thomas said about year round school: "If you're checking in every time they come back . . . You're able to implement catch-up lessons on the fly, which are more effective for student retention."

So there you have it—if Year Round school makes sense for a community, it should be adopted. There aren't any arguments that hold up about whether it works, only whether it's necessary. Parents and administrators should keep in mind how tangible retention benefits are, and make the logistics work however they can.

Reader Response for the High-Scoring Sample Essay

This essay effectively advances a qualified argument that year-round schooling may have benefits for specific communities, but should be implemented based on community needs rather than financial or logistical concerns. The student chose to organize the essay by examining the needs of each stakeholder in turn—first school administrators, then students, then parents. The writer also appropriately incorporates her own perspective about long summer breaks. The student demonstrates effective strategies by incorporating the sources in relationship to one another, not merely summarizing or making reference to them. For instance, the student notices commonalities between Sources A and D and extends her reasoning with the more philosophical Source C. The student also notes some weaknesses in the arguments proposed by administrative or school-centered sources, by citing student concerns and parent priorities. Synthesis of other sources is more implicit than explicitly quoted, but still combines the author's own perspective with that of the teachers and students represented in the sources. Although the student's prose is somewhat informal and contains various flaws, the essay is concise and easy to follow for a reader.

Middle-Scoring Sample Essay

As the great teaching philosopher Dr. Maria Montessori once said, "What we all desire for ourselves, namely, not to be disturbed in our work, not to find hindrances to our efforts." It may not sound like it, but summer vacation can actually be a hindrance to many students! Yes, we all like to be free from school and get to stay up late and sleep in, but consider how much harder we have to work—and how hard teachers have to work (Source D). According to Ms. Thomas, "Shorter breaks means kids remember more." If our work is to learn as much as we can, even breaks should be designed to help us do that.

The State of California has developed guidelines that should be useful to all schools that want to consider Year Round education—typically this means 60 days of school and 20 days of vacation (Source A). Some schools even have multiple tracks to make the most of resources like buildings, classrooms and teacher energy level. It's not just about facilities, though, it's also better for kids to learn from, sometimes. It's also good because they can still get lunch at school! Personally I prefer school lunch in the summer because I don't even have to think about what to get.

In conclusion, there are pluses and minuses to year round school that teachers should remember, and kids shouldn't get so upset about it. If it happens at your school, there are good things about it that you can focus on. You may thank your principal later.

Reader Response for the Middle-Scoring Sample Essay

This essay adequately takes a stance on year-round education, centers a student perspective, and also explains the logistics of implementing the year-round format for a school. The essay responds to the prompt appropriately, although briefly, by identifying key ideas and engaging with them. (for example, Source C, which presents an educational philosophy, and Source D, which contains the views of teachers) The writer responds with the student's own perspective ("If our work is to learn as much as we can, even breaks should be designed to help us do that"). The development of the writer's reasoning and evidence could be stronger, for example, the use of "I prefer school lunch" is not as persuasive as the previous example, which cited the fact that lower income families can't afford lunches. The essay concludes by addressing students directly, which clarifies the writer's perspective. The writer could have done more to indicate his audience earlier in the essay, because it wasn't clear if he was speaking to administrators or students. The writer's sentence-level control is largely successful but could be more polished and ambitious. The prose is generally clear, and the argument is sustained for the duration of the essay.

Low-Scoring Sample Essay

The important thing to remember about school calendars is that kids like routine and they don't like new things. Schools shouldn't institute new plans without thinking first what will happen to the kids, and then how will it affect them. If I woke up tomorrow and had to go to school all year around I would wonder why the school did it and not like it at all because I like to go away to Camp Summersides, and you can't do that unless you go for the whole summer. I mean you can but it's less fun and different people are there for the shorter time. Think about the holidays too. Some states do this but lots of states don't. That's why we shouldn't do it either, it shows schools don't think about kids.

Reader Response for the Low-Scoring Sample Essay

This essay fails to produce meaningful analysis or synthesis of the sources provided, though it does demonstrate the author's perspective on year-round schooling and takes an opinionated stance. The writer didn't make references to sources or support her opinion with reasoning or evidence, and includes a number of irrelevant statements that do not respond to the prompt appropriately (for example, the digression about Camp Summersides, or "Think about the holidays too"). Perhaps the writer ran out of time or struggled to connect with the prompt, but she could have accomplished more with an outline that reflected source use instead of this incomplete fragment. The language is simplistic, and contains errors like run-on sentences. The sentence-level prose does not show an ability to write effectively for an audience.

Question 2

High-Scoring Sample Essay

This 1905 letter from American author Mark Twain to the Reverend J.H. Twichell quickly establishes a striking juxtaposition between a light, affectionate tone towards its recipient and a bleak attitude towards its topic. Despite the fact that Twain's letter comes as a disagreement with a position Twichell has previously taken, it's clear from the outset that the two men are close friends. Twain opens his argument with what he refers to as "a Pudd'nhead maxim"—a reference to a line spoken by the title character of his novel *Puddn'head Wilson*—implying the Twichell was familiar with Twain's body of work and would have understood the reference. As the letter continues, Twain—ever the comedic writer—pokes gentle fun at Twichell, concluding the letter with the ironically generous statement "N.B. No charge for these informations." Twain appears to apply the maxim he uses to frame the letter, "When a man is a pessimist before 48 he knows too much; if he is an optimist after it he knows too little," to insult Twichell's intelligence ("It is with contentment, therefore, that I reflect that I am better and wiser than you.") However, this insult is facetious. Mark Twain was born in the mid 1830s, and by the time of this letter both he and Twichell would have been nearly 70—far older than the age of 48, and therefore pessimistic. If anything, Twain is accusing his friend of being a dreamer, or overly inclined to see the good in others and in society.

Twain reserves harsher criticism for the honesty of members of the Senate, as well as ordinary citizens whose desires to be honest are complicated by lust for money and material progress. "When a person is disloyal to any confessed duty, he is plainly and simply dishonest, and knows it..." Twain writes. "Judged by this standard—and who will challenge the validity of it?—there isn't an honest man in Connecticut, nor in the Senate, nor anywhere else. I do not even except myself..." Twain goes on to argue that failure to fulfill any aspect of one's duty, in case withholding a book he knows he ought to publish, as a kind of dishonesty, and employs a rhetorical style of asking questions, as if he were having a philosophical debate or even a Socratic dialogue in the same room as Twichell, as opposed to carrying on a written correspondence. "Joe, you seem to be dealing in 'bulks', now; the 'bulk' of the farmers and U.S. Senators are 'honest,'" he writes, "As regards purchase and sale with money? Who doubts it? Is that the only measure of honesty? Aren't there a dozen kinds of honesty which can't be measured by the money-standard?" This rhetorical structure creates the premise of a philosophical debate, as opposed to a mere exchange of viewpoints, and invites Twichell to extrapolate on the larger societal pulls that cause the decline of fundamental honesty among men and politicians.

To make his own position on this clear, Twain uses repetition of parts of the phrase "steady progress from age to age of the coming of the kingdom of God and righteousness." The words "age to age," or some variation upon them, appear 3 times in the letter, as a refrain and always in reference to the unstoppable advance of industrial progress and the societal obsession with getting rich it yields. "Money-lust has always existed," he clarifies, "but not in the history of the world was it ever a craze, a madness, until your time and mine." By repeating the phrase "age to age" over the course of the letter, Twain uses dramatic rhetoric to create a kind of drumbeat of dread, and instills in the reader the feeling of being unable to escape progress, even if its results are just as oppressive as they are innovative.

Reader Response for the High-Scoring Sample Essay

This essay effectively analyzes the rhetorical techniques present in the work, including the contrast between content and tone, the context of many of Twain's references, his teasing insults for his friend, and his critical take on members of the Senate. The writer articulates the distinctions between Twain's ideas and his sarcastic or "facetious" choice of rhetoric. It presents a clear introduction to frame the circumstances of the letter, followed by a paragraph that examines the way Twain writes to his friend. The third paragraph studies Twain's attitude toward the Senate, not only providing examples, but analyzing them in a relevant, insightful way. The writer also identifies the refrain of "age to age" and how that factors into the argument Twain is ultimately talking about the inevitability of progress. The essay successfully showcases the student's own interpretation with a thoughtful analysis of Twain's rhetoric.

Middle-Scoring Sample Essay

In this letter, Mark Twain responds to an argument he's having with the Reverend J.H. Twichell, who argues that politicians are honest. In responding "I reflect that I am better and wiser than you," Twain is adopting a bombastic rhetoric in order to underscore the vast number of factors Twichell has simplified or failed to take into account altogether in his position that "the 'bulk' of the farmers and U.S. Senators are honest...as regards purchase and sale with money. For example, Twain argues, "Treason is treason—and there's more than one form of it; the money-form is but one of them." When industry progress causes men to take value away from being men of their word and put value towards being materially successful, they open themselves up to corruption and the potential to betray their friends, family and even country.

Twain knows that in order for readers to agree with him that they are open to such corruption, he needs to make his tone less lecture-like and more conversation. "Am I honest? I give you my word of honor (private) I am not," he writes, employing empathetic rhetoric in an attempt to appeal to the ethos of the reader. This tactic, along with the little pockets of humor he intersperses in the text, helps soften the otherwise bleak attitude of men's ability to be honest in an age of progress and lust for wealth.

Reader Response for the Middle-Scoring Sample Essay

The writer has identified some important rhetorical techniques present in the text, but has misunderstood or omitted several critical examples of others—for example, interpreting Twain's "I reflect that I am better and wiser than you" as bombast and not sarcasm. The writer misinterprets the purpose of the text when discussing Twain's intention for readers—this is a letter, not a public document. What the writer calls Twain's rhetoric of empathy is not an entirely accurate reading of Twain's tone. The writer's mention of the use of humor as a rhetorical tool is an interesting point, but the writer did not fully develop the argument or provide any specific examples of Twain's perception of men's bleak attitude or potential for corruption. The final paragraph begins with an assumption about what Twain knows about readers—more could have been accomplished by analyzing the effect of Twain's argument rather than speculating about his intentions. The response does manage to convey the student's ideas even if it is insufficiently developed.

Low-Scoring Sample Essay

While Mark Twain's friend argues that politicians and people in general have become more honest than they used to be, Twain writes in this letter that people have always been liars and they haven't changed even though they have so much technology and industry helping to make the society richer and develop new jobs. Twain also argues that people naturally get more pessimistic as they get older, and therefore they are inclined to lie more as they do not value the honor of being a man of their word the way they used to when they were younger. Twain thinks his friend is stupid and naive for believing otherwise and he argues that there is no point in furthering social problems to help people be honest and work together because society has changed so much but still at heart they are all liars who will always prioritize their own interests over the interests of the group.

Reader Response for the Low-Scoring Sample Essay

This writer has retained some of the basic information from the letter, but has misinterpreted much of it and is also confused about the meaning of the maxim at the beginning of the passage. Twain's opening lines are about knowledge, not necessarily honesty. The writer has not identified any rhetorical tools used by Twain in this letter, nor has he used any specific passages—instead the writer used paraphrase and summary to make inferences that are then not sufficiently supported by the text. The writing is rambling and unclear, and the writer has not made distinctions between his analysis of the text and the close-reading of the text itself. For example, the last run-on sentence doesn't contain support for any of its observations, so it's hard to know what is the author's perception specifically from the text.

Question 3

High-Scoring Sample Essay

According to Aristotle, humans work in order to have leisure. His philosophy states that without the unpleasantness of hard work, the pleasure of being idle would be meaningless. Indeed, it seems that in many ways, humans were designed to work often and hard: even when we are given the opportunity to be idle, we more often than not use our free time to create work of our own. We run triathlons, break hot dog-eating contest world records, and write thousand page long novels, not because financial necessity compels us to do so, but because of our basic human drive to see whether it can be done.

When Russell speaks about idleness, he does not speak from the perspective of someone who has adopted a lifestyle of maximum lifestyle and ease. From a young age, he ".. acquired a conscious which has kept me working hard, down to the present moment," he clarifies, "but although my conscious has controlled my *actions*, my *opinions* have undergone a transformation." This suggests that his essay "In Praise of Idleness" is less focused on the logistics of being idle and more focused on the psychological and practical impact hard work might have on a person.

For an example, let's imagine a person who lives well below the poverty line gets a job in a factory making hats for $2 per hat. Since his goal is to make as much money as possible and lift himself out of poverty, he wishes to make as many hats as possible. Yet due to the laws of supply and demand, the more hats the person makes, the greater the supply of hats will be. As long as the demand for hats remains the same, the value of each hat will decrease. Karl Marx develops this theory—the theory of surplus value—in his critique of political economy, stating that the hatmaker's hard work paradoxically fuels the cycle that keeps him in poverty, and that he therefore lacks control and power over the kind of work he does.

Ironically, the best conditions under which to accomplish self-selected, productive work are those in which the worker has no financial need to do any work at all. In her essay "A Room of One's Own," Virginia Woolf argues that a woman must have money and her own space in order to successfully become a writer, impressing the key point that the reason why so few women became successful writers prior to the early 20th century is because of their perceived poverty and lack of power in society.

The social implications of work make sense in the context of Russell's claim that there is nothing inherently virtuous about working hard, since so many aspects of working-class employment have nothing to do with nobleness and everything to do with keeping entry-level workers in a cycle of poverty. Yet humans are nearly always driven to work of some kind, whether that work cause financial gain or otherwise, so perhaps a qualification on Russell's claim is necessary. A separation of virtuosity from work comes not from a state of idleness, but rather from the freedom to choose the kind of work one spends time doing.

Reader Response for the High-Scoring Sample Essay

This essay successfully reflects the writer's perspective on the value of work and leisure. He begins by invoking Aristotle, and paraphrasing his philosophy, then following it with his own examples to define leisure. Then the writer moves toward answering the prompt by analyzing Russell's self-represented experience to determine the relevance of his perspective. The writer supports his perspective with individual examples, Karl Marx, and Virginia Woolf, which sufficiently addresses the prompt by invoking readings and observations. The essay's strength lies in the way the author incorporates different perspectives to examine the moral and societal advantages of work, and taking a critical stance toward the association of work with nobility as opposed to survival. The prose is well-developed and demonstrates an appropriate control of rhetorical techniques, a sophisticated level of thought, and a strong grasp of relevant readings and synthesis moves.

Middle-Scoring Sample Essay

Everyone would prefer to be idle instead of working all day. Yet if we lived in a society where no one was compelled to work in order to benefit the society, our quality of life would drop way down. If we believe it's more virtuous for us to be idle and pursue the things that make us happy, we then need to grant the same liberty towards everyone else in our society. Then the people whose work increases our happiness during our leisure time will no longer be doing their jobs. The people who get paid to pave the roads, clean up the parks, sell groceries etc will no longer be there, resulting in a community that is much more difficult to live in. This is why Russell's position is elitist—he only considers this theory for himself, with no regard to how it would impact the community around him.

The importance of work dates back to John Locke's social contract, which states that all citizens give up their private freedoms in exchange for the safety and security of living in a society. One of the freedoms one gives up is a measure of one's time in the form of work. This is why hard work is considered virtuous—because it signifies giving up one's time in order to enhance the good of the society over the good of the self. Russell's essay is single-minded and fails to take into account this aspect of virtuosity in work.

Reader Response for the Middle-Scoring Sample Essay

The writer has closely read the passage in the assignment and has begun to develop an argument against Russell's claim, but fails to fully develop her position. The writer begins with generalizations—"everyone would prefer to be idle ..." for example—and uses a slippery-slope argument without specifically invoking individual scholars or writers to support her perspective. In the second paragraph, the writer does mention John Locke, and successfully interprets one of his ideas in a relevant way ("it signifies giving up one's time in order to enhance the good of the society over the good of the self."). The author also introduces a counterargument to respond to Russell's essay, but doesn't fully explain what Russell was arguing or presenting the source for an unfamiliar reader. The writer could have done more to introduce Russell's text or could have responded with other outside sources or with his own observations in a more thoughtful way. The writer's use of supporting evidence is thin, and the prose, while adequate, is not particularly compelling.

Low-Scoring Sample Essay

Bertrand Russell thinks that it's a mistake that people think work is so great and that they should consider that maybe the best thing for citizens is to make their own decisions about what they spend their time doing instead of spending hours and hours a day on their jobs. He thinks that maybe the real virtue is not in work but in being able to choose how you spend your time, even if it means doing nothing. Russell has been brought up to believe in the importance of work, so he's just now as an adult beginning to questions why we value work so highly over things like imagination and play. He feels betrayed by the people who taught him the importance of work because he has wasted so much of his life working in a meaningless job he hates.

Reader Response for the Low-Scoring Sample Essay

This essay does begin by introducing Bertrand Russell's argument, both his broad main idea and paraphrasing some of his supportive material as provided in the prompt. However, the writer focuses on explaining the text without coming up with her own opinion on the material. The author does not bring in outside sources to comment for or against Russell's position, and she does not structure her essay into a clear, organized format. There is no argument being presented by the author, though she does summarize Russell appropriately. The essay is inadequate to respond to the prompt, and there is nothing in the prose that might elevate a short submission to a higher score level.

Practice Test 3

Chapter 6

ANSWER SHEET PRACTICE TEST 3

Section I: Multiple Choice

1. Ⓐ Ⓑ Ⓒ Ⓓ Ⓔ	15. Ⓐ Ⓑ Ⓒ Ⓓ Ⓔ	29. Ⓐ Ⓑ Ⓒ Ⓓ Ⓔ	43. Ⓐ Ⓑ Ⓒ Ⓓ Ⓔ
2. Ⓐ Ⓑ Ⓒ Ⓓ Ⓔ	16. Ⓐ Ⓑ Ⓒ Ⓓ Ⓔ	30. Ⓐ Ⓑ Ⓒ Ⓓ Ⓔ	44. Ⓐ Ⓑ Ⓒ Ⓓ Ⓔ
3. Ⓐ Ⓑ Ⓒ Ⓓ Ⓔ	17. Ⓐ Ⓑ Ⓒ Ⓓ Ⓔ	31. Ⓐ Ⓑ Ⓒ Ⓓ Ⓔ	45. Ⓐ Ⓑ Ⓒ Ⓓ Ⓔ
4. Ⓐ Ⓑ Ⓒ Ⓓ Ⓔ	18. Ⓐ Ⓑ Ⓒ Ⓓ Ⓔ	32. Ⓐ Ⓑ Ⓒ Ⓓ Ⓔ	46. Ⓐ Ⓑ Ⓒ Ⓓ Ⓔ
5. Ⓐ Ⓑ Ⓒ Ⓓ Ⓔ	19. Ⓐ Ⓑ Ⓒ Ⓓ Ⓔ	33. Ⓐ Ⓑ Ⓒ Ⓓ Ⓔ	47. Ⓐ Ⓑ Ⓒ Ⓓ Ⓔ
6. Ⓐ Ⓑ Ⓒ Ⓓ Ⓔ	20. Ⓐ Ⓑ Ⓒ Ⓓ Ⓔ	34. Ⓐ Ⓑ Ⓒ Ⓓ Ⓔ	48. Ⓐ Ⓑ Ⓒ Ⓓ Ⓔ
7. Ⓐ Ⓑ Ⓒ Ⓓ Ⓔ	21. Ⓐ Ⓑ Ⓒ Ⓓ Ⓔ	35. Ⓐ Ⓑ Ⓒ Ⓓ Ⓔ	49. Ⓐ Ⓑ Ⓒ Ⓓ Ⓔ
8. Ⓐ Ⓑ Ⓒ Ⓓ Ⓔ	22. Ⓐ Ⓑ Ⓒ Ⓓ Ⓔ	36. Ⓐ Ⓑ Ⓒ Ⓓ Ⓔ	50. Ⓐ Ⓑ Ⓒ Ⓓ Ⓔ
9. Ⓐ Ⓑ Ⓒ Ⓓ Ⓔ	23. Ⓐ Ⓑ Ⓒ Ⓓ Ⓔ	37. Ⓐ Ⓑ Ⓒ Ⓓ Ⓔ	51. Ⓐ Ⓑ Ⓒ Ⓓ Ⓔ
10. Ⓐ Ⓑ Ⓒ Ⓓ Ⓔ	24. Ⓐ Ⓑ Ⓒ Ⓓ Ⓔ	38. Ⓐ Ⓑ Ⓒ Ⓓ Ⓔ	52. Ⓐ Ⓑ Ⓒ Ⓓ Ⓔ
11. Ⓐ Ⓑ Ⓒ Ⓓ Ⓔ	25. Ⓐ Ⓑ Ⓒ Ⓓ Ⓔ	39. Ⓐ Ⓑ Ⓒ Ⓓ Ⓔ	53. Ⓐ Ⓑ Ⓒ Ⓓ Ⓔ
12. Ⓐ Ⓑ Ⓒ Ⓓ Ⓔ	26. Ⓐ Ⓑ Ⓒ Ⓓ Ⓔ	40. Ⓐ Ⓑ Ⓒ Ⓓ Ⓔ	54. Ⓐ Ⓑ Ⓒ Ⓓ Ⓔ
13. Ⓐ Ⓑ Ⓒ Ⓓ Ⓔ	27. Ⓐ Ⓑ Ⓒ Ⓓ Ⓔ	41. Ⓐ Ⓑ Ⓒ Ⓓ Ⓔ	55. Ⓐ Ⓑ Ⓒ Ⓓ Ⓔ
14. Ⓐ Ⓑ Ⓒ Ⓓ Ⓔ	28. Ⓐ Ⓑ Ⓒ Ⓓ Ⓔ	42. Ⓐ Ⓑ Ⓒ Ⓓ Ⓔ	

Section II: Free Response

Question 1

Question 2

Question 3

PRACTICE TEST 3

Section I: Multiple Choice

Time: 1 Hour • 55 Questions

Directions: This section consists of selections from prose passages and questions on their content, form, and style. After reading each passage, choose the best answer to each question and then fill in the corresponding circle on your answer sheet.

Questions 1–14. Read the following passage carefully before you decide on the answers to the questions.

Francis Bacon was an English philosopher and scientist who lived from 1561–1626. The following is an excerpt from his essay "Of Truth."

WHAT is truth? said jesting Pilate, and would not stay for an answer. Certainly there be, that delight in giddiness, and count it a bondage to fix a belief; affecting free-will in thinking, as well as in acting. And though the sects of philosophers of that kind be gone, yet there remain certain discoursing wits, which are of the same veins, though there be not so much blood in them, as was in those of the ancients. But it is not only the difficulty and labor, which men take in finding out of truth, nor again, that when it is found, it imposeth upon men's thoughts, that doth bring lies in favor; but a natural, though corrupt love, of the lie itself. One of the later school of the Grecians, examineth the matter, and is at a stand, to think what should be in it, that men should love lies; where neither they make for pleasure, as with poets, nor for advantage, as with the merchant; but for the lie's sake. But I cannot tell; this same truth, is a naked, and open day-light, that doth not show the masks, and mummeries, and triumphs, of the world, half so stately and daintily as candle-lights. Truth may perhaps come to the price of a pearl, that showeth best by day; but it will not rise to the price of a diamond, or carbuncle, that showeth best in varied lights. A mixture of a lie doth ever add pleasure. Doth any man doubt, that if there were taken out of men's minds, vain opinions, flattering hopes, false valuations, imaginations as one would, and the like, but it would leave the minds, of a number of men, poor shrunken things, full of melancholy and indisposition, and unpleasing to themselves?

One of the fathers, in great severity, called poesy vinum daemonum, because it fireth the imagination; and yet, it is but with the shadow of a lie. But it is not the lie that passeth through the mind, but the lie that sinketh in, and settleth in it, that doth the hurt; such as we spake of before. But howsoever these things are thus in men's depraved judgments, and affections, yet truth, which only doth judge itself, teacheth that the inquiry of truth, which is the love-making, or wooing of it, the knowledge of truth, which is the presence of it, and the belief of truth, which is the enjoying of it, is the sovereign good of human nature. The first creature of God, in the works of the days, was the light of the sense; the last, was the light of reason; and his sabbath work ever since, is the illumination of his Spirit. First he breathed light, upon the face of the matter or chaos; then he breathed light, into the face of man; and still he breatheth and inspireth light, into the face of his chosen. The poet, that beautified the sect, that was otherwise inferior to the rest, saith yet excellently well: It is a pleasure, to stand upon the shore, and to see ships tossed upon the sea; a pleasure, to stand in the window of a castle, and to see a battle, and the adventures thereof below: but no pleasure is comparable to the standing upon the vantage ground of truth (a hill not to be commanded, and where the air is always clear and serene), and to see the errors, and wanderings, and mists, and tempests, in the vale below; so always that this prospect be with pity, and not with swelling, or pride. Certainly, it is heaven upon earth, to have a man's mind move in charity, rest in providence, and turn upon the poles of truth.

1. What is the primary purpose of the passage?

A. To warn against the dangers of lying

B. To develop an argument about why people enjoy lying more than telling the truth

C. To explain that in earlier times, lying was less common than telling the truth, but dishonesty has grown in popularity

D. To argue that without the pleasure of lying, one's life is meaningless

E. To argue that without the pleasure of telling the truth, one's life is meaningless

2. Which of the following is the closest meaning of "bondage" as it is used in line line 2?

A. Imprisonment

B. Requirement

C. Repercussion

D. Reason

E. Difficulty

3. What is the relationship between the first paragraph and the second paragraph of this passage?

A. The first paragraph establishes the dangers of lying, and the second paragraph explains the benefits.

B. The first paragraph offers evidence that more people lie today than they used to, and the second paragraph explains *why* they lie.

C. The first paragraph speaks in abstract terms, and the second paragraph offers specific evidence to support those claims.

D. The first paragraph enumerates the pleasures of lying, and the second paragraph explores the benefits of telling the truth.

E. The first paragraph discusses the commonplace nature of lying, and the second paragraph states the case that this is especially the case among pearl-sellers.

4. The author's tone can best be described as

   A. melancholy.

   B. playful.

   C. hysterical.

   D. condemnatory.

   E. scientific.

5. In line 22, what does "vinum daemonum" most likely mean in context?

   A. Fear of an authority, to keep a person from lying despite their desire to do so once inspired by poetry

   B. The wine of the devil, because poetry stimulates the imagination to go beyond the truth

   C. Critical thinking, because reason should always prevail over imagination

   D. A dreamer's spirit, because reading poetry is essentially a waste of time

   E. Delight in lying, because always telling the truth decreases one's intelligence

6. In lines 29–30, to what does the "sovereign good of human nature" refer?

   A. The ability to be moral despite enjoying lying

   B. Finding pleasure in the belief of truth

   C. The fact that humans are incarnations of divine imagination

   D. The fact that humans retain truth more easily than they retain lies

   E. The fact that humans have great imaginations and therefore enjoy lying

7. To which of the following items does the author compare the truth in the first paragraph?

   A. A pearl

   B. A mask

   C. A mummy

   D. A man's shrunken mind

   E. A flower

8. From the passage, we can infer that the author would NOT agree with which statement?

   A. Though the truth is sometimes less pleasurable to believe than a lie, it is usually more rewarding.

   B. Certain philosophers have advocated free will over a belief in the truth, but that opinion is less popular than it once was.

   C. We should pity those people who stand upon the vantage point of truth to view their lives, because they do not know the pleasures of imagination and white lies.

   D. People can love a lie, though that love is inherently problematic.

   E. The lies we believe are more damaging to us than those we simply hear but know are lies.

9. The phrase "The poet . . . and to see the errors, and wanderings, and mists, and tempests, in the vale below" (lines 34–41) is an example of which rhetorical device?

   A. Metaphor

   B. Syllogism

   C. Simile

   D. Irony

   E. Alliteration

10. The author probably used the phrase "in great severity" in line 22 to illustrate which of the following?
   A. The fact that giving in to emotion over reason was considered inexcusable for most of philosophical history
   B. The fact that the fathers were generally very strict about the laws of human conduct
   C. The fact that favoring the pleasures of lying deprives one of the deeper, if more difficult to achieve, pleasures of believing truth
   D. The fact that God expressly forbids poetry
   E. The fact that God expressly forbids truth-telling

11. Which of the following stylistic features does the author use to conclude the passage?
   A. Religious imagery
   B. Animal imagery
   C. Humor
   D. Repetition for emphasis
   E. Pastoral imagery

12. What, according to the author, was the last creation of God?
   A. Curiosity
   B. The human ability to reason
   C. Light
   D. The human ability to lie
   E. Pearls

13. In lines 15–16 of the passage, which rhetorical technique does the author use when stating, "but it will not rise to the price of a diamond, or carbuncle, that showeth best in varied lights"?
   A. Simile
   B. Analogy
   C. Allusion
   D. Rhetorical question
   E. Irony

Questions 14–25. Read the following passage carefully before you decide on the answers to the questions.

Mary Wollstonecraft was an English writer who lived from 1759–1797 and is credited with writing one of the first major feminist texts, A Vindication on the Rights of Woman, *published in 1792. This is an excerpt from the introduction to that book.*

My own sex, I hope, will excuse me, if I treat them like rational creatures, instead of flattering their FASCINATING graces, and viewing them as if they were in a state of perpetual childhood, unable to stand alone. I earnestly wish to point out in what true dignity and human happiness consists—I wish to persuade women to endeavour to acquire strength, both of mind and body, and to convince them, that the soft phrases, susceptibility of heart, delicacy of sentiment, and refinement of taste, are almost synonymous with epithets of weakness, and that those beings who are only the objects of pity and that kind of love, which has been termed its sister, will soon become objects of contempt.

Dismissing then those pretty feminine phrases, which the men condescendingly use to soften our slavish dependence, and despising that weak elegancy of mind, exquisite sensibility, and sweet docility of manners, supposed to be the sexual characteristics of the weaker vessel, I wish to show that elegance is inferior to virtue, that the first object of laudable ambition is to obtain a character as a human being, regardless of the distinction of sex; and that secondary views should be brought to this simple touchstone.

This is a rough sketch of my plan; and should I express my conviction with the energetic emotions that I feel whenever I think of the subject, the dictates of experience and reflection will be felt by some of my readers. Animated by this important object, I shall disdain to cull my phrases or polish my style—I aim at being useful, and sincerity will render me unaffected; for wishing rather to persuade by the force of my arguments, than dazzle by the elegance of my language, I shall not waste my time in rounding periods, nor in fabricating the turgid bombast of artificial feelings, which, coming from the head, never reach the heart. I shall be employed about things, not words! and, anxious to render my sex more respectable members of society, I shall try to avoid that flowery diction which has slided from essays into novels, and from novels into familiar letters and conversation.

These pretty nothings, these caricatures of the real beauty of sensibility, dropping glibly from the tongue, vitiate the taste, and create a kind of sickly delicacy that turns away from simple unadorned truth; and a deluge of false sentiments and over-stretched feelings, stifling the natural emotions of the heart, render the domestic pleasures insipid, that ought to sweeten the exercise of those severe duties, which educate a rational and immortal being for a nobler field of action.

The education of women has, of late, been more attended to than formerly; yet they are still reckoned a frivolous sex, and ridiculed or pitied by the writers who endeavour by satire or instruction to improve them. It is acknowledged that they spend many of the first years of their lives in acquiring a smattering of accomplishments: meanwhile, strength of body and mind are sacrificed to libertine notions of beauty, to the desire of establishing themselves, the only way women can rise in the world—by marriage. And this desire making mere animals of them, when they marry, they act as such children may be expected to act: they dress; they paint, and nickname God's creatures. Surely these weak beings are only fit for the seraglio! Can they govern a family, or take care of the poor babes whom they bring into the world?

14. Which rhetorical device does the author employ in the first paragraph of the passage?

A. Speculation

B. Irony

C. Juxtaposition

D. Allusion to another text

E. Parenthetical asides

15. The word "epithets" in line 7 most closely fits which definition, in context?

A. Opponents

B. Champions

C. Labels

D. Apologists

E. Families

16. Which of the following is NOT a major point addressed in the passage?

A. Men ascribe softer, more sensitive attributes to femininity, which ultimately makes women objects of contempt.

B. Women's education is even more neglected than it was in previous decades, due to the fact that teachers do not take women seriously.

C. Women are not trained to cultivate strength in either their bodies or their minds.

D. Women, unlike men, are not encouraged to develop their characters as human beings.

E. The author aims to be useful, not eloquent.

17. Why, in lines 23–24, does the author wish to avoid wasting her time "fabricating the turgid bombast of artificial feelings"?
   A. As a woman, she has been extensively trained in the art of rhetoric and literary composition.
   B. She knows a minimalistic style is more compelling to her audience.
   C. She believes sincerity is more important than elegance.
   D. Time constraints limit the length of her essay.
   E. She fears that to display too much emotion will appear typically feminine.

18. From the context of the passage, which of the following can we infer about the author?
   A. She believes women should not be allowed to take painting and music lessons, because it reduces them to animals in the eyes of their male counterparts.
   B. She feels that women are naturally more frivolous than men, and should not receive lesser education simply due to circumstances outside their control.
   C. She believes that women prefer to have their charms flattered, and are offended by those who treat them like rational creatures.
   D. She believes that women have the strength and virtue to raise families, as opposed to being relegated to an eternal state of semi-childhood.
   E. She believes that men naturally employ more flowery language in writing essays and novels, and therefore strives to avoid that style in her own writing.

19. Lines 17–19 ("This is a rough sketch ... felt by some of my readers.") reflect which of the following sentiments?
   A. The author presumes that many of her readers have had experiences similar to the ones she is describing.
   B. The author believes a scientific analysis of the behavior of women as a whole can teach us more about which characteristics are inherently feminine.
   C. Energetic emotions are not helpful when positing rational arguments.
   D. The author aims to teach women the benefits of establishing good character.
   E. The author suppresses her own feelings and emotions because she does not want to seem overly feminine.

20. Which of the following is NOT an example of voice in the passage?
   A. "My own sex, I hope, will excuse me, if I treat them like rational creatures, instead of flattering their FASCINATING graces." (line 2)
   B. "These pretty nothings, these caricatures of the real beauty of sensibility, dropping glibly from the tongue." (lines 29–30)
   C. "They dress; they paint, and nickname God's creatures. Surely these weak beings are only fit for the seraglio." (lines 44–45)
   D. "The education of women has, of late, been more attended to than formerly." (line 36)
   E. "Dismissing then those pretty feminine phrases, which the men condescendingly use to soften our slavish dependence." (lines 10–11)

21. This passage uses all the following stylistic features EXCEPT:

A. Compound sentences

B. Litotes

C. Understatement

D. Parallelism

E. Irony

22. In lines 41–42, the author uses the phrase "to the desire of establishing themselves, the only way women can rise in the world—by marriage" to illustrate which of the following points?

A. Marriage is the highest goal to which any person, man or woman, can aspire.

B. Until our society evolves to the extent that women can enjoy the same rights as men, marriage is a good way for women to move forward in society.

C. The constraints of society dictate that women may only aim to marry well, when in reality they are capable of achieving a much broader spectrum of goals.

D. Women desire to establish themselves by any means necessary, and marriage is a good way in which to accomplish this.

E. Women usually value getting ahead in society and their careers over their family lives.

23. The author's tone is best categorized as

A. hysterical and irate.

B. mocking but sincere.

C. melancholy and disinterested.

D. energized and optimistic.

E. boastful and condescending.

24. The author develops this passage by moving from

A. establishing a goal to illustrating examples.

B. personal experience to universal experience.

C. constructing an argument to presenting a counterargument.

D. recording field notes to extrapolating evidence.

E. positing an argument to relating a similar argument formed by a contemporary.

25. What is the purpose of the final sentence of the passage?

A. Facetious: the author adopts a sarcastic tone to illustrate women's insecurities about their own abilities

B. Rhetorical: the author asks a question to invite the reader to consider the fact that despite the delicate sentiments commonly attributed to femininity, women regularly raise families and run households

C. Concern: the author worries that women may not be equipped for the tasks society expects them to perform

D. Conclusion: the author summarizes the points already addressed in the passage

E. Alarm: the author addresses a major problem in society today and is shocked that no one else has identified it yet

Questions 26–34. Read the following passage carefully before you decide on the answers to the questions.

Henri Bergson was a Parisian philosopher and essayist who lived from 1859 to 1941. The following is an excerpt from an essay titled "On Laughter: An Essay on the Meaning of the Comic," which was published in 1900 in a three-essay collection called Laughter.

What does laughter mean? What is the basal element in the laughable? What common ground can we find between the grimace of a merry—andrew, a play upon words, an equivocal situation in a burlesque and a scene of high comedy? What method of distillation will yield us invariably the same essence from which so many different products borrow either their obtrusive odour or their delicate perfume? The greatest of thinkers, from Aristotle downwards, have tackled this little problem, which has a knack of baffling every effort, of slipping away and escaping only to bob up again, a pert challenge flung at philosophic speculation. Our excuse for attacking the problem in our turn must lie in the fact that we shall not aim at imprisoning the comic spirit within a definition. We regard it, above all, as a living thing. However trivial it may be, we shall treat it with the respect due to life. We shall confine ourselves to watching it grow and expand. Passing by imperceptible gradations from one form to another, it will be seen to achieve the strangest metamorphoses. We shall disdain nothing we have seen. Maybe we may gain from this prolonged contact, for the matter of that, something more flexible than an abstract definition,—a practical, intimate acquaintance, such as springs from a long companionship. And maybe we may also find that, unintentionally, we have made an acquaintance that is useful. For the comic spirit has a logic of its own, even in its wildest eccentricities. It has a method in its madness. It dreams, I admit, but it conjures up, in its dreams, visions that are at once accepted and understood by the whole of a social group. Can it then fail to throw light for us on the way that human imagination works, and more particularly social, collective, and popular imagination? Begotten of real life and akin to art, should it not also have something of its own to tell us about art and life?

26. In line 5, the phrase "obtrusive odour" most likely refers to which of the following?
    - A. The bad smell of stale perfume
    - B. A metaphor for human failure to perceive quality
    - C. A metaphor for imitations of humor that fail to grasp what it is about humor that causes human response
    - D. A metaphor for the ineffable quality that triggers laughter
    - E. The scent of the basal element of laughter

27. What reasoning does the author provide for philosophers' inability to articulate what it is that causes laughter?
    - A. The problem baffles philosophy, being more intuitive than logical.
    - B. The quality of "being laughable" has not received a proper definition.
    - C. The problem has not yet been tackled by a sufficiently great thinker.
    - D. Philosophers disdain the quality of "being laughable" as a hoax.
    - E. Philosophers are not interested in the problem because it is too simple.

28. In line 20, the phrase "it has a method in its madness" utilizes which of the following stylistic devices?
    - A. It alludes to Shakespeare, suggesting that the quality of laughability is understood by all who experience it, but defies logical reasoning.
    - B. It is a metaphor for insanity, implying that those who react to laughability are insane.
    - C. It is hyperbole, because laughter does not cause madness.
    - D. It is understatement, because laughability is a commonly discussed philosophical issue.
    - E. It is sarcasm, because laughter obviously has no rhyme or reason to it.

29. Which of the following most closely describes the author's relationship to the quality of laughability?
    - A. The author believes that laughability must be defined in order to be truly appreciated.
    - B. The author seeks to pin down laughability in order to eradicate it, because the ineffable quality of laughability is a detriment to mankind.
    - C. The author seeks to watch laughability as it grows and changes, and thereby learn things about the nature of humanity in general.
    - D. The author believes that a laughing reaction indicates eccentricity, and therefore those who recognize the quality of laughability must be committed to asylums.
    - E. The author wishes to identify the formula of laughability in order to profit from it.

30. Which of the following is true of the rhetorical style of the passage in general?

A. The passage uses epithets to pinpoint the specific nature of laughability.

B. The passage uses simile to create a greater understanding of what causes laughability.

C. The passage personifies laughability in order to normalize its eccentricities and define its terms.

D. The passage begins and ends with rhetorical questions on the nature of laughability.

E. The passage begins and ends with ironic statements intended to mock those who enjoy laughing.

31. What is the author's intended audience?

A. Scientists who seek to find chemical evidence of laughability

B. A close friend or acquaintance previously familiar with the author's work

C. A general audience interested in the nature of laughter

D. Philosophers experienced in the literature exploring the nature of laughter

E. Comedians looking for new material

32. Which of the following best describes the author's tone in this passage?

A. Critical and overconfident

B. Curious and meandering

C. Scientific and data-driven

D. Intimate and audience-focused

E. Hyperbolic and outraged

33. Which of the following best describes the trajectory of the passage?

A. The author begins with an inquiry into who has examined the philosophy of laughter previously, and ends with an admonishment for the lack of scientific evidence utilized in the study of laughter.

B. The author begins with a general question about the nature of laughter and ends with the acknowledgment that basal laughter may have much to teach humans about society.

C. The author begins with specific evidence about the nature of what makes something laughable and ends with a general conclusion about what kinds of laughable qualities different aspects of the population find humorous.

D. The author begins with a personal anecdote and ends with scientific evidence that supports his findings.

E. The author begins by dismissing the importance of laughter and then moves on to argue that the ability to reason is far more important and the study of laughter is a waste of time.

34. From the context of the passage, which of the following can we NOT infer about the author?

A. The author is fascinated by the study of laughter, but resigned to the fact that laughability may not be easily defined.

B. The author prefers certain types of humor to others.

C. The author believes in the importance of studying laughability to learn more about human nature.

D. The author believes that humans can easily tell the difference between cheap imitations of humor and true laughability.

E. The author doesn't blame previous philosophers for not answering this question sufficiently, as the question may not ultimately have an answer.

Questions 35–43. Read the following passage carefully before you decide on the answers to the questions.

Edwin Bryant was an American author and editor who lived from 1805–1869. In this account from his book, What I Saw in California, *Bryant chronicles his journey through the American West in 1846–1847, well before the Gold Rush. The following is an excerpt from a chapter describing the missionary settlements in Northern California.*

Presidios.—The necessity of protecting the apostolic predication was the obligatory reason for forming the presidios, which were established according to circumstances. That of San Diego was the first; Santa Barbara, Monterey, and San Francisco were built afterwards. The form of all of them is nearly the same, and this is a square, containing about two hundred yards in each front, formed of a weak wall made of mud-bricks. Its height may be four yards in the interior of the square, and built on to the same wall. In its entire circumference are a chapel, storehouses, and houses for the commandant, officers, and troops, having at the entrance of the presidio quarters for a *corps-de-garde*.

These buildings in the presidios, at the first idea, appear to have been sufficient, the only object having been for a defence against a surprise from the gentiles, or wild Indians in the immediate vicinity. But this cause having ceased, I believe they ought to be demolished, as they are daily threatening a complete ruin, and, from the very limited spaces of habitation, must be very incommodious to those who inhabit them. As to the exterior of the presidios, several private individuals have built some very decent houses, and, having evinced great emulation in this branch of business, I have no doubt but in a short time we shall see very considerable towns in California.

At the distance of one, or at the most two miles from the presidio, and near to the anchoring-ground, is a fort, which has a few pieces of artillery of small calibre. The situation of most of them is very advantageous for the defence of the port, though the form of the walls, esplanades, and other imperfections which may be seen, make them very insignificant.

The battalion of each presidio is made up of eighty or more horse soldiers, called *cuera*; besides these, it has a number of auxiliary troops and a detachment of artillery. The commandant of each presidio is the captain of its respective company, and besides the intervention, military and political, he has charge of all things relating to the marine department.

The missions contained in the territory are twenty-one. They were built at different epochs: that of San Diego, being the first, was built in 1769; its distance from the presidio of the same name is two leagues. The rest were built successively, according to circumstances and necessity. The last one was founded in the year 1822, under the name of San Francisco Dolores, and is the most northern of all.

The edifices in some of those missions are more extensive than in others, but in form they are all nearly equal. They are all fabricated of mud-bricks, and the divisions are according to necessity. In all of them may be found commodious habitations for the ministers, storehouses to keep their goods in, proportional granaries, offices for soap-makers, weavers, blacksmiths, and large parterres, and horse and cattle pens, independent apartments for Indian youths of each sex, and all such offices as were necessary at the time of its institution. Contiguous to and communicating with the former is a church, forming a part of the edifices of each mission; they are all very proportionable, and are adorned with profusion.

The Indians reside about two hundred yards distant from the above-mentioned edifice. This place is called the rancheria. Most of the missions are made up of very reduced quarters, built with mud-bricks, forming streets, while in others the Indians have been allowed to follow their primitive customs; their dwellings being a sort of huts, in a conical shape, which at the most do not exceed four yards in diameter, and the top of the cone may be elevated three yards. They are built of rough sticks, covered with bulrushes or grass, in such a manner as to completely protect the inhabitants from all the inclemencies of the weather. In my opinion, these rancherias are the most adequate to the natural uncleanliness of the Indians, as the families often renew them, burning the old ones, and immediately building others with the greatest facility. Opposite the rancherias, and near to the mission, is to be found a small garrison, with proportionate rooms, for a corporal and five soldiers with their families. This small garrison is quite sufficient to prevent any attempt of the Indians from taking effect, there having been some examples made, which causes the Indians to respect this small force. One of these pickets in a mission has a double object; besides keeping the Indians in subjection, they run post with a monthly correspondence, or with any extraordinaries that may be necessary for government.

35. Which of the following is NOT a major point in the passage?

A. The author's observations of the topographical and social status of the territory of Northern California

B. The lifestyles of the native people living in Northern California

C. The construction of missions in Northern California

D. The importance of communications between missions and native communities in Northern California

E. How a person might go about recreating a settlement like the one the author describes

36. What is the tone of the passage?

A. Scandalized and vindictive

B. Observant and measured

C. Poetic and rhetorical

D. Critical and sarcastic

E. Boastful and self-assured

37. In the first line of the passage, "apostolic predication" most likely refers to

A. religious practices.

B. communication with the natives.

C. the businesses of soap-making, basket-weaving, and blacksmithing.

D. recording the events that transpire.

E. reverence for the natural world.

38. Which of the following most closely defines the relationship between paragraph 6 and paragraph7?
    - A. Paragraph 6 describes the establishment of the missionary community, and paragraph 7 details its interactions with the native community.
    - B. Paragraph 6 describes the establishment of the missionary community and the business it creates, and paragraph 7 details the native community's interaction with that business.
    - C. Paragraph 6 details the importance of forming a missionary community, and paragraph 7 describes the native response to that community's inception.
    - D. Paragraph 6 details the logistics of establishing a missionary community, and paragraph 7 juxtaposes that community against the existing native community standards.
    - E. Paragraph 6 discusses the framework of the native community, and paragraph 7 details the ways in which the missionary community borrows from it.

39. To what does the author attribute the regular burning to the ground of native rancherias?
    - A. Protest regarding white missionaries establishing a community so close to theirs
    - B. Religious mandates
    - C. General uncleanliness
    - D. A greater connection with nature than with the comforts of society
    - E. The fact that the native community is careless with fire

40. Which of the following may represent the author's intended audience?
    - A. Those considering a trip to Northern California and curious about the lifestyle and topography there
    - B. Those concerned with the religious practices of California's natives
    - C. Those who believe that Christian missionaries should be more widespread in California and wish to see what a conflict between missionaries and California natives looks like
    - D. A personal family friend or acquaintance with no knowledge of California but with an interest in the author's personal adventures
    - E. A reader interested in the biography of the author

41. Which of the following can we infer about the author's position?
    - A. The author prioritizes detailing the landscape and customs of Californians over his personal reflections.
    - B. The author prioritizes personal reflection over the development of a sense of the landscape and customs of Californians.
    - C. The author believes that the natives should leave California because of their uncleanliness.
    - D. The author supports Christian missionaries but thinks their structures are flawed.
    - E. The author believes that Christian missionaries should significantly reduce their presence in California.

42. In line 35, the word "edifices" most likely means

A. religious structures in place to preserve Christianity.

B. divisions to separate the various structures of the compound.

C. bulwarks to keep the Native Californians from invading the building.

D. buildings used to house residents and local shops.

E. social practices in place to keep the compound from burning to the ground.

43. Which of the following does the author NOT use to depict the landscape in Northern California?

A. Listing of physical structures

B. Metaphor regarding the dissonance between natives and Western Christians

C. Depictions of the kinds of work people do in the compound

D. General instruction on how to recreate the society built in Northern California

E. Description of the military presence in the missionaries

Questions 44–55. Read the following passage carefully before you decide on the answers to the questions.

Samuel Butler, an English novelist who lived from 1835–1902, is also known for his translations of The Iliad *and* The Odyssey. *The following essay was published in a collection called* Essays on Life, Art and Science.

I have been asked to speak on the question how to make the best of life, but may as well confess at once that I know nothing about it. I cannot think that I have made the best of my own life, nor is it likely that I shall make much better of what may or may not remain to me. I do not even know how to make the best of the twenty minutes that your committee has placed at my disposal, and as for life as a whole, who ever yet made the best of such a colossal opportunity by conscious effort and deliberation? In little things no doubt deliberate and conscious effort will help us, but we are speaking of large issues, and such kingdoms of heaven as the making the best of these come not by observation.

The question, therefore, on which I have undertaken to address you is, as you must all know, fatuous, if it be faced seriously. Life is like playing a violin solo in public and learning the instrument as one goes on. One cannot make the best of such impossibilities, and the question is doubly fatuous until we are told which of our two lives—the conscious or the unconscious—is held by the asker to be the truer life. Which does the question contemplate—the life we know, or the life which others may know, but which we know not?

Death gives a life to some men and women compared with which their so-called existence here is as nothing. Which is the truer life of Shakespeare, Handel, that divine woman who wrote the "Odyssey," and of Jane Austen—the life which palpitated with sensible warm motion within their own bodies, or that in virtue of which they are still palpitating in ours? In whose consciousness does their truest life consist—their own, or ours? Can Shakespeare be said to have begun his true life till a hundred years or so after he was dead and buried? His physical life was but as an embryonic stage, a coming up out of darkness, a twilight and dawn before the sunrise of that life of the world to come which he was to enjoy hereafter. We all live for a while after we are gone hence, but we are for the most part stillborn, or at any rate die in infancy, as regards that life which every age and country has recognised as higher and truer than the one of which we are now sentient. As the life of the race is larger, longer, and in all respects more to be considered than that of the individual, so is the life we live in others larger and more important than the one we live in ourselves. This appears nowhere perhaps more plainly than in the case of great teachers, who often in the lives of their pupils produce an effect that reaches far beyond anything produced while their single lives were yet unsupplemented by those other lives into which they infused their own.

44. Which of the following rhetorical devices does the author NOT employ in this passage?

A. Parallelism

B. Metaphor

C. Simile

D. Antiphrasis

E. Analogy

45. Based on context, what is the purpose of this passage?

A. To deliver a speech on the question of how to make the most out of life

B. To deliver a speech on the question of how to achieve immortality after death

C. To make the argument that Shakespeare lived a fuller life after his death

D. To caution young people who take life too seriously to appreciate its inherent facetiousness

E. To develop the argument that the importance of life is greater than any given individual

46. In lines 15–16, to which of the following does the question "Which does the question contemplate—the life we know, or the life which others may know, but which we know not" refer?

A. Whether it is better to achieve happiness in life, or achieve immortal recognition after death

B. Whether it is the accomplishments that we are aware of or the accomplishments that are recognized after death that measure the success of our life

C. Whether we should count the measure of our success in our vocations, or in our personal lives

D. Whether we should count toward the measure of our lives the people we impact on a professional level, or merely on a personal level

E. Whether a person is qualified to instruct others on how to live a happy life if he is unhappy in his own

47. Which of the following best describes the trajectory of the passage?

A. The passage develops an argument from personal experience, then uses statistics to support that argument.

B. The passage argues that the measure of life may take place either before or after death, then poses a counterargument.

C. The passage argues that the measure of life may take place either before or after death, then provides examples.

D. The passage begins with a general overview, then focuses on the author's experience.

E. The passage develops a blueprint by which every man can live a fulfilled life.

48. In line 24, what does the author mean by "embryonic stage"?

A. The time before birth, when a person comes up out of the darkness and begins a finite quest to make the most of life

B. The time spent before realizing how to philosophize about life

C. In Shakespeare's case, the time he spent alive, since his true life did not begin until his work gained popularity after his death

D. The time in which it becomes clear that a life will be "stillborn," and never achieve fulfillment

E. The time in which a person is ignorant of the importance of living a meaningful life

49. In comparison with the rest of the passage, the tone of paragraph 2 is

A. more scientific and fact-based.

B. dreamier and more curious.

C. more swayed by personal experience.

D. geared toward experienced philosophers.

E. more critical and angrier.

50. The relationship between the second and third paragraphs can be most accurately defined by which of the following?

A. The second paragraph establishes that no person's life bears fundamental similarity to another, and the third paragraph argues that this means that living a good life cannot be taught.

B. The second paragraph argues that life is ad-libbed as a person goes along, and the third paragraph argues that no person will remain in others' memories long after death anyway.

C. The second paragraph posits two lives—the conscious and the unconscious life—and the third paragraph describes circumstances under which a person might experience his true life well after death.

D. The second paragraph argues that life is worth living only if one can make an impact on others, and the third paragraph provides specific examples of how that can be accomplished.

E. The second paragraph argues that there is no use in trying to live a meaningful life, as no one can control how he is perceived after death, and the third paragraph provides examples.

51. Based on this passage, the author would be most likely to agree with which of the following statements?

A. Death is the great equalizer, and therefore how one lives life does not matter too much.

B. In death we are provided the opportunity to correct everything we did poorly in life, so no one should be afraid to make mistakes.

C. For some people, such as Shakespeare, death truly begins after life, and life is but a nascent stage during which one may develop the assets for which one will be remembered.

D. Teachers cannot effectively change the lives of their students; therefore, people working as teachers should also cultivate alternate methods for gaining immortality once they die.

E. What happens to us in our afterlives is a result of how we spend our time on earth.

52. Which of the following is the author's intended audience?

A. A diary or close acquaintance, because the passage is personalized to specific and intimate correspondence

B. A speech to a curious audience of general knowledge, because the passage explains each concept without assuming any prior knowledge of philosophy

C. A team of experienced philosophers who are expected to interpret the author's argument with little development

D. A group of artists who seek immortality after death

E. An audience seeking a light-hearted counterpoint to the serious question of how to live a meaningful life

53. According to this passage, what does the author believe about teachers?

A. The author believes teachers can help their students learn early how to make the most out of life, thereby causing their students to lead fuller and productive lives.

B. The author believes teachers cannot live full and productive lives without also cultivating an artistic life outside of teaching.

C. The author believes that teachers are poised to have lives that go on beyond their conscious lives, because of the impact they have on their students.

D. The author is a former teacher who found that the time spent studying for standardized tests made the study of philosophy impractical.

E. The author's personal philosophies have been widely influenced by his teachers in grade school.

54. In line 11, what does the word "fatuous" most closely mean?

A. Deadly

B. Silly

C. Complicated

D. True

E. Erroneous

55. The passage can be described most accurately as which of the following types of writing?

A. Narrative

B. Persuasive

C. Legal

D. Philosophical

E. Satirical

STOP!
IF YOU FINISH BEFORE THE TIME IS UP,
YOU MAY CHECK YOUR WORK IN THIS SECTION ONLY.

Section II: Free Response

Total Time: 2 Hours, 15 minutes

> **Directions:** The following prompt is based on the accompanying sources. This question requires you to synthesize a variety of sources into a coherent, well-written essay. When you synthesize sources, you refer to them to develop your position and cite them accurately. Your argument should be central; the sources should support the argument. Avoid merely summarizing sources. Remember to attribute both direct and indirect references.

Question 1
Suggested Time—40 Minutes

Many leading educational experts agree that exposure to visual and performing arts like drama, music, and dance has a positive effect on child and adolescent development. Some districts want to take it even further and require students to take at least one arts class every year they're in school. Do you think it's a valuable addition to the curriculum?

Carefully read the following six sources, including the introductory information for each source. Then synthesize and incorporate at least three of the sources into a coherent and well-written essay in which you develop a position on whether arts requirements would benefit students at your school, or even beyond high school in college.

Your argument should be the main focus of the essay. Use the sources to inform and strengthen your argument. Avoid merely summarizing the sources. Indicate clearly which sources you are drawing from, whether through direct quotation, paraphrase, or summary. You may cite the sources as Source A, Source B, etc. or by using the descriptions in parentheses.

Source A (Stinson)

Source B (Kentucky news article)

Source C (Rubinthal)

Source D (Lasky)

Source E (Quotes)

Source F (Corkery)

Source A

The Vitality of Public Arts Programming
Belinda Stinson, U.S. Education News

A 2002 study by the Arts Education Partnership was one of the first conclusive evaluations of the impact of arts education on public school education. Researchers found that students who had a chance to explore arts like drama and music had higher reading, writing, and math scores than peers who only focused on traditional academic subjects. The partnership analyzed 62 studies and cross-referenced them with academic achievement, standardized testing achievement, social skills and student-reported motivation.

"There's no guarantee students enrolled in arts classes will magically get straight As," said Henry Luston, the head coordinator for the report, "But we certainly see the influence on lower-income students who have a chance to express themselves, or students who need remedial instruction, who build self esteem by engaging in a less evaluative activity at school."

Many school administrative officials and even teachers are dismissive of the value of arts education, and consider it "expendable" when school budget season rolls around. The partnership insists drama is especially valuable for helping students perceive and understand social relationships and complex emotions, cultivates sustained thought, and augments their abilities to comprehend narrative storytelling. Music education is correlated with improvement in math skills, reading and cognition, SAT verbal scores and even language skills for English-Language Learners. Dance boosts students' creativity, originality, flexibility, and self-expression. Students demonstrate increased confidence and persistence as well. The visual arts, say researchers, lead to improvement in quality and structure of writing, more complex reading and interpretive skills, and reasoning abilities. Combining the arts foments interdisciplinary learning, skills, and collaboration.

Source B

Kentucky Governor Calls for Arts Cuts, STEM investment

Responding to a general trend towards evaluating high schools and universities on the earnings potential of graduates, as opposed to the breadth and depth of their course offerings or the diversity of their student body, the governor of Kentucky recently announced as part of his budget plan that the state would be subsidizing universities and public schools that offer increased emphasis on STEM careers in the sciences, technology, engineering, and math. In his remarks to the General Assembly, the governor said, "The net result of putting public tax dollars into education is to ensure that we actually are graduating people that can go into the work force." The implication was that students of the Humanities—literature, the arts—are not being prepared for meaningful contributions to society or the economy. Tennessee has considered similar measures recently, which involves tying higher education funding to various performance measures related to employment and income. "There will be more incentives to electrical engineers than French literature majors, there just will," said the governor, "All the people in the world who want to study French literature can do so they're just not going to be subsidized by the taxpayers like engineers will be, for example." Critics of the governor's plan suggest that budgeting agencies are not best equipped to determine what majors will be most successful or necessary 5 or 10 years down the road, and warn that restricting humanities funding shuts out lower-income and nontraditional students who may not be able to afford the expensive private universities that will be the last bastions of humanities majors, if other states follow Kentucky's example.

Source C

Should the Arts Be Required?
Matilda Rubinthal

When I was in fourth grade, the orchestra teacher came around to every class with one of each kind of stringed instrument—she brought a cello, a viola, and a violin. She left the bass at home, she joked, because it would have had to be strapped on the roof of her car. I plunked each instrument when it was my turn, and decided rather than go with the most popular, I would go with the underdog. I would become a violist.

In a way maybe I'm the wrong person to ask about whether arts should be required. I joined orchestra that year, I also joined the chorus, and tried out for every school play that I could for the next 8 years. I found a home in the arts that I never found anywhere else. The people who doubt the benefits of arts programs aren't going to be persuaded by an arts lover!

Let me tell you instead about the kids I met from other classes, other grades, other academic tracks. Charlie was a talented gymnast and class clown who settled down and learned to focus in Mr. K's theater classes—he took those skills off to study business and economics, and owns a string of small businesses now! Sally was a shy and introverted classmate I befriended in a Spanish class and encouraged to try out for chorus with me. She found her voice and got so good at public speaking that now she's teaching fourth graders! David always had a calculator in his hand and a textbook on his lap—he loved physics more than anybody else in our grade, but he struggled to see how to apply all the formulas he understood so well. His guidance counselor nudged him into joining us in the orchestra, and he found learning to read music and play as part of an ensemble unlocked creative problem solving abilities he hadn't known he was missing! He's a leading engineer and consultant at a major aeronautics company today.

As for me? I'm still in chorus, I still go to plays, though I haven't touched my viola in a while. I became a writer, because it was the best way to express all the things I saw and heard around me, to make sense of them. I would have wound up here anyway, because I was lucky to have family to support and encourage me. But Sally and David and Charlie needed something only arts could have given them, and if they hadn't been available, who knows if they'd have found it when they needed it.

Source D

Let STEM Be STEM?
Dr. Wendy Lasky, head of the Math department at Tanya McCall Middle School

Every fall I have meetings with parents at the beginning of the school year. We go over a typical student schedule—a science, a math, an English class, gym, history, and an elective. We have a number of offerings at our school—theater, chorus, orchestra, visual art, band, wood shop, home ec, anthropology, journalism, statistics, philosophy, and others. Students are required to take an arts elective, a humanities elective and something hands on. Every year there are at least a couple of parents protesting, "My child is going into a STEM career! Why should they have to join chorus or help out backstage at the school play? They don't have time for philosophy!"

I get their concerns. College admissions are more competitive now than ever, and parents are eager for their kid to get as many classroom hours in their prospective field as possible. They may look back on their school performances with dread, or think their kid is just too awkward or tone deaf to make it worthwhile. But I also have students who are determined to become actors, politicians, English teachers, rock stars. They still have to take math. They still have to take civics. They have to take biology, chemistry, and physics too, because that's what education should do—it should expose you to all the strands of knowledge that there are, that you have time for, so that your brain can do what brains do best and bring that knowledge together in new and unexpected ways. If you gave your toddler only blue play-dough, how would she learn to mash it with yellow and make green? If you let your child walk down only one street in your neighborhood, how would he learn to explore? It was Albert Einstein who said, "Logic will get you from A to B. Imagination will take you everywhere."

Source E

Quotes from Prominent American Scholars and Leaders

"Life without industry is guilt; industry without art is brutality."
—*John Rushkin*

"The Arts and Sciences, essential to the prosperity of the State and to the ornament of human life, have a primary claim to the encouragement of every lover of his country and mankind."
—*George Washington*

"I must study politics and war, that my sons may study mathematics and philosophy … in order to give their children the right to study painting, poetry, music and architecture."
—*John Q. Adams*

Source F

Letter to the Editor
Tim Corkery, PTA President

The head of our math department, Dr. Lasky, recently published an Op-Ed in these pages I feel compelled to respond to. My son and daughter Benny and Ruby are 7th and 8th graders at McCall this year, and I am dismayed that each of them must sacrifice the chance to take advanced algebra, physics, or chemistry to take an arts class or waste time interviewing neighbors about their paper routes. We are preparing them for a crowded, underresourced world, and they need to be equipped with as much knowledge that will be relevant to that world, as soon as possible. If they are a year ahead in their sciences when they leave middle school, they can fit in an extra AP class in each branch, and that will translate to college credit!

Being ahead of the game in their college pre-requisites will let them advance to higher level classes more quickly, which will qualify them for labs and internships. More internships means better applications for entry level jobs, where they can do the important work of grappling with the problems of the world! I want the best for my children, and if they had an aptitude for a literary career or any interest in music or could do more with a paint brush than make a mess, then of course I would support them to balance their future career prospects with the arts. If they made them happy. But they don't! Both of them have been outside in the dirt building things since they were toddlers, and have never shown any interest or talent outside of physical science and mathematics. So it's my job as their dad to make the way as smooth as possible. As the great Helen Keller once said, "Many persons have a wrong idea of what constitutes true happiness. It is not attained through self-gratification but through fidelity to a worthy purpose." Benny says he wants to build sustainable buildings that run on solar power and grow their own food. Ruby wants to figure out how to make a whole body transplant. I'm not saying they'll always want to do that, or even that what they dream about is possible, but they're going to figure out for themselves a lot faster if they're exposed to the sciences in meaningful ways as soon and as long as possible. Please consider implementing more flexibility in elective policies. I'll be proposing this district-wide at the next school board meeting.

GO ON TO THE NEXT PAGE.

Question 2
Suggested Time—40 Minutes

The following passage is taken from Mary Church Terrell's 1906 speech "What It Means To Be Colored In Capital of the U.S." In her speech, the author develops an argument that, despite the fact that Washington, D.C. has adopted the nickname "The Colored Man's Paradise," racism is still rampant in the city.

Read the passage carefully. Then, develop a well-written essay in which you analyze the author's position and examine the rhetorical tools she uses to convey her point.

Washington, D.C., has been called "The Colored Man's Paradise." Whether this sobriquet was given to the national capital in bitter irony by a member of the handicapped race, as he reviewed some of his own persecutions and rebuffs, or whether it was given immediately after the war by an ex-slaveholder who for the first time in his life saw colored people walking about like free men, minus the overseer and his whip, history saith not. It is certain that it would be difficult to find a worse misnomer for Washington than "The Colored Man's Paradise" if so prosaic a consideration as veracity is to determine the appropriateness of a name.

For fifteen years I have resided in Washington, and while it was far from being a paradise for colored people when I first touched these shores it has been doing its level best ever since to make conditions for us intolerable. As a colored woman I might enter Washington any night, a stranger in a strange land, and walk miles without finding a place to lay my head. Unless I happened to know colored people who live here or ran across a chance acquaintance who could recommend a colored boarding-house to me, I should be obliged to spend the entire night wandering about. Indians, Chinamen, Filipinos, Japanese and representatives of any other dark race can find hotel accommodations, if they can pay for them. The colored man alone is thrust out of the hotels of the national capital like a leper.

As a colored woman I may walk from the Capitol to the White House, ravenously hungry and abundantly supplied with money with which to purchase a meal, without finding a single restaurant in which I would be permitted to take a morsel of food, if it was patronized by white people, unless I were willing to sit behind a screen. As a colored woman I cannot visit the tomb of the Father of this country, which owes its very existence to the love of freedom in the human heart and which stands for equal opportunity to all, without being forced to sit in the Jim Crow section of an electric car which starts form the very heart of the city– midway between the Capital and the White House. If I refuse thus to be humiliated, I am cast into jail and forced to pay a fine for violating the Virginia laws....

As a colored woman I may enter more than one white church in Washington without receiving that welcome which as a human being I have the right to expect in the sanctuary of God....

Unless I am willing to engage in a few menial occupations, in which the pay for my services would be very poor, there is no way for me to earn an honest living, if I am not a trained nurse or a dressmaker or can secure a position as teacher in the public schools, which is exceedingly difficult to do. It matters not what my intellectual attainments may be or how great is the need of the services of a competent person, if I try to enter many of the numerous vocations in which my white sisters are allowed to engage, the door is shut in my face.

From one Washington theater I am excluded altogether. In the remainder certain seats are set aside for colored people, and it is almost impossible to secure others.…

With the exception of the Catholic University, there is not a single white college in the national capitol to which colored people are admitted.… A few years ago the Columbian Law School admitted colored students, but in deference to the Southern white students the authorities have decided to exclude them altogether.

Some time ago a young woman who had already attracted some attention in the literary world by her volume of short stories answered an advertisement which appeared in a Washington newspaper, which called for the services of a skilled stenographer and expert typewriter.… The applicants were requested to send specimens of their work and answer certain questions concerning their experience and their speed before they called in person. In reply to her application the young colored woman … received a letter from the firm stating that her references and experience were the most satisfactory that had been sent and requesting her to call. When she presented herself there was some doubt in the mind of the man to whom she was directed concerning her racial pedigree, so he asked her point-blank whether she was colored or white. When she confessed the truth the merchant expressed … deep regret that he could not avail himself of the services of so competent a person, but frankly admitted that employing a colored woman in his establishment in any except a menial position was simply out of the question.…

Not only can colored women secure no employment in the Washington stores, department and otherwise, except as menials, and such positions, of course, are few, but even as customers they are not infrequently treated with discourtesy both by the clerks and the proprietor himself.…

Although white and colored teachers are under the same Board of Education and the system for the children of both races is said to be uniform, prejudice against the colored teachers in the public schools is manifested in a variety of ways. From 1870 to 1900 there was a colored superintendent at the head of the colored schools. During all that time the directors of the cooking, sewing, physical culture, manual training, music and art departments were colored people. Six years ago a change was inaugurated. The colored superintendent was legislated out of office and the directorships, without a single exception, were taken from colored teachers and given to the whites.…

Now, no matter how competent or superior the colored teachers in our public schools may be, they know that they can never rise to the height of a directorship, can never hope to be more than an assistant and receive the meager salary therefore, unless the present regime is radically changed....

Strenuous efforts are being made to run Jim Crow cars in the national capital....

Representative Heflin, of Alabama, who introduced a bill providing for Jim Crow street cars in the District of Columbia last winter, has just received a letter from the president of the East Brookland Citizens' Association "indorsing the movement for separate street cars and sincerely hoping that you will be successful in getting this enacted into a law as soon as possible." Brookland is a suburb of Washington.

The colored laborer's path to a decent livelihood is by no means smooth. Into some of the trades unions here he is admitted, while from others he is excluded altogether. By the union men this is denied, although I am personally acquainted with skilled workmen who tell me they are not admitted into the unions because they are colored. But even when they are allowed to join the unions they frequently derive little benefit, owing to certain tricks of the trade. When the word passes round that help is needed and colored laborers apply, they are often told by the union officials that they have secured all the men they needed, because the places are reserved for white men, until they have been provided with jobs, and colored men must remain idle, unless the supply of white men is too small....

And so I might go on citing instance after instance to show the variety of ways in which our people are sacrificed on the altar of prejudice in the Capital of the United States and how almost insurmountable are the obstacles which block his path to success....

It is impossible for any white person in the United States, no matter how sympathetic and broad, to realize what life would mean to him if his incentive to effort were suddenly snatched away. To the lack of incentive to effort, which is the awful shadow under which we live, may be traced the wreck and ruin of score of colored youth. And surely nowhere in the world do oppression and persecution based solely on the color of the skin appear more hateful and hideous than in the capital of the United States, because the chasm between the principles upon which this Government was founded, in which it still professes to believe, and those which are daily practiced under the protection of the flag, yawn so wide and deep.

GO ON TO THE NEXT PAGE.

Question 3
Suggested Time—40 Minutes

From personal blogs to YouTube channels to Twitter feeds, the Internet provides a platform for all people to express their viewpoints to a large audience. In a carefully crafted essay, consider how the Internet has changed the landscape of public discourse. Use appropriate evidence from your reading, experience, or observations to support your argument.

STOP!
IF YOU FINISH BEFORE THE TIME IS UP,
YOU MAY CHECK YOUR WORK IN THIS SECTION ONLY.

ANSWER KEY AND EXPLANATIONS

Section I: Multiple Choice

1. B	12. B	23. B	34. B	45. A
2. A	13. B	24. A	35. D	46. B
3. D	14. B	25. B	36. B	47. C
4. B	15. C	26. C	37. A	48. C
5. B	16. B	27. A	38. D	49. B
6. B	17. C	28. A	39. C	50. C
7. A	18. D	29. C	40. A	51. C
8. C	19. A	30. D	41. A	52. B
9. A	20. D	31. C	42. B	53. C
10. C	21. B	32. B	43. B	54. B
11. A	22. C	33. B	44. D	55. D

1. **The correct answer is B.** The author aims to make a philosophical investigation into why people seem to enjoy the pleasures of lying over the pleasures of telling the truth. Choice A is incorrect because the author's tone is contemplative, and does not necessarily seek to form any value judgments about honesty versus lying. Choice C is incorrect because the author's only comment on how the popularity of lying has changed over time occurs in the first paragraph, when he addresses some philosophers who earlier in history made the case for free will over complete honesty. Choice D is incorrect because, while he argues that lying has some appeal to the imagination, the pleasure of truth-telling is deeper and longer lasting. Choice E is incorrect because, although the author believes in the virtues of telling the truth, there is nothing to indicate a connection between honesty and a meaningful life—the author is more focused on the pleasures both lying and honesty bring a person.

2. **The correct answer is A.** In the first line, the author states that there are some people who view truth-telling as being excessively limiting, or a kind of imprisonment. *Bondage* is defined as "enslavement" or "imprisonment," so Choices B, C, D, and E are all incorrect because none denote any form of imprisonment.

3. **The correct answer is D.** It accurately describes the relationship between the paragraphs in questions. Paragraphs two and three establish a juxtaposition, or contrast, between the pleasures of lying and the pleasures of telling the truth. Choice A is incorrect because the second paragraph does not address the benefits of lying, but rather the benefits of telling the truth. Choice B is incorrect because, although the first paragraph briefly mentions an outdated school of philosophical thought that condones lying, the primary point of the passage is about the pleasure both lying and truth-telling bring. Choice C is incorrect

because both paragraphs speak primarily in abstract generalities. Choice E is incorrect because the second paragraph does not speak about lying or what kind of person lies the most, but rather moves on to discuss the phenomenon of truth-telling.

4. **The correct answer is B.** Of the choices listed, *playful* is the best answer, because the author adopts a light tone to reflect the fact that lying is, for many, a form of play. Choices A and C are incorrect because *melancholy* and *hysterical* do not accurately describe the tone of the passage, which neither expresses a gloomy outlook on its subject nor is it overly emotional. Choice D is incorrect because the author does not pass harsh value judgments on those who lie; he instead seeks to examine the reasons people enjoy being dishonest. Choice E is incorrect because the author uses abstract generalities instead of specific points of reason and data or technical language.

5. **The correct answer is B.** In context, the phrase refers to the inspirational effect lying has on the imagination. Choice A is incorrect because the passage focuses on how poetry affects lying, not on how authorities may combat that phenomenon. Choice C is incorrect because the sentence addresses imagination, not critical thinking. Choice D is incorrect because the author does not argue for or against reading poetry. Choice E is incorrect because at no point in the passage does the author establish a connection between telling the truth and intelligence.

6. **The correct answer is B.** In the compound sentence in line 29, the subject of the phrase is "the belief of truth." Therefore, the author states that human capacity to believe in the truth is evidence of the good of human nature. Choices A, C, D, and E are all asserted elsewhere in the passage, but are incorrect answers here because in this sentence they are not evidence of the "sovereign good of human nature."

7. **The correct answer is A.** The author compares the result of truth-telling to a pearl because it looks best in daylight, thereby implying that while lying can have some more exciting properties "by night," or in the imagination, the truth is more reliable. Choices B, C, and D are all incorrect because the author compares lying, not truth-telling, to a "mask," a "mummy" and "a man's shrunken mind." Choice E is incorrect because the author does not use a metaphor involving flowers at any point in the passage.

8. **The correct answer is C.** In the second paragraph, the author uses the metaphor of standing on a vantage point and clearly seeing the valley below to illustrate the pleasures of truth-telling, so we can infer that he does not believe that such people should be pitied. Choice A is incorrect, since the author argues that truth-telling is reliable, like the price of a pearl, and our ability to believe the truth ultimately represents the best qualities of human nature, we can infer that the author would argue that truth-telling is ultimately more rewarding than lying. Choice B is incorrect because the author mentions the decline of the philosophical belief in lying as free will in the first paragraph. Choices D and E are both directly stated in the second paragraph, so we can assume the author agrees with these statements.

9. **The correct answer is A.** This description is a metaphor, or a non-literal description to help the reader better understand the clarity and joy of honesty. Choice B is incorrect because a syllogism involves using two statements assumed to be true in order to form a conclusion, and that is not the structure of this sentence. Simile (choice C) is a tempting choice because of its similarity

to metaphor, but similes, unlike metaphors, are constructed using connecting words and phrases such as *like* and *as if to*, neither of which are present in this sentence. Choice D is incorrect because the sentence does not use irony, or the deliberate expression of something using language that typically means the opposite of what the author uses it to mean. Choice E is incorrect because alliteration is a repetition of certain letters or sounds over the course of a phrase (such as "curious crocodiles"), and that rhetorical tool is not used in this sentence.

10. **The correct answer is C.** The use of *severity* in this sentence implies an understanding the fathers had that the pleasures of telling the truth are ultimately more rewarding than the pleasures of lying. Choice A is incorrect because, in the first paragraph, the author says that in fact in previous years philosophers sometimes condoned lying as an expression of free will, and this contradicts Choice A. Choice B is incorrect because no additional information is given about the fathers, so we cannot be sure if they were generally strict. Choices D and E are both incorrect because the passage expresses no opinion on whether aspects of lying or truth-telling are forbidden by God.

11. **The correct answer is A.** The author ends the passage by comparing the ultimate rewards of truth-telling to the pleasures of heaven. Choices B and E are both incorrect. Animal imagery, or the depiction of animals in order to further the reader's point, is not present anywhere in the passage. Pastoral imagery (choice E) is present in the second paragraph when the author creates a metaphor of a truth-teller standing at the top of a hill and looking with clarity down at the innocent, pristine valleys below—however, this imagery is not present at the end of the passage. Choice C is incorrect because the tone at the end of the passage is sincere and exalting, not humorous. Choice D is incorrect because the author does not repeat any words, phrases, or sentences at the end of the passage.

12. **The correct answer is B.** In the second paragraph, the author states that human reason was God's last creation. Curiosity and the ability to lie (choices A and D) are not addressed in the passage. Light (choice C) was created by God, but it was not the last act of creation. *Pearls* (choice E) refers to a metaphor used elsewhere in the passage but which does not appear in this sentence.

13. **The correct answer is B.** The author uses the juxtaposition of a pearl and a carbuncle to illustrate the difference between a lie and the truth. Choice A is incorrect because the sentence does not use connecting words such as *like* or *as*. Choice C is incorrect because, while the sentence does use metaphorical language, it directly states the comparison, and allusion involves using language to call something to the reader's mind by referring to another work of art. Choice D is incorrect because the author does not pose any questions in this sentence. Choice E is incorrect because the author does not make use of irony, or the use of language which typically means the opposite of what the author is using it to mean, in order to express his point.

14. **The correct answer is B.** The author begins the passage by stating that she hopes that the women she is addressing will forgive her for treating them like rational human beings, when in fact the meaning behind the sentence is that women are tired of *not* being treated like rational human beings. Choice A is incorrect—while it may appear as if the author is speculating that she may anger women in the following passage, this speculation is facetious, or tongue-in-cheek. Choice C is incorrect because juxtaposition

involves the comparison of one thing against another, and while the author arguably establishes that women are treated one way but should be treated another, she does not *compare* those two methods of treatment until later on in the passage. Choice D is incorrect because there is no evidence that the author is alluding to another text in this sentence. Choice E is incorrect because the author does not make use of parentheses or similar asides in this sentence.

15. **The correct answer is C.** *Epithet* most closely means "nickname," "moniker," or "label." Choices A, B, D, and E are incorrect because *opponents* most closely means "rivals," *champions* most closely means "winners," *apologists* most closely means "those who seek to defend a viewpoint, especially a controversial one," and *families* means "related groups." Therefore, Choice C is clearly the best option.

16. **The correct answer is B.** The author clearly states that women's education has improved somewhat, and therefore the assertion that it is even more neglected than it was in previous decades is NOT true. Choices A, C, D, and E are all explicitly stated in the passage and therefore all four choices are incorrect, since the question asks which of the statements are NOT a major point in this passage.

17. **The correct answer is C.** Since she states that she aims to be useful instead of elegant, it is clear that the author values sincerity and usefulness over skillful turns of phrase. While Choice A is likely true, it is an incorrect answer because it does not address the reason the author attempts to avoid overly eloquent language. Choice B is incorrect because the author does not directly state in the passage that audiences prefer a minimalistic style. Choice D is incorrect because the author does not mention time constraints in the passage. Choice E is incorrect, because although, as in Choice A, it is likely true, it does not address the direct reason for her wish to avoid eloquent language.

18. **The correct answer is D.** In the last paragraph, the author expresses her belief that the subjugation of women implies a belief that they are stuck in an eternal semi-childhood. Choice A is incorrect because the author does not directly speak out against women taking painting and music lessons. Choices B and C are incorrect because they directly contradict statements that the author makes in the passage. Choice E is incorrect because the author states that women are often flowery in their language because they have often been taught to speak and write in an elegant manner, but does not address the ways in which men are taught to speak and write.

19. **The correct answer is A.** In the sentence, the author states that if she appears aggravated by the subject matter, her female readers will likely understand why, because they have had similar experiences. Choice B is incorrect because the author does not address the role that scientific analysis may play in learning more about the true nature of women. Choice C is incorrect because, while we can infer that the author believes that strong emotions do not help her be of use in solving the problem of injustices toward women, it is not stated in this sentence. Choice D is incorrect because the author does not indicate that teaching women better character is her goal. Choice E is incorrect because, similar to Choice C, the author likely believes that emotional writing is not useful: however, in this sentence she argues that her female readers will likely understand if she betrays emotion.

20. **The correct answer is D.** It is the only choice in which the author expresses a fact

without expressing an opinion on that fact. Choices A, B, C, and E all represent opinions and rhetorical devices used to express those opinions, and therefore they are example of the author's voice.

21. **The correct answer is choice B.** A litote is the expression of a viewpoint using an ironic negative ("you won't be sorry," for example, meaning that you'll be glad). Choice A is incorrect because the passage uses several compound sentences, or sentences that include multiple independent clauses. Choice C is incorrect because the passage uses ironic understatement to express the author's voice. Choice D is incorrect because parallelism, or the rhythmic use of grammatically similar words or phrases, appears in the passage in instances such as "I shall disdain to cull my phrases or polish my style." Choice E is incorrect because the author employs irony, or the deliberate use of a word to describe something, meaning the opposite of its traditional definition, at the beginning of the passage, when she writes "My own sex, I hope, will excuse me, if I treat them like rational creatures, instead of flattering their FASCINATING graces."

22. **The correct answer is C.** The sentence in lines 38–42) illustrates that society gives women the illusion that they can succeed only through marriage, when in fact women can succeed in any number of ways when they are treated fairly. Choice A is incorrect because the author does not address marriage as a goal for people in general; she speaks about it only in terms of how it relates to the subjugation of women. Choice B is incorrect because the author does not offer an opinion as to whether women should get married as a way of doing the best they can until society's treatment of women improves. Choice D is incorrect because, while the author may believe women desire to establish themselves in society by any means necessary, she does not directly state as much. Choice E is incorrect because the author does not talk about whether career or family is more important to women in this passage.

23. **The correct answer is B.** The author employs mocking, ironic rhetoric, but it is clear that she also cares very sincerely about her subject. Choice A is incorrect, though it may be a tempting choice, because while the author may be angry and emotional about the subject of the passage, she states that she wishes to be useful and therefore not employ emotional and eloquent language. Choice C is incorrect because, while she may be angry, she is not melancholy, and neither is she disinterested—that is, engaged in the subject but unbiased or impartial. Choice D is incorrect because, while the author may be optimistic about the progress of women in society, she does not explicitly state this. Choice E is incorrect because the author does not boast in this passage.

24. **The correct answer is A.** The author begins by establishing her goal (to avoid being forced into a limiting definition of femininity and establishing her character as a human being) and moves on to provide examples of how being defined by femininity, in her view, limits women's characters. Choice B is incorrect because the author does not use personal examples. Choice C is incorrect because the author does not form a counter-argument: she devotes the entire passage to one argument. Choice D is incorrect because the author focuses primarily on abstract generalizations instead of collecting and citing specific data and forming ideas from that data. Choice E is incorrect because the author does not cite any other writers or philosophers when forming her argument.

25. **The correct answer is B.** The passage ends with a question that invites the reader to consider the problems of viewing women

as incapable. Choice A is incorrect because the tone it describes appears in the passage, but not in the final sentence. Choice C is incorrect because, while the author feigns concern, asking "Can they govern a family, or take care of the poor babes whom they bring into the world?" she is not *genuinely* concerned because she believes that society does not give women credit for their capability. Choice D is incorrect because the author leaves the passage open-ended as an invitation to her readers to consider their own thoughts on the matter. Choice E is incorrect because, as in choice C, the author feigns alarm at the thought of (supposedly) defenseless, incapable women being tasked with running homes and raising children, when in fact she believes that women are entirely capable of these things.

26. **The correct answer is C.** The author uses the phrase "obtrusive odour" to symbolize attempts at humor that miss the mark. Choice A is incorrect because it is a literal interpretation of a phrase that is used metaphorically. Choice B is incorrect because the author argues that it is not humans' inability to grasp humor, but rather the humor lacking the basic quality of laughability, that causes bad attempts at humor to fail. Choice D is incorrect because, while the passage is describing the mysterious quality of laughter, this particular metaphor applies specifically to attempts at humor that are cheap imitations instead of the real thing. Choice E is incorrect because the basal elements of true humor do not have a literal scent.

27. **The correct answer is A.** The author argues that philosophers have had difficulty nailing down the basic properties of true laughability because these properties are driven by instinct as opposed to reason. Choice B is incorrect because the author argues that many have tried, unsuccessfully, to give laughability a proper definition because it defies simple description and cannot be so easily identified. Choice C is incorrect because the author states that "The greatest of thinkers, from Aristotle downwards, have tackled this little problem," yet the problem still persists. Choice D is incorrect because at no point in the passage does the author imply that philosophers do not believe that the problem is genuine and worthy of consideration. Choice E is incorrect because, on the contrary, the author argues that the problem is too complex and too ineffable to be easily solved.

28. **The correct answer is A.** The phrase "it has a method in its madness" references Shakespeare's *Hamlet*, which deals with another ineffable problem: romantic love. This implies that, although the problem of laughability defies human reasoning, it has a logic of its own. Therefore, choice B is incorrect, since there is some form of logic to what makes something funny. Choice C is incorrect because the "madness" refers to the logic of the laughter itself, not that of those who experience it. Choice D is incorrect because understatement, or the presentation of a concept as less important than it actually is, does not apply here because the author is not understating the mystery of laughter. Choice E is incorrect because there is no indication that the tone is sarcastic.

29. **The correct answer is C.** The author states "We shall confine ourselves to watching it grow and expand," implying he wishes to learn more about laughability without attempting to force it into a definition. Choice A is incorrect because it is the opposite of this statement. Choice B is incorrect because the author expresses no desire to eradicate humor. Choice D is incorrect because, since the author has established that there is a kind of logic to laughter, he does not believe that laughter or those who appreciate it are insane. Choice

E is incorrect because the author makes no mention of wishing to profit from understanding laughter.

30. **The correct answer is D.** The passage both begins and ends with a question intended to invite the reader to consider the nature of laughability. Choice A is incorrect because the author argues that it is impossible to apply epithets, or labels, to something as ineffable as laughability. Choice B is incorrect because simile, or the comparison of two subjects using connecting phrases such as "like" or "as," is not present in the passage in terms of helping to define the nature of laughability. Choice C is incorrect because the author does not employ personification, or the representation of a non-human figure as having human qualities, to help understand laughter. Choice E is incorrect because the author's tone does not seek to mock those who appreciate laughability.

31. **The correct answer is C.** Choices A and D are incorrect because the passage does not use any overly scientific or philosophical language, and the reader need not understand any scientific or philosophical concepts prior to reading this passage in order to understand its meaning. The author does not use an informal tone, nor does he reference his reader as a specific person, so Choice B is an unlikely answer. Choice E is incorrect because there is no evidence that the author intends comedians to be his primary audience. That leaves us with choice C—a general audience interested in the nature of laughter.

32. **The correct answer is B.** The author exhibits curiosity about the nature of laughter and is content to examine instances of laughability and learn more about human nature from them, in lieu of an exact definition of laughability; therefore, the tone can be described as meandering. Choice A is incorrect because the author does not criticize laughter in this passage, nor does he criticize other philosophers who have been unable to come up with an exact definition for laughability. Choice C is incorrect because the author does not reference data in this passage. Choice D is incorrect because the author is writing for a general reader, and does not directly interact with his reader. Choice E is incorrect because the author does not express any outrage, nor does he exaggerate his point.

33. **The correct answer is B.** The author begins the passage with an inquiry into the nature of what makes something laughable, but after acknowledging that laughability has no firm definition, he settles for learning more about basal laughter in order to learn more about human nature. Choice A is incorrect because the author does not admonish past researchers for a lack of data, since he states that data cannot possibly apply to something as basic as laughability. Choice C is incorrect because the author does not offer specific evidence in this passage; the passage consists primarily of abstract generalizations. Choice D is incorrect because the passage is not autobiographical. Choice E is incorrect because the author does not dismiss the importance of laughter, and in fact makes the point that while we may not be able to understand it, laughability has a logic unto itself.

34. **The correct answer is B.** Since the question asked which option could NOT be inferred about the author from reading the paragraph, let's look at our choices: We already know that the author has explicitly stated choice A in the passage; therefore that option is incorrect. Choice C is also incorrect, since the author argues that we cannot strictly define laughability, but it is still worth studying as a measure of human nature. choice D is incorrect because at the beginning of the

passage the author uses the analogy of fine perfume versus an offensive odor to describe the instinctual way in which humans tell the difference between true laughability and its imitation. Choice E is incorrect because the beginning of the passage acknowledges that many great philosophers have approached this question and been unable to solve it because it may not have a concrete solution. That leaves us with Choice B, which is correct, because while the author presumably has a sense of humor, he does not address his personal tastes in humor in this passage and therefore we cannot infer this statement from the context.

35. **The correct answer is D.** The author does not describe the nature of relations between the missionary community and the native community in this passage. Instead, he focuses on a geographical description of the California landscape in which the missionary community has settled, so choice A is incorrect. Choices C and E are also important points in the author's description of how the mission established itself and how others might do the same, so they are both incorrect. Choice B is also incorrect because the passage goes on to describe the customs of the natives in Northern California.

36. **The correct answer is B.** The author observes and describes his surroundings in this passage in a measured tone with little emotion. Choice A is incorrect because the author does not appear scandalized, or shocked, by either the establishment of the missionary community or the customs of the natives. Choice C is incorrect because the author uses plain language and fairly simple sentences. Choice D is incorrect because the author expresses little voice in the passage and does not employ any rhetorical techniques that would indicate sarcasm, such as irony or understatement. Choice E is incorrect because, while the author *may* be self-assured and overconfident, it is impossible to tell that from this passage because he does not speak biographically at any point or brag about his community.

37. **The correct answer is A.** In context, the phrase "apostolic predication" most likely refers to the religious practices which, since they differed from those practiced by the natives, made it necessary for the missionaries to construct structures called *presidios*. Choices B and E are incorrect because if the phrase referred to communication with the natives or appreciation for the natural world, it would not make sense that it would be necessary to build walls and structures in order to facilitate that communication or appreciation. Choice C is incorrect because the practices of basket-weaving and soap-making are not brought up until a later paragraph in the passage. Choice D is incorrect because it is not necessary to build barriers and compounds in order to record events.

38. **The correct answer is D.** The sixth paragraph discusses life in the missionary, and the seventh paragraph addresses the native community that exists nearby, comparing the two communities' habits. Choice A is partially correct, but does not address this comparison. Choice B is incorrect because there is no indication that the natives patronize the missionaries' businesses. Choice C is incorrect because the author does not offer many details on the natives' response to the missionaries' arrival. Choice E is incorrect because the author does not mention any native cultural traditions that the missionaries imitate.

39. **The correct answer is C.** The author states his opinion that "these rancherias are the most adequate to the natural uncleanliness of the Indians, as the families often renew them, burning the old ones, and immediately

building others." Therefore, Choices A, B, D, and E are incorrect, since the author offers only one reason why the natives periodically burn down their housing structures.

40. **The correct answer is A.** The passage primarily addresses the geography, structure, and daily life in Northern California, presumably to give an audience considering a trip there a sense of what it's like. Choice B is incorrect because the author does not go into detail about the religious practices of the natives. Choice C is incorrect because the author does not indicate an opinion on whether missionaries should spread further. Choice D is incorrect because the author speaks in relatively formal language, and the passage is not structured like a letter. Choice E is incorrect because the passage does not speak at all about the author's personal life or opinions, beyond that fact that he is in Northern California at a missionary building.

41. **The correct answer is A.** Since the author speaks not at all about himself, and almost completely about the nature of his surroundings, we can infer that his goal is to educate his readers about missionary life in Northern California. Choice B is incorrect because there is no personal reflection in this passage. Choice C is incorrect because the author does not offer an opinion on whether the natives should leave California for any reason. Choice D is incorrect because the author does not offer an opinion on whether he supports Christian missionaries. For the same reason, choice E is also incorrect.

42. **The correct answer is B.** The "edifices" in context refer to barriers within the compound to allocate various rooms and sections. Choice A is incorrect because the edifices in these sentences are literal, physical structures, not religious practices. Choice C is incorrect because these edifices are separate from protective barriers outside the compound: they are described as being inside the building, and primarily organizational, not protective. Choice D is incorrect because the edifices refer to *barriers* as opposed to separate building units. Choice E is incorrect because, as is the case with choice A, these edifices are physical, not societal, barriers.

43. **The correct answer is B.** The author does not directly address any dissonance between the Western missionaries and the natives, and does not employ any rhetorical devices to depict any such dissonance. Choice A is incorrect because the author lists different kinds of physical structures over the course of the passage, such as the *presidios*, missions and *rancherias*. Choice C is incorrect because the author describes the employment of people in the compound, such as basket-weaving and soap-making. Choice D is incorrect because the author offers a detailed description of how the missionary established its community. Choice E is incorrect because the author describes the military presence and how they create defense barriers for the missionary.

44. **The correct answer is D.** Antiphrasis, or the ironic use of a word to mean its opposite in order to achieve a humorous effect, is not present in this passage. The author uses parallelism, or the use of grammatically similar phrases in a sentence, in the third paragraph, when he states, "His physical life was but as an embryonic stage, a coming up out of darkness, a twilight and dawn before the sunrise." The author uses metaphor, or the comparison of a subject to something which does not literally apply to it, in the same sentence, when he states that in Shakespeare's case physical life was "a twilight and dawn" before the sunrise of the life he lived in his literature. The author uses simile, or a similar comparison that uses connecting words such as *like* or *as*

when he states "Life is like playing a violin solo in public" in the second paragraph. The author uses analogy in the third paragraph, when he compares most people's lives to stillborn infancy, since they live during their physical lives and do not live on afterwards. Therefore, there are examples of choices A, B, C, and E in the passage, but none of D.

45. **The correct answer is A.** The passage begins with the statement "I have been asked to speak on the question how to make the best of life." Choice B is incorrect because the author argues that only a small fraction of the population achieves this definition of immortality, and therefore it is not a reasonable goal for the majority of people. Choice C is incorrect because, while the author does indeed make the argument that Shakespeare lived a full life after his death, this is an example of the broader point that some people cannot be truly said to have started living until well after they physically die. Choice D is incorrect because the author asserts in the first sentence of the second paragraph that facing the question of how to make a meaningful life is, if faced seriously, fatuous, or silly. Choice E is incorrect because, while the author does state that the importance of life is greater than individual people, this is not a primary point of the passage.

46. **The correct answer is B.** The question in lines 15–16 asks whether the life that we should be trying to make meaningful is the one we physically live or the one we may enjoy after we die. Choice A is incorrect because the author does not seek to answer which is the better life, per se, but rather which kind of life has a greater measure of meaningfulness to the human race in general. Choice C is incorrect because, although the author does bring up the question of meaningfulness in work versus meaningfulness in personal life, he does not do so until the following paragraph. Choice D is similar to choice C, but focuses on the impact we have on other *people*, not just on the world and on ourselves. Again, this question does arise in the passage, but not until later. Choice E is incorrect because it is a question that is addressed earlier in the passage, but not one that emerges in this particular sentence.

47. **The correct answer is C.** After establishing the two kinds of meaningful lives, the author goes on to explain how figures such as Shakespeare achieved meaning after death and describes the ways in which we may make meaning in our physical lives. Choice A is incorrect because the author does not open the passage with a personal anecdote. Choice B is incorrect because the author does not use the second half of the passage to debate whether or not a meaningful life may occur either before or after death; he used the entire passage to explain his theory that either kind of meaningful life is possible. Choice D is incorrect because the passage does not focus on the author's experience at any point in the passage: he speaks in abstract generalizations or in terms of historical examples the entire time. Choice E is incorrect because the passage states that no person can tell another person the perfect and correct way to live his own life.

48. **The correct answer is C.** As it is used in the text, the "embryonic stage" was the stage in which Shakespeare was physically alive, because he had not yet achieved the true life in literature he was given after death. Choice A is incorrect, because the author is speaking metaphorically, not literally about the time a human spends in the womb before birth. Choice B is incorrect because in Shakespeare's case, he was not unaware of how to make a meaningful life during his physical life—he simply had not yet achieved immortality through literature. Choice D is incorrect because, in Shakespeare's case,

his life was not "stillborn" simply because he had an "embryonic stage." Choice E is incorrect because, as in choice B, the "embryonic stage" is not a comment on a person's ignorance about philosophy and the meaning of life; it simply represents a time when that person has not yet achieved his or her life's true meaning.

49. **The correct answer is B.** In the first paragraph, the author establishes his premise and the difficulties in advising another person on how to have a meaningful life. The second paragraph is more contemplative and questioning, and makes use of rhetorical devices like metaphor and rhetorical questioning. Choice A is incorrect because the second paragraph does not cite data or statistics, nor does it use technical language. Choice C is incorrect because it does not borrow from the author's own personal experience. Choice D is incorrect because the paragraph does not have an overly philosophical tone, nor does it use premises or words that an average person would not understand. Choice E is incorrect because the tone does not indicate that the author is angry in any way.

50. **The correct answer is C.** The second paragraph establishes the juxtaposition between life during physical life and life after physical death, and the third paragraph offers examples, such as Shakespeare, Handel, and Jane Austen to describe how one might live more fully after one's physical death. Choice A is incorrect because, while the passage does make the point that no life bears fundamental similarity to another, this point comes in the first paragraph, not the second. Furthermore, the idea that living of a good life cannot be taught is not present in the third paragraph. Choice B is incorrect because, although the simile the author uses in the second paragraph comparing life to a public violin solo indicates that he likely does believe that life is ad-libbed, the third paragraph does not argue that no one lives on in others' memories after death—in fact, it argues the opposite. Choice D is incorrect because while the second paragraph does imply that making an impact on others can help a person achieve life after death, the primary point of the paragraph is to illustrate that some people live primarily before they physically die and other people live primarily afterward. Choice E is incorrect because it is the opposite of the paragraph's argument that many people live fully after death.

51. **The correct answer is C.** Since Shakespeare's physical life was but an "embryonic stage," according to the author, his true life began after death. Choice A is incorrect because the author argues, contrary to the statement in choice A, that in fact many people live on in death. Choice B is incorrect because the author argues that a majority of people do not live on in death, and he does not say anything to indicate that after we die we can fix the mistakes we made in life. Choice D is incorrect because the author argues in the final paragraph that teachers achieve lives beyond their own through the students they impact, which is the opposite of what this statement argues. Choice E is incorrect because the author does not address an afterlife, but instead uses *life* to refer to how we are known on Earth.

52. **The correct answer is B.** Since the author begins the passage by addressing a group of people and the tone is not specialized, we can infer that the passage is intended for an audience of general knowledge. Choice A is incorrect because the passage is not intimate or specific enough to be intended for a diary or just one person. Choice C is incorrect because the language and terms are not overly philosophically advanced, implying that the passage is meant for the general reader to understand. Choice D is incorrect because there is nothing in the

passage to indicate it is especially meant for artists, although artists might well be interested in the subject. Choice E is incorrect because, while the author does state that a serious look at the meaning of life is inherently fatuous, or silly, it is not an especially comical passage.

53. **The correct answer is C.** The author cites teachers among the examples of those people who go on to live full lives after their physical lives are over. Choice A is incorrect because, while the statement that teachers can help their students get a head start on understanding life is likely true, it is not the point of the sentence. Choice B is incorrect because the author argues the opposite: teaching is worthwhile and meaningful in itself. Choice D is incorrect because the author does not state whether he is a former teacher. Choice E is incorrect because the author does not reference his own teachers.

54. **The correct answer is B.** The word *fatuous* can be defined as "silly." *Deadly* is defined as "mortally dangerous," *complicated* is described as "complex" or "not simple," *true* is defined as "factual," "right," or "correct"; and *erroneous* is defined as "wrong" or "incorrect." Therefore, choices A, C, D, and E are all incorrect.

55. **The correct answer is D.** The tone of the passage is philosophical. Choice A is incorrect because the author speaks about ideas, as opposed to telling a story. Choice B is incorrect because the passage is not intended to convince its reader of any single conclusion. Choice C is incorrect because the passage does not employ legal terms or subject matter. Choice E is incorrect because the passage does not contain much sarcasm, irony, condescension, mocking, or other rhetorical tools that would lead one to believe the author intends to disprove or deride his subject.

Section II: Free Response

Question 1

High-Scoring Sample Essay

No less of a luminary than President John Quincy Adams once said that he studied politics and war so that his children could study math and philosophy, and his grandchildren could spend their time on "painting, poetry, music, and architecture" (Source E). With that in mind let's consider the question of whether schools should require their students to take at least one arts class during their academic careers.

The responses seem to be different depending on what age group is under discussion. For young children, the answer seems nearly unanimous—the arts are good for self-expression, boost test scores, build fundamental skills, and establish life-long patterns of enthusiasm (Source A). But as early as middle school, the argument becomes more contested. Helicopter parents like the one in Source F insist their little engineers must study only math and science or they'll fall behind all the other students and never achieve their dreams of changing the scientific landscape forever! Obviously I think this idea is a little silly. We all study things in middle school that may not seem immediately useful, or that we study because they make us good citizens or more well-rounded, not just because we like them (Source D). I myself learned how to plan, shop for, cook, and write thank you notes for a dinner party in home ec, and how to make a bridge that supports five—but not six—text books. Was this educational? Of course! Do I expect to develop it into a career? Not so much.

In high school and even college the debate gets more heated. High school students have to get ready for college, and college students have to get ready for their careers. A Kentucky governor even proposed amending his state budget so that colleges get rewarded for producing STEM majors over humanities students (Source B). This seems like a bad policy, because while jobs are important, we don't always know exactly how what we study will inform our career path. Humanities skills—communication, critical thinking, problem-solving, collaboration—transfer easily to multiple disciplines. STEM knowledge is less flexible and less portable. It's still important, but it may be better to wait until you are certain that's what you want to spend your life on before you focus your studies entirely on that!

Ultimately that's why I come down on the side of supporting mandatory arts education. It's only one class! But it might show you something important, and it also speaks to our ideals as a society in a way that financially penalizing high schools and colleges for making space for humanities scholars just doesn't. Parents and politicians alike should remember that our ideals go back a lot further than their revenue accounts, and preserve arts education in public schools.

Reader Response for the High-Scoring Sample Essay

This essay effectively provides an argument that synthesizes multiple sources, using them together to find additional meaning and developing the argument logically. For example, the writer begins with a theoretical/principle-based discussion based on a John Quincy Adams quote. Then the writer pivots with a clear transition to applying that theoretical question to how that shows up in school policy. The writer begins by examining differences in attitudes toward mandatory arts education based on age, and then reviewing the arguments about why arts education is considered important for each group. The writer tackles this in two paragraphs—one about elementary and middle schools, and then one about high school and college. The essay concludes with the writer's own perspective, and directs the argument specifically at parents and policy-makers. The writer uses sources appropriately to examine both the reasons for incorporating arts education and why some stakeholders might prefer more career-based or STEM study options. The essay successfully explains the writer's reasoning, accounts for multiple perspectives, and achieves clarity at the sentence and structural level.

Middle-Scoring Sample Essay

Partnerships with arts programs can be really beneficial for schools and students. Schools get the chance to offer more interesting classes, and students get to break up the monotony of their scheduled classes. People say that it helps to express ourselves and that we learn lessons that apply to real life in other ways (Source A). But other people think the arts are a waste of time (Source B), and while I don't agree it's a waste, I do agree it shouldn't be mandatory.

Like Mr. Cookery said in Source F, his kids aren't into the arts, they really like science and they need to be really good at them in order to make a difference. Why shouldn't school get them started earlier to be informed and motivated? I think this is a compelling argument, because college is really competitive and if you or your kids want to achieve big things, you want as much experience as possible. I really like playing lacrosse, and I would be annoyed if the school said instead of doing that after school, I had to try out for a play. I might be able to get a scholarship, and I should be allowed to decide how I spend my time!

Like I said, I think arts should be available. Like Matilda Rubinthal said, they help people discover things they didn't know they needed. I played trumpet for a while, and enjoyed working with a group, and developing my ear training. But what about the things they would have discovered in extra hard math and science classes, if that's what they like? (Source C). I also developed more respect for my abilities as a creative problem solver by taking an engineering course, and took that confidence back onto the lacrosse field! People should consider whether arts are necessary or just great to have. I would rather only take one rather than one every year.

Reader Response for the Middle-Scoring Sample Essay

This essay adequately presents a qualified argument in support of arts education—taking exception to the idea that it should be mandatory, but also supporting the idea that it is important and should be widely available. The writer integrates sources mostly appropriately, with a few places where those ideas could be more developed or more accurately introduced (for example, using "People say" for source A and source B rather than presenting the author or stakeholder in each text. The writer supports his interpretation with personal experience in adequate ways—mentioning his experience playing lacrosse, playing trumpet, and taking an engineering class to demonstrate the value of choice over compulsory course restrictions. This reflects the writer's understanding of the pro and con arguments, and backs up his decision to introduce his own modified perspective. The writer's prose at the sentence level could use more polish to effectively demonstrate mastery of rhetorical strategies, as the language is not consistently formal enough for an academic context. The writing is generally clear.

Low-Scoring Sample Essay

I love the arts so much, when I was younger I got to play instruments and sing and it was so important to how I grew up. On the other hand not everybody enjoys that. Some people would rather spend time on things like science because they think it will help them when they grow up more or just like it better, which is fine for them, but if I have to take gym shouldn't they have to take chorus or something? I don't get why it's a debate and not just the rules.

Reader Response for the Low-Scoring Sample Essay

This essay is insufficiently developed beyond the writer's own experience—it doesn't feature any discernible source use or broader context for why the conversation about mandatory arts education is relevant, and fails to consider multiple points of view in a thoughtful way. The writer asks rhetorical questions, but it's not a deliberate choice that the writer uses to explain or extend his own argument. On the sentence level, the writer is struggling to communicate clearly, and fails to put forth a concrete argument, instead signaling that the writer doesn't understand the prompt sufficiently.

Question 2

High-Scoring Sample Essay

From the first paragraph of Mary Church Terrell's 1906 speech "What It Means To Be Colored In Capital of the U.S." onward, it is evident that Terrell's intended audience is white, and her objective is to offer some perspective into the bias she suffers as a black person living in Washington, D.C. To achieve this objective, she adopts an explanatory rhetoric, depicting in detail circumstances which are part of the day-to-day black experience, but of whose injustices a white person might be unaware, or towards which the white community may not have given much thought. "As a colored woman I may walk from the Capitol to the White House, ravenously hungry and abundantly supplied with money....without finding a single restaurant in which I would be permitted to take a morsel of food, if it was patronized by white people, unless I were willing to sit behind a screen," she writes. "I cannot visit the tomb of the Father of this country, which owes its very existence to the love of freedom in the human heart...without being forced to sit in the Jim Crow section of an electric car..." In grounding her descriptions of injustices committed against her to mundane, everyday facts, Terrell effectively depicts a clear picture of how racism in D.C. impacts even the smallest aspects of her daily life, including all of the errands, chores and outings that the white people she is addressing can undertake without any consideration for the logistics.

This methodical account of how daily life is more difficult for black people than for their white counterparts compels a white audience to envision themselves in Terrell's position. If her speech had focused on the atrocities of slavery or lynch mobs, a white audience might be horrified, but it would be more difficult for them to empathize, as they would have no personal context via which to place themselves in Terrell's shoes. The daily injustices of being unable to eat when one is hungry, and having to sit in a certain section on public transportation, are more accessible, and for Terrell, using small-scale examples allows her to use the powerful rhetorical tool of eliciting empathy.

Since Terrell's focus in this speech is not individual people but the common plight of black people suffering prejudice in America, she employs the synecdoche "the colored man" to signify the problems all people of color face. "The colored man alone is thrust out of the hotels of the national capital like a leper," she writes, referring not just to a single incident but what might happen to any black person who chooses to walk into a D.C. hotel.

"It is certain that it would be difficult to find a worse misnomer for Washington than 'The Colored Man's Paradise,'" Terrell writes wryly, "if so prosaic a consideration as veracity is to determine the appropriateness of a name." The irony of D.C.'s nickname 'The Colored Man's Paradise' is not lost on Terrell, and she develops a compelling rhetorical argument by juxtaposing the American values of freedom and equality against the realities of life for black people living in America. Her language reflects this contrast. At the end of her speech, comprised nearly entirely of a list of the day-to-day instances that negatively impact black people's everyday lives, Terrell's language shifts into metaphor. "And surely nowhere in the world do oppression and persecution based solely on the color of skin appear more hateful and hideous than in the capital of the United States," she concludes, "because the chasm between the Principles upon which the government was founded, in which it still professes to believe, and those which are daily practiced under the protection of the flag, yawn so wide and so deep." Here the discrepancy between depictions of racism and an explanation of the hypocritical value system in the capital of the United States is mirrored by a notable shift in the language from mundane to metaphorical. Terrell uses rhetorical incongruence to allude to the larger societal incongruence of widespread racism in a city built on the values of freedom and equality.

Reader Response for the High-Scoring Sample Essay

The writer has provided a clear, organized analysis of rhetorical devices used in the text to produce her own interpretive argument ("This methodical account of how daily life is more difficult for black people than for their white counterparts compels a white audience to envision themselves in Terrell's position"). The first paragraph begins by summarizing the main ideas of Mary Church Terrell's essay, using quotes appropriately, as well as including interpretive moves of the author's own to frame it ("Terrell effectively depicts a clear picture ..."). In the next paragraph, the writer considers different rhetorical strategies he or she could have used that would have been less effective in order to support the writer's interpretation of the effectiveness of the author's arguments. The next paragraphs identify literary devices like synecdoche and metaphor to close-read the rhetoric used by the author of the text under analysis. Though the essay contains some minor rhetorical and organizational issues, it is a thoughtful and controlled analysis of Terrell's rhetorical techniques.

Middle-Scoring Sample Essay

Mary Church Terrell uses motivational rhetoric to convince a white audience that they should be doing more to further racial inequalities in their own city. She believes that it is only through an extreme change in the way white people think about racism in D.C. that black youth can have a fair shot making their lives in the nation's capital. "To the lack of incentive to effort, which is the awful shadow under which we live, may be traced the wreck and ruin of score of colored youth." Terrell seeks to solve the problem of disenfranchisement of black youth by using rhetoric that appeals to the ethos of her white audience: while many white people are afraid of black youths, Terrell addresses the aspects of the lives of young black men that funnel them into an adulthood with few prospects and daily systemic oppression in a city that claims to cherish the values of freedom and equality.

Terrell employs irony as a rhetorical tool to state that D.C. is not, in fact, a black person's paradise—in fact, nothing could be further from the truth. She speculates on how the name came to be, and whether it was "… given immediately after the war by an ex-slave holder who for the first time in his life saw colored people walking about like free men, minus the overseer and the whip." Humor is a powerful tool in counterbalancing difficult subjects, and Terrell's ironic and dark sense of humor in this essay provides additional reflection into the hypocrisy of D.C. and America in general.

Reader Response for the Middle-Scoring Sample Essay

This essay is an adequate effort to close-read Terrell's essay and draw out an interpretive argument. The writer included introductory sentences for several points ("Terrell seeks to solve the problem…"; "Terrell employed irony…") but struggles to adequately follow up on many of them. The writer discusses the irony and humor present in Terrell's essay but doesn't provide examples from the text in which Terrell demonstrates those techniques, although the writer did employ the text to provide evidence for some interpretations (for example, when illustrating how racism has influenced young residents of D.C. and how the "paradise" moniker came to be assigned to the city after the Civil War). The writer misunderstood portions of the speech, which impacts the writer's ability to interpret the text. The prose is adequate but not fully developed or demonstrative of a wide range of rhetorical techniques.

Low-Scoring Sample Essay

Racism in America is as common as shopping malls. We may have abolished Jim Crow laws and made it illegal to turn away customers from restaurants for being black, but it's amazing how much in common Terrell's experience of being black in America has with the experience of being black in America today especially because she phrased her speech so simply and directly it sounds like it could have been a modern-day speech with only a few alterations. I thought it was horrible to read her experience with trying to get a job and the guy over the phone asking her directly if she was white or black, then having to look for menial work that was already scarce to begin with. That was so unfair and the truth is it's still unfair to be black in America, we just have subtler injustices and structures in place to keep black people from advancing these days.

Reader Response for the Low-Scoring Sample Essay

This essay struggles to fulfill the requirements of the prompt. While the writer did start to compare Terrell's experience in 1906 to the black experience in America today ("it's amazing how much in common Terrell's experience of being black in America has with the experience of being black in America today"), he did not finish developing that thread with specific examples or his own interpretation. The writer also failed to organize his essay into any discernible structure—he could have begun with an introduction to present the source, a more specific close-reading of the rhetorical techniques in the text, and a conclusion that offers a more complete interpretation of the effects of those techniques on the essay as whole.

Question 3

High-Scoring Sample Essay

The advent of YouTube has provided a forum unlike any that previously existed in society, and over the course of the last 10–15 years, those who enjoy YouTube content have been able to watch first hand as the website's participants and celebrities have found their footing as contributors to a global conversation. The beauty of YouTube is this: whatever you want to watch, from makeup tutorials to political commentary to videos of people playing video games while talking about it—you can find it on YouTube, quickly and for free. Likewise, within the limits of the law, those who start their own YouTube channels can upload pretty much whatever they'd like, as the format of what a YouTube video can and should be is drastically more relaxed than that of a sitcom or reality television show.

Education television programs that had existed long before the advent of YouTube, such as *How Stuff Works* and *Bill Nye The Science Guy*, found new ways to reconnect with an older audience that had watched them on TV as well as accessing a younger generation who might not have seen their original programs, but could discover them through old and new YouTube content. Notably, the community aspect of YouTube offers these TV personalities a way to connect with viewers that television never has: they can communicate with their viewers directly by responding to comments and holding live Q&As to directly address viewer questions.

However, perhaps the most important aspect of YouTube is the creation of an entirely new persona: someone who makes video content crafted especially for YouTube, which would not have fit into the formats of any existing television programs. One example is the advent of the vlog, which is a video diary, typically using fairly low production, in which a YouTube personality carries a camera and brings their audience along with them as they go about their daily routine. This allows viewers to feel more intimately connected with the channel they are watching, as if the YouTube personality they are watching is as much their friend as they are an entertainer.

One such example is Jenna Marbles, a YouTube personality who creates relatively short comedic videos. With over 17 million subscribers, several auxiliary weekly projects such as a podcast and a weekly YouTube Top 15 countdown and a line of merchandise featuring her dogs and most memorable YouTube moments, Marbles has simultaneously created and monetized her brand as a YouTube persona. Her videos, while not strictly educational, are highly personal, and typically feature her daily routine and are shot inside her house. While this may seem like a simple formula, Marbles' openness and intimate relationship with her viewers has amassed her millions of devoted fans and an annual income estimated at over $500,000 annually.

What Marbles gets right—and what YouTube does best—is a combination of TV-style entertainment and a kind of long-distance friendship with her viewers. She frequently makes specific videos because her fans have asked her to—examples would be her take on the Jimmy Kimmel classic "Reading Mean Comments" and her attempt to sew a Disney princess dress for her boyfriend in "Jenna's Ratchet Fashion Boutique: My Boyfriend." In an age where entertainment is participatory, not passive (as it would be for a fan of *Friends* or *Real Housewives*, for example,) YouTube lends an openness and ease of communication that makes Marbles' fans feel that they truly know her. This speaks to a truth about how the Internet has changed the way people interact with their idols today. The more open lines of communications exist over platforms like YouTube, the more accessible the person on the other side of the screen becomes.

Reader Response for the High-Scoring Sample Essay

This essay begins with a strong introduction that explains the importance of YouTube as a media source that provides a wide variety of content. The writer addresses multiple effects of public discourse over the Internet, including specific examples, such as Bill Nye and *How Stuff Works*, as well as newer performers like Jenna Marbles or components of late night TV talk shows. The writer develops an argument for why different kinds of careers and personalities emerge as the way we consume entertainment changes—that YouTube has given rise to more open and easy communications, and that this makes entertainers more accessible and audiences more devoted. The prose is clear and organized, though the significance of the author's argument could be more explicitly fleshed out.

Middle-Scoring Sample Essay

For many, the Internet is a soapbox from which to shout from. Resources like blogs were intended to allow anyone who had something to say do so, as opposed to public discourse only being accessible to people who published books or filmed movies and television shows, or went into politics or became famous in conventional ways. But expressly because of the ease with which you can use the Internet to communicate, it's less like an active center for public discourse and more like a shouting contest. There are too many people who want to speak and not enough people who are actually qualified to do so.

Therefore while the Internet is great in theory for those who want to make their voices heard, it's actually very difficult to take seriously anything you read on the Internet because there's no way to know if it's true. Take Wikipedia. Anyone can edit it and even though there are moderators fact checking it, there's no way they can keep up with how many people are adding information to every page every day. One example is the Wikipedia page for the folk band "Old Crow Medicine Show." They are a pretty popular band, but if you just looked at their Wikipedia page and didn't know anything else about them you would think they were bigger than the Beatles because they have one crazy fan who keeps adding all this stuff to their Wikipedia page to make them sound way more popular than they actually are and since the Internet values free speech and public discourse there's nothing for the moderators to do except to continue fact checking every article this fan puts up on their page.

Extreme fandom isn't new, but the Internet lets it really get out of hand. It allows crazy fans to stalk and harass their idols, make tribute websites and Instagrams, and just maintain a much larger presence than they'd be able to do if the Internet didn't give them all these channels to make themselves heard.

Reader Response for the Middle-Scoring Sample Essay

This essay adequately takes a position on the online media offerings discussed in the prompt, and the negative effects some aspects of the discourse can have on viewers and internet users. The essay begins with the observation that "There are too many people who want to speak and not enough people who are actually qualified to do so." The writer provides examples of the positives and negatives of websites like Wikipedia and the way anonymous users can update it. The writer argues that the Internet allows people to have access to those they admire in harmful ways. The writer has some interesting points, but relies too heavily on personal opinion and not enough on evidence, e.g. specific performers, websites, or sources, let alone outside readings. The essay develops its points but abandons the discussion of how to evaluate sources online that it began in the second paragraph. The prose is clear but not particularly polished or well crafted.

Low-Scoring Sample Essay

I love how easy it is on the Internet to talk to strangers. Anytime you have a question you can just go on Reddit. I meet most of my friends in chat forums and it makes so much sense because you just go to a thread that you're interested in and right away you meet people who are interested in the same things you're interested in. I live in Baltimore and one of my best friends lives in New York so there is no way we would have met in real life but we are both really interested in pressing wildflowers so we met in a forum for talking about pressing wildflowers and then eventually we met in real life. People say that's dangerous and also there is that show *Catfish* where people meet people from the Internet and they turn out to be different from what they said they are but I think that this actually happens way less in real life than you'd think it does if you never experienced it and only watched it on TV. Obviously the ones they put on TV are the most extreme cases but I think in general it is a really, really good and efficient way to meet people who share your interests and I will continue to do it.

Reader Response for the Low-Scoring Sample Essay

This essay is logically organized but insufficiently developed. While the writer is enthusiastic about the topic, the essay reads less like an argument in favor of public discourse over the Internet and more as a case study for meeting friends online. The writer mentions examples of Internet forums but does not thoroughly explain any of them—the prompt asks writers to include evidence from readings or other areas of observation (for example, specific online publications or other sites beyond social media). The prose is informal for an academic context, and doesn't adequately answer the prompt.

NOTES

NOTES